I0050375

Disconnected

Disconnected

Exploring the Decline of Social Networks

Milan Frankl

BEP

BUSINESS EXPERT PRESS

Leader in applied, concise business books

Disconnected: Exploring the Decline and Fall of Social Networks

Copyright © Business Expert Press, LLC, 2025

Cover design by Brent Beckley

Interior design by Exeter Premedia Services Private Ltd., Chennai, India

All rights reserved. No part of this publication may be reproduced, stored in a retrieval system, or transmitted in any form or by any means—electronic, mechanical, photocopy, recording, or any other except for brief quotations, not to exceed 400 words, without the prior permission of the publisher.

First published in 2025 by
Business Expert Press, LLC
222 East 46th Street, New York, NY 10017
www.businessexpertpress.com

ISBN-13: 978-1-63742-746-0 (paperback)
ISBN-13: 978-1-63742-747-7 (e-book)

Business Expert Press Service Systems and Innovations in Business and Society Collection

First edition: 2025

10 9 8 7 6 5 4 3 2 1

Description

Disconnected: Exploring the Decline of Social Networks **examines the future of social networks, highlighting their transformation from community builders to sources of misinformation and frustration**. Using interdisciplinary insights, it uncovers the complex interplay of technological, social, and cultural factors behind this shift. It discusses the impact on individuals, businesses, and society, proposing pathways to a healthier digital environment.

The book delves into the fascinating journey of social networks, tracing their evolution from tools that fostered community building to platforms that can sometimes spread misinformation. It explores how privacy issues are crucial in shaping user experiences and trust. *Disconnected* also examines the phenomenon of algorithmic polarization, where algorithms create echo chambers and contribute to the spread of disinformation.

The author explores the social and cultural factors that influence social networks. Additionally, he includes case studies that highlight the real-world impacts of social networks on individuals, businesses, and society as a whole.

Readers will discover practical solutions that offer pathways to creating a healthier digital environment, enable recognition of misinformation and privacy issues more effectively, and gain strategic insights that will help navigate and influence the future of social networks.

Contents

CHAPTER 1

Purpose and Scope of the Book

The evolution of social networks has been a topic of interest since its inception, especially as connection and communication shifted online.

In *disconnected*, we explore the evolution of social networks, once seen as the high point of online connectivity. We examine privacy issues and popular polarization, revealing how social platforms evolved from community builders to sources of misinformation.

Using interdisciplinary insights, we uncover the complex interplay of technological, social, and cultural factors leading to this shift. We present through debates on the effect of this shift on individuals, businesses, and society, proposing pathways to a healthier digital environment.

What Is a Social Network?

Social media networks

A social network is a social structure made up of individuals or organizations (called *nodes* or *actors*) that are connected by one or more types of interdependency or relationships, such as friendship, kinship, interests, financial exchange, or relationships of beliefs, knowledge, or prestige.

Some key points about social networks include:

- Nodes (individual actors, people, or groups) and the ties or connections (relationships or interactions) between these nodes.
- Ties can be of different types like friendship, family, interests, beliefs, knowledge sharing, and so on.
- Social networks allow for the exchange, transfer, or flow of resources (tangible or intangible) between the nodes.
- Social networks can exist at multiple levels—interpersonal, intraorganizational, or interorganizational networks.
- Social network analysis studies the structure and patterning of these networks and relationships.

Online social networks, like Facebook, Twitter, and many others, are virtual platforms that enable the formation of social networks facilitated by internet and web technologies.

Social networks exhibit properties like clustering, reciprocity, and centrality, that influence how resources flow through the network.

In essence, a social network represents the web of relationships and connections that exist between different actors, enabling the transfer of resources, knowledge, influence, and other social commodities within that network structure.

Both offline and online platforms can facilitate the formation and analysis of such social networks.

Historical Background

Social media platforms have evolved from hopeful spaces, initially praised for their ability to encourage worldwide connections and enable meaningful engagements, into environments filled with misinformation and disinformation.* A key factor driving this change is the uncontrolled spread of inaccurate or deceptive information within these online environments. The structure of social media networks, which prioritizes popularity and engagement measures rather than truthfulness and dependability, unintentionally encourages the dissemination of exaggerated or unconfirmed content. Furthermore, the emergence of algorithm-driven internet search engines has led to intellectual seclusion due to algorithms (which make assumptions based on users' selections) and echo chambers† formed by users, wherein they are primarily exposed to information that conforms to their existing beliefs and preferences. This selective exposure reinforces preconceived ideas and contributes to societal polarization, as dissenting perspectives are increasingly marginalized or disregarded. Additionally, the anonymity and perceived distance provided by online interactions empower individuals to spread misinformation or engage in harmful behavior without concern for consequences. This trend, combined with the lack of accountability measures inherent in many social networks, creates an environment conducive to the rapid dissemination of falsehoods and the amplification of divisive rhetoric.

Moreover, the business strategies employed by social media corporations, such as targeted advertising based on user data, worsen the spread of misinformation by prioritizing user engagement and attention over the accuracy of content. This commercial focus often encourages sensationalism and clickbait, resulting in an abundance of deceptive or provocative material crafted to attract clicks and shares. As a result, the pervasiveness of misinformation and the decline in trust in social networks have led to widespread discontent among users, who are inundated with contradictory narratives and struggle to distinguish truth from falsehood. This erosion of trust not only diminishes the reliability of social networks as sources of trustworthy information but also presents significant societal obstacles, including the deterioration of democratic dialogue, the

---

* Misinformation is false information spread without bad intent, while disinformation is false information deliberately created and spread to mislead and manipulate.
† An echo chamber is a media environment that amplifies or reinforces preexisting beliefs inside a closed system, isolating participants from opposing views.

amplification of societal fractures, and the undermining of public health endeavors.

In summary, the evolution of social networks into environments ripe with misinformation and discontent is a complex occurrence influenced by a combination of technological, social, and economic elements. Tackling these issues necessitates a collaborative endeavor involving stakeholders from various fields to redefine the purpose of social networks in fostering informed discussions, enhancing digital literacy, and protecting the credibility of online engagements.‡

Chapter 1 endnote references§

---

‡ Mass polarization, or popular polarization, occurs when an electorate's attitudes toward political issues, policies, celebrities, or other citizens are neatly divided along party lines.
§ How to Protect Against Disinformation on Social Media, https://us.norton.com/blog/emerging-threats/election-disinformation-and-social-media; MIT Research Finds Shifting Attention to Accuracy Can Reduce Spread of Fake News, https://mitsloan.mit.edu/press/what-can-be-done-to-reduce-spread-fake-news-mit-sloan-research-finds-shifting-peoples-attention-toward-accuracy-can-decrease-online-misinformation-sharing; How to Combat Fake News and Disinformation, www.brookings.edu/articles/how-to-combat-fake-news-and-disinformation/; Wikipedia: Social Network, https://en.wikipedia.org/wiki/Social_network; Britannica: Network Sociology, www.britannica.com/topic/network-sociology.

CHAPTER 2

The Rise of Social Media

A Global Phenomenon

Social media has transformed the way people connect, communicate, and share information. Some key insights about its rise and dominance include its profound impact on shaping public discourse, its ability to democratize access to information and amplify diverse voices, and its role in reshaping traditional notions of privacy and personal expression.

Global social networks

Early Beginnings

At the core, the features that define a social media platform are (i) profiles for users, (ii) the ability for users to upload content constantly, and (iii) the ability for users to discuss content and connect with other users.

The journey of social media began in the early 2000s. Myspace, launched on August 1, 2003, was the pioneer, reaching a million monthly active users around 2004. This milestone marked the birth of social media as is known presently (in 2024). Other platforms like Facebook, YouTube, and Reddit followed suit, each with its unique trajectory.

Facebook, created in 2004 by Mark Zuckerberg with four other Harvard College students and roommates Eduardo Saverin, Andrew McCollum, Dustin Moskovitz, and Chris Hughes, remains the largest social media platform in the world. Facebook had 3.07 billion users in early 2024. Other social media platforms, including YouTube and WhatsApp, also had over one billion users each.

These numbers are high: as of January 2024, there were 5.35 billion internet users worldwide, which amounted to 66.2 percent of the global population. Of this total, 5.04 billion, or 62.3 percent of the world's population, were social media users. This means social media platforms more than two-thirds of all internet users.

Social media has changed the world. The rapid and vast adoption of these technologies is changing how some people find partners, access information from the news, and organize to demand political change.

Social Media Started in the Early 2000s

There were, of course, earlier, much smaller predecessors of social networking websites. The first recognizable social media site, in the format we know presently, was Six Degrees—a platform created in 1997 that enabled users to upload a profile and make friends with other users. It was followed by more successful sites based on the *social-circles network model* such as Friendster, Myspace, LinkedIn, XING, and Facebook.

While some large social media sites, such as Facebook, YouTube, and Reddit, have been around for ten or more years, others are much newer.

TikTok, for example, launched in September 2016. By mid-2018, it had already reached half a billion users. To put this in perspective: TikTok gained, on average, about 20 million new users per month over this period.

Once-dominant platforms have disappeared. In 2008, Hi5, Myspace, and Friendster were close competitors to Facebook, yet by 2012 they had virtually no market share. The case of Myspace is remarkable, considering that in 2006 it temporarily surpassed Google as the most visited website in the United States.

Most social media platforms that survived the last decade have shifted significantly in what they offer users. Twitter, for example, didn't allow users to upload videos or images initially. Since 2011 this has been possible, and in 2024, more than 50 percent of the content viewed on Twitter (X) includes images and videos.

Facebook dominated the social media market for a decade. With more than three billion users, Facebook continues to be the most popular social media platform in 2024 followed by YouTube (2.7 billion), Instagram (2.3 billion), WhatsApp (2 billion), and WeChat (1.3 billion). One can find more detailed information on this topic online at www.statistista .com.

Social Media Diversity

The social media landscape is diverse, with several platforms enjoying widespread popularity. Some of the most prevalent social media platforms include:

1. **Facebook:** despite facing some challenges, Facebook remains one of the most widely used social media platforms globally. It offers a range of features, including social networking, messaging, and content sharing.
2. **Instagram:** owned by Facebook, Instagram has grown rapidly in popularity, especially among younger demographics. It focuses on photo and video sharing, with features like stories and reels.
3. **X (Twitter)** remains a popular platform for real-time news updates, discussions, and networking. Its character-limited format encourages concise communication and has become a key tool for public figures, journalists, and organizations.
4. **LinkedIn** is widely used for professional networking, job searching, and career development. It is particularly popular among professionals, recruiters, and businesses for networking and recruitment purposes.

5. **YouTube** is the leading platform for video content, offering a vast range of videos on various topics, including entertainment, education, and tutorials. It has a significant user base in developed countries for both content consumption and creation.

6. **Snapchat** is known for its ephemeral messaging features, including disappearing photos and videos. It is popular among younger demographics for casual communication and sharing moments.

7. **TikTok** has quickly risen in popularity, especially among younger generations, for short-form video content. Its algorithm-driven feed and creative tools have contributed to its rapid growth.

In China, the most prevalent social media platforms are primarily domestically developed because of government restrictions on foreign platforms. **WeChat**, operated by **Tencent**, is one of the most popular social media apps, offering messaging, social networking, and payment services. **Weibo** is another widely used Chinese microblogging platform.

In Russia, **VKontakte** is a dominant social media platform, often compared to Facebook. It offers similar features such as messaging, social networking, and content sharing. Additionally, **Odnoklassniki** (OK.ru) is popular, especially among older demographics, and **Telegram**, a messaging app, has gained significant traction.

These platforms are often used for various purposes, including social networking, content creation and consumption, communication, and professional networking, reflecting the diverse ways people engage with social media in developed countries.

Who Uses Social Media?

Some social media sites are particularly popular among specific population groups. The aggregate numbers mask heterogeneity across user demographics.

The following two diagrams present a distribution of social media usage by age groups. The age percentages are estimates based on various studies and surveys conducted on social media usage patterns across different age groups. These figures can vary based on factors such as geographic location, socioeconomic status, and individual preferences. Additionally, the popularity of specific platforms among different age groups may change over time with the introduction of new technologies and shifts in cultural norms.

Uses of social media around the world vary widely depending on regional preferences. For Snapchat and Instagram, the *age gradient* is exceptionally steep—the popularity of these platforms drops much faster with age. Most people under 25 use Snapchat (73%), while only 3 percent of people over 65 use it. Since these platforms are relatively new, it is hard to know how much of this age gradient results from a *cohort effect*. In other words, it is unclear whether today's young people will continue using Snapchat as they age. If they do, the age gradient will narrow. For some platforms, the gender differences are substantial. The share of women who used Pinterest was three times as high as that of men using this platform. For Reddit, it was the other way around: the share of men was twice as high.[*]

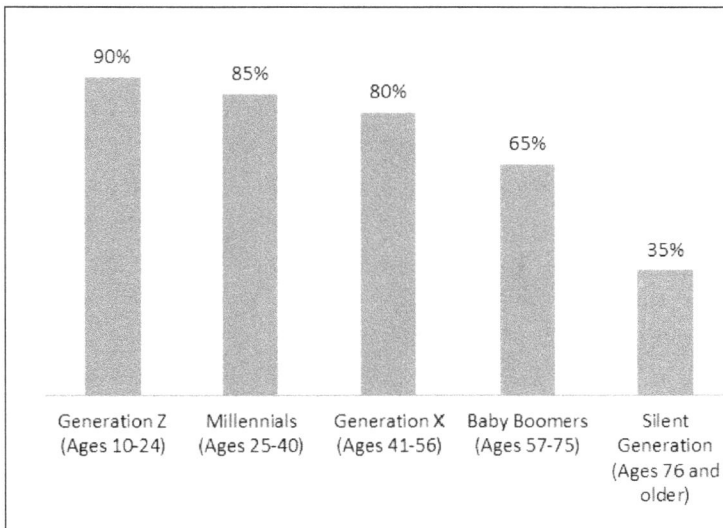

Percent of users within the whole user population

---

[*] The distribution of age groups varies significantly across countries and regions and has changed over time as countries go through demographic transitions.

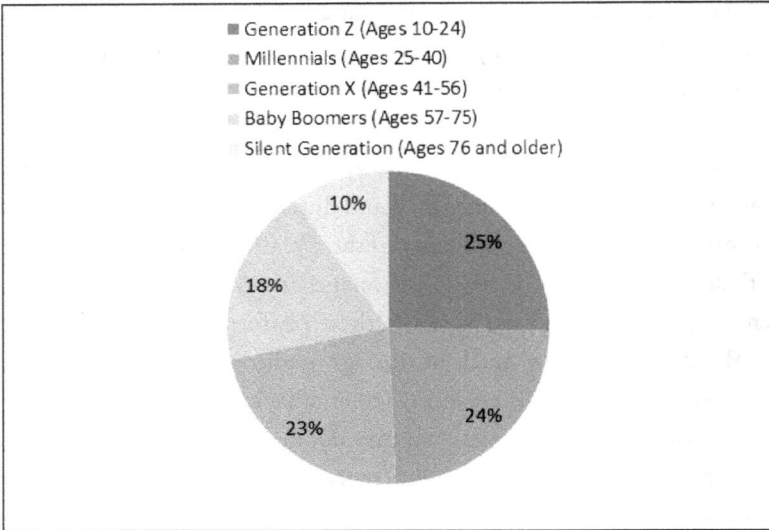

Legend:
- Generation Z (Ages 10-24)
- Millennials (Ages 25-40)
- Generation X (Ages 41-56)
- Baby Boomers (Ages 57-75)
- Silent Generation (Ages 76 and older)

Pie chart values: 25%, 24%, 23%, 18%, 10%

Percent of users within each age group population

In rich countries where access to the internet is nearly universal, the vast majority of young adults use it. For example, the average for the OECD (Organization for Economic Cooperation and Developmen) is close to 90 percent. *[OECD stands for the Organization for Economic Cooperation and Development, an international alliance of governments that works to promote economic growth, prosperity, and sustainable development]*

If today's young adults continue using social media throughout their lives, then it is likely that social media will continue growing rapidly as internet adoption expands throughout lower-income countries.

The rise of social media in rich countries has come together with an increase in the time spent online. The increase in social media worldwide use over the last decade has resulted in a large increase in the time people spend online.

In the United States, adults spend more than six hours daily on digital media (apps and websites accessed through mobile phones, tablets, computers, and other connected devices such as game consoles). This growth has been driven almost entirely by additional time spent on smartphones and tablets.

According to a survey from the Pew Research Center, adults aged 18 to 29 in the United States are more likely to get news indirectly via social media than directly from print newspapers or news sites. They also report being online *almost constantly.*

In the United States, the number of social media users is anticipated to cross 313 million in 2024 with 90 percent of the total U.S. population using social media actively. Facebook is the most popular social media platform in the United States, with 74.2 percent of adults using it. Social media's growth in the United States is comparable—in speed and, to some extent, reach—to most modern communication-enabling technologies, including computers, smartphones, and the internet.

The rise of social media is an extraordinary example of how quickly and drastically social behaviors can change: something that is today part of the everyday life of one-third of the world population was unthinkable less than a generation ago. Rapid changes like those brought about by social media always spark fears about possible negative effects. Specifically, in the context of social media, a key question is whether these new communication technologies are harming our mental health (see endnote references—Our World in Data).

In summary, social media's impact is profound, shaping how some people partner, access news, and advocate for change. From Myspace to TikTok, the journey continues, connecting billions of people across the globe.

Why People Use Social Networks

Below is a breakdown of why people use social networks across different age groups:

1. **Generation Z (ages 10 to 24):**[†]
   - **Social connection:** Generation Z primarily uses social networks to connect with friends, classmates, and peers. They value platforms that facilitate instant communication and enable them to share experiences and interact with others in real time.

[†] The specific year range is sometimes contested, but various online sources give the year range starting in 1997 to 2012.

- **Self-expression:** social media serves as a platform for Generation Z to express themselves creatively through posts, photos, videos, and memes.[‡] They seek validation and feedback from their online communities, shaping their identities in the digital realm.
- **Entertainment:** Generation Z engages with social networks as a source of entertainment, consuming viral content, following influencers, and participating in challenges and trends on platforms like TikTok and Snapchat.

2. **Millennials (ages 25 to 40):**[§]
   - **Networking:** Millennials use social networks for professional networking and career advancement. Platforms like LinkedIn are popular among this demographic for connecting with colleagues, recruiters, and industry professionals.
   - **Information sharing:** Millennials utilize social media to share updates about their lives, such as milestones, achievements, and travel experiences. They also use platforms like Facebook and Twitter to stay informed about current events, news, and trends.
   - **Social activism:** many Millennials are passionate about social causes and use social media to raise awareness, advocate for change, and mobilize support for various issues such as climate change, social justice, and human rights.

3. **Generation X (ages 41 to 56):**[¶]
   - **Keeping in touch:** Generation X values social networks as a means of staying connected with family members, old friends, and acquaintances. They use platforms like Facebook to share updates about their lives, communicate with loved ones, and reminisce about past experiences.

[‡] Memes are a form of cultural transmission that spread rapidly online, often through social media platforms. They can take various forms such as images, videos, GIFs, and viral sensations.

[§] Millennials are people who were born between 1981 and 1996.

[¶] Generation X refers to people born between the mid-1960s and about 1980.

- **Professional development:** Generation X professionals utilize social media for career-related purposes, such as job hunting, skill development, and industry networking. They may also use platforms like Twitter to follow thought leaders and stay updated on industry news and trends.

4. **Baby Boomers (ages 57 to 75):****
- **Family communication:** Baby Boomers often use social networks to keep in touch with family members, particularly those who live far away. They share photos, updates, and messages with loved ones, fostering a sense of closeness and connection.
- **Information sharing:** Baby Boomers utilize social media to share news articles, recipes, health tips, and other useful information with their social circles. They may also engage with community groups and forums to exchange advice and support with peers.

5. **Silent Generation (ages 76 and older):**††
- **Family connection:** members of the Silent Generation use social networks to connect with family members, especially grandchildren and great-grandchildren. They enjoy seeing photos and updates from loved ones and may use platforms like Facebook to send birthday wishes and share memories.
- **Community engagement:** some members of the Silent Generation participate in online communities and forums related to their hobbies, interests, and pastimes. They may join groups dedicated to topics such as gardening, knitting, or genealogy, where they can connect with like-minded individuals and share advice and experiences.

In summary, reasons for using social networks are based on common motivations observed among different age groups, but individual preferences and behaviors may vary. Additionally, technological literacy,

---

** Baby Boomers are people born between 1946 and 1964.
†† The Silent Generation refers to people born between 1928 and 1945, following the Greatest Generation and preceding the Baby Boomers.

cultural norms, and personal experiences can influence how individuals engage with social media across different age demographics.

Year	Users (billions)	Globally, people spend an average of 2 hours and 23 minutes per day on social media platforms, primarily on mobile devices (98% of usage time). The most popular activities include watching videos, reading news, and interacting with friends and family.
2017	2.80	
2024	5.16	
2027	5.84 (projected)	

Growth of social media users globally over the past decade

Chapter 2 endnote references[‡‡]

‡‡ 1. Countries with high GDP per capita are often considered richer and more developed. This metric divides a country's GDP by its population, providing a per-person income figure. Higher GDP per capita typically indicates greater prosperity.

2. Digital media contrasts with print media (including books, newspapers, and magazines) and other traditional or analog media (including TV, movies, and radio).

3. According to a survey from Pew Research, 36 percent of adults 18 to 29 in the United States say they "often get news via social media," which is higher than the share saying they "often get news via other platforms," such as news sites, TV, radio or print newspapers. From the same survey, we also know that 48 percent of adults 18 to 29 say they go online almost constantly, and 46 percent say they go online multiple times daily.

4. Esteban Ortiz-Ospina (2019)—"The Rise of Social Media" Published online at OurWorldInData.org; Statista.com (Worldwide digital population 2024 Published by Ani Petrosyan, Jan 31, 2024); Canadians' assessments of social media in their lives (statcan.gc.ca).

Social Media and Wellbeing, https://ourworldindata.org/social-media-wellbeing; Facebook Statistics, www.demandsage.com/facebook-statistics/; Data and Statistics: www.demandsage.com/category/data-statistics/; Instagram Statistics: www.statista.com/topics/1882/instagram/#dossier-chapter2; Mobile Social Network Statistic, www.statista.com/topics/2478/mobile-social-networks/#topicOverview; YouTube User Statistics, www.globalmediainsight.com/blog/youtube-users-statistics/; WeChat Statistics, www.usesignhouse.com/blog/wechat-stats.

CHAPTER 3

Most Common Social Networks

In this chapter, we review the history, usage, and evolution of prevalent social media platforms.

As of January 2024, some of the most common social networking platforms include (in alphabetical order):

Facebook	A widely used platform for personal and business connections, offering various features like sharing updates, photos, and videos.
Instagram	Popular for sharing photos and short videos, known for its visual-centric approach.
LinkedIn	Primarily used for professional networking and job searching.
Pinterest	Used for discovering and saving ideas, particularly visual content.
Reddit	A community-driven platform with various forums (subreddits) for discussions on diverse topics.
Snapchat	Known for its ephemeral content, especially among younger users.
TikTok	Gained popularity for short-form, creative videos, and trends.
WhatsApp	A messaging app with a large global user base.
X (Twitter)	Focused on real-time updates, discussions, and short-form content.
YouTube	A video-sharing platform with a vast user base for uploading and watching videos.

Some less common or niche social networking platforms include:

Diaspora	A decentralized social network emphasizing user control over their data and privacy.
Ello	Positioned as an ad-free alternative to mainstream platforms, focusing on creative and artistic communities.
Goodreads	Geared toward book enthusiasts, providing a platform for readers to share book recommendations and reviews.
Mastodon	A decentralized social network with a focus on user privacy and control is often used as an alternative to Twitter.

(Continued)

(*Continued*)

MeWe	Promotes itself as a privacy-focused alternative to mainstream platforms, offering ad-free experiences.
Nextdoor	Focused on local communities, allowing neighbors to connect and share information.
Quora	While primarily a question-and-answer platform, it has social networking elements where users can follow topics and engage in discussions.
Ravelry	Geared toward the knitting and fiber arts community, providing a platform for sharing projects, patterns, and ideas.
Steemit	Built on blockchain technology, users are rewarded with cryptocurrency for creating and curating content.
Vero	An ad-free social network emphasizing user privacy and chronological content presentation.

News consumption on social media

% of U.S. adults who get news from social media ...

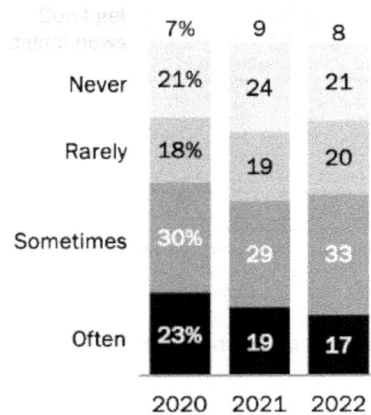

	2020	2021	2022
Don't get digital news	7%	9	8
Never	21%	24	21
Rarely	18%	19	20
Sometimes	30%	29	33
Often	23%	19	17

Note: Figures may not add up to 100% due to rounding.
Source: Survey of U.S. adults conducted July 18-Aug. 21, 2022.

PEW RESEARCH CENTER

News consumption on social media

Facebook Messenger: A Social Media Pioneer

Facebook logo

As a globally renowned social networking platform, Facebook has significantly transformed the landscape of online communication and social interaction since its inception. Founded by Mark Zuckerberg along with his college roommates Eduardo Saverin, Andrew McCollum, Dustin Moskovitz, and Chris Hughes in February 2004, Facebook emerged from the dormitories of Harvard University with the initial purpose of connecting college students. Its rapid growth and evolution over the years have led to its prominence as one of the most influential companies in the technology sector. Facebook, the world's largest social networking platform, has evolved from a Harvard dorm room project to a global phenomenon with billions of users worldwide.

Founding and Early Years (2004 to 2006)

Mark Zuckerberg, then a sophomore at Harvard, launched *TheFacebook* as a platform exclusively for Harvard students. The website's popularity quickly spread to other Ivy League institutions and eventually expanded to universities across the United States and Canada. In June 2004, the domain name was changed to *facebook.com*, reflecting its broader appeal beyond Harvard. The platform's interface allowed users to create personal profiles, connect with friends, and share messages and photos within their network. In September 2006, Facebook opened its platform to anyone aged 13 and older with a valid email address, fueling its rapid growth and global expansion.

Expansion and Global Reach (2006 to 2010)

The introduction of the News Feed in September 2006 transformed the way users consumed content on the platform, providing a personalized stream of updates from friends, family, and pages they followed. Facebook further expanded its offerings with the introduction of features such as photo sharing, events, groups, and messaging, solidifying its position as a comprehensive social networking platform.

Strategic partnerships and investments further fueled its expansion, including a $240 million investment from Microsoft in 2007, valuing the company at $15 billion. Facebook's international expansion began in 2008, with localized versions launched in various countries, marking the beginning of its global reach.

As Facebook's user base grew the platform introduced new features and functionalities to enhance user experience and engagement.

Monetization and Innovation (2010 to 2015)

The early 2010s witnessed Facebook's focus on monetization, introducing targeted advertising and sponsored content to generate revenue. The company went public in May 2012, with one of the most anticipated initial public offerings (IPOs) in history, raising $16 billion and valuing the company at over $100 billion.

The IPO provided Facebook with the financial resources to pursue strategic acquisitions and investments, including the landmark acquisition of Instagram in April 2012 for approximately $1 billion and WhatsApp in 2014*, expanding its portfolio and user base.

Facebook also prioritized monetization efforts, introducing advertising solutions such as sponsored posts, targeted ads, and promoted content to generate revenue from its massive user base.

Diversification and Challenges (2015 to 2018)

In subsequent years, Facebook diversified its offerings and expanded its reach into new areas, including virtual reality (VR), artificial intelligence (AI), and

---

* Facebook acquired WhatsApp for $19 billion in cash and stock in February 2014.

messaging services. The acquisition of Oculus VR in March 2014 signaled Facebook's entry into the burgeoning VR market, while the launch of the Messenger Platform and WhatsApp Business demonstrated its commitment to providing communication solutions for businesses and individuals.

However, this period also saw Facebook facing increasing scrutiny and criticism regarding privacy concerns, data breaches, and its role in spreading misinformation and fake news. These challenges prompted regulatory investigations and calls for increased oversight of the platform.

Focus on Privacy and Community (2018 to Present)

In response to criticism and concerns about privacy and data security, Facebook has prioritized initiatives to enhance user privacy, transparency, and community well-being. The introduction of features such as Privacy Checkup, Off-Facebook Activity, and Clear History allows users to control their privacy settings and manage their data more effectively.

Facebook also implemented measures to combat misinformation, hate speech, and harmful content on its platform, including the establishment of independent oversight boards and partnerships with fact-checking organizations.

Recent Developments

In 2021, the company rebranded itself as Meta Platforms, reflecting its broader focus on building the metaverse and advancing VR technologies.

In response to mounting pressure, Facebook has taken steps to address concerns regarding privacy and misinformation, implementing stricter policies, and investing in technologies to improve content moderation and data protection.

As Facebook continues to evolve and innovate, its impact on society, communication, and technology remains profound, shaping the way people connect and interact in the digital age.

Facebook's Positive Outlook

The future positive outlook for **Facebook** includes a blend of technological innovation, connectivity, and ambitious goals.

Some of the key aspects of Facebook's future positive outlook include:

- Internet.org, Facebook's initiative to bring online services to underserved areas, has expanded significantly. The company released open-source blueprints for telecommunications infrastructure and is testing Terragraph, which delivers data 10 times faster than existing Wi-Fi networks.
- Aquila, a project to design, build, and launch an aircraft that beams down Internet access from 65,000 feet, could have been a game-changer. It was stopped in 2018.

Facebook has also invested in the following:

- Augmented Reality (AR): Facebook has made several announcements about its ambitions for AR and VR through new product launches, research, and funding opportunities.
- VR: Facebook has invested in developing technology for the future of VR, including developing a brain–computer interface that will let people type with just their minds.
- AI: Facebook is investing in AI to create a more connected world and is building new technology for the future of AR/VR, including speech and audio AI.

Facebook's long-term goal is to transition into a metaverse company rather than a social media company, and investments in AI and VR are a step toward that goal.

Facebook's Negative Outlook

Despite its widespread popularity, Facebook is facing several challenges:

1. **Privacy concerns:**
   - Facebook has been embroiled in numerous privacy scandals. The Cambridge Analytica incident, where user data were

harvested without consent, raised serious questions about
Facebook's data protection practices.

- Users worry about their personal information being misused,
leading to growing concerns about privacy and trust.

2. **Misinformation and fake news:**

- Facebook has struggled to combat the spread of
misinformation and fake news on its platform. False
information can influence public opinion, and elections, and
even incite violence.

- The company faces criticism for not doing enough to prevent
the dissemination of harmful content.

3. **Mental health impact:**

- Research on the impact of social media, including Facebook,
on mental health has yielded mixed results. While some
studies find no significant negative effects, others link
excessive social media use to feelings of loneliness, anxiety,
and depression.

- The platform's addictive nature and constant comparison
with others' curated lives can contribute to mental health
issues.

4. **Political polarization:**

- Facebook's algorithms prioritize content based on user
engagement. This unintentionally creates echo chambers,
reinforcing users' existing beliefs and contributing to
political polarization.

- The platform has been criticized for amplifying extreme
views and dividing society.

5. **Regulatory scrutiny:**

- Governments worldwide are scrutinizing Facebook's
practices. Antitrust investigations, calls for breaking up the
company, and demands for more transparency are mounting.

- Stricter regulations could impact Facebook's business model
and operations.

6. **Declining user engagement:**
   - Some reports suggest that younger users are shifting away from Facebook in favor of other platforms like Instagram, TikTok, and Snapchat.
   - Maintaining user engagement and relevance is crucial for Facebook's long-term success.

What Might Trigger the Decline of Facebook?

Several factors that could potentially contribute to the decline of Facebook include:

- Changing user preferences: if users shift toward other platforms that better align with evolving preferences or values, it could impact Facebook's user base.
- Privacy concerns: ongoing concerns about user privacy and data security may lead to a decline in user trust and usage. Changes in privacy policies, such as Apple's move to require iPhone users to consent to being tracked by advertisers, have also had a significant impact on Facebook's advertising revenue
- Competition: increased competition from emerging platforms that offer unique features or address specific needs could draw users away from Facebook.
- Regulatory changes: stringent regulations or legal challenges related to privacy, antitrust, or other issues could affect Facebook's operations.
- Technological shifts: rapid advancements in technology, such as the rise of new communication mediums, could alter the landscape of social networking.
- Leadership changes: changes in leadership or corporate strategy may influence the platform's direction and user engagement.
- Increased distrust: Facebook has faced numerous scandals and criticisms over the years, which have led to a growing distrust

of the platform. This includes issues related to data privacy, misinformation, and the company's handling of user data.

- Increased discord: the platform has been criticized for its role in spreading misinformation and fostering negative discourse. This has led some users to leave the platform in search of more positive online environments.
- Increased disinterest: with the rise of other social media platforms like TikTok, users, particularly younger demographics, may be shifting their attention away from Facebook. This could lead to a decline in user engagement and, consequently, advertising revenue.

Facebook's Future Outlook

Facebook, now known as Meta, has been a dominant force in the social media landscape for over a decade. As it approaches three billion monthly active users (MAU), the future of Facebook is a topic of intense interest.

User Growth

Facebook's user base continues to grow, albeit at a decelerating rate. In 2022, Facebook's global MAU had increased by 6.2 percent. However, experts predict that Facebook's user growth rate will decrease to 0.7 percent in 2024 and further slow to 0.6 percent in 2025. This deceleration is not surprising given that nearly 6 in 10 people aged 13 and above outside of China already use Facebook every month.

In the United States, the number of Facebook users is forecasted to increase by 5.04 percent between 2024 and 2028. Globally, Facebook's reach is projected to grow to 75.79 percent of people around the world by 2027.

Revenue Streams

Facebook's primary revenue stream is advertising. In 2020, advertising revenue was $84.169 billion, a 21 percent increase from the previous year. However, Facebook's revenue growth has been slowing. In the first quarter of 2023, total revenue was expected to be in the range of $26 to $28.5 billion, potentially marking a drop from the second quarter of 2021, when sales came in at $29.1 billion.

The average revenue per user (ARPU) varies significantly by geography. In the third quarter of 2021, ARPU in the United States and Canada was USD 52.34, in Europe it was USD 16.50, in Asia-Pacific, it was USD 4.30, and for the *Rest of the World*, it was USD 3.14.

Conclusion

In conclusion, while Facebook's user growth is slowing, it still maintains a steady increase. The platform's revenue growth is also decelerating, but it continues to generate substantial income from advertising. The future of Facebook will likely depend on its ability to innovate and adapt to changing market conditions, as well as its success in monetizing its vast user base. The company's recent rebranding to Meta and its focus on the metaverse indicate its ambition to remain at the forefront of technological innovation. However, only time will tell if these strategies will ensure its continued growth and relevance in the ever-evolving digital landscape.

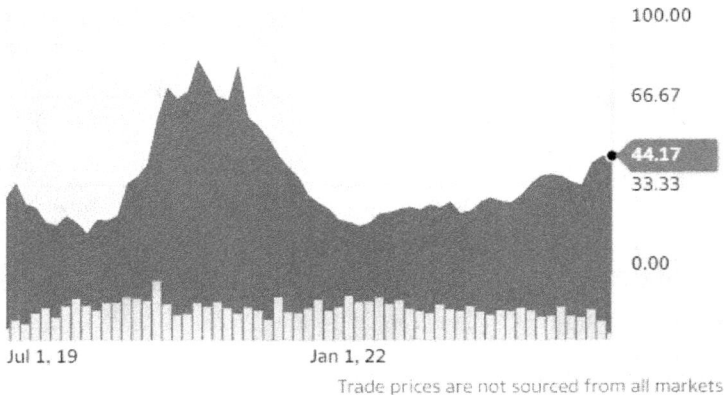

Meta share price fluctuation over the past five years

However, predicting the future of such a large and complex platform is inherently uncertain.

Facebook endnote references[†]

[†] These URLs present an overview of Facebook, tips and tricks for using its features effectively, important statistics about Facebook's user base and engagement, guides on leveraging Facebook for business marketing and branding, as well as best practices for businesses utilizing the platform. They provide a comprehensive understanding of Facebook's capabilities and usage.

Title: "Facebook—Wikipedia," https://en.wikipedia.org/wiki/Facebook; Title: "Facebook Tips and Tricks You Should Know," www.cnet.com/tech/services-and-software/facebook-tips-and-tricks/; Title: "37 Facebook Stats That Matter to Marketers in 2023," https://blog.hootsuite.com/facebook-statistics/; Title: "How to Use Facebook for Business: 12 Facebook Marketing Tips," www.businessinsider.com/guides/tech/facebook; Title: "How to Use Facebook for Business: The Complete Guide www.socialmediaexaminer.com/how-to-use-facebook-for-business/. Data Sources as of July 2024 (1) "Facebook at 20: All Grown Up With 3 Billion Users - Statista," www.statista.com/chart/5380/facebook-user-engagement/. (2) "Digital 2022: The Potential Future of Facebook—DataReportal," https://datareportal.com/reports/digital-2022-future-of-facebook. (3) "Facebook User Growth (2021–2025)—Oberlo," www.oberlo.com/statistics/facebook-user-growth. (4) "Global Social Networks Growth 2025 | Statista," www.statista.com/statistics/1401614/global-social-media-growth/; (5) "How Does Facebook Make Money? Here's 8 Revenue Streams," https://expertbeacon.com/how-does-facebook-make-money/. (6) "Meta—Meta Reports Fourth Quarter and Full Year 2021 Results—Facebook," https://investor.fb.com/investor-news/press-release-details/2022/Meta-Reports-Fourth-Quarter-and-Full-Year-2021-Results/default.aspx. (7) "Track Facebook Analytics, Future Predictions, & Facebook … - Social Blade," https://socialblade.com/facebook/. (8) "Facebook Reports Fourth Quarter and Full Year 2020 Results," https://investor.fb.com/investor-news/press-release-details/2021/Facebook-Reports-Fourth-Quarter-and-Full-Year-2020-Results/default.aspx. (9) "TikTok to Rank as the Third Largest Social Network, 2022 Forecast Notes," https://techcrunch.com/2021/12/20/tiktok-to-rank-as-the-third-largest-social-network-2022-forecast-notes/.

Instagram: An Ubiquitous Photo-Sharing Platform

Instagram logo

Instagram, a leading photo and video-sharing social networking platform, has captivated users worldwide with its visually immersive experience and emphasis on storytelling since its inception.

Founded by Kevin Systrom and Mike Krieger in October 2010, Instagram has undergone a remarkable journey from its humble beginnings to becoming a cultural phenomenon and an indispensable tool for self-expression, community-building, and digital marketing.

A Snapshot of Instagram's Evolution

Instagram, the ubiquitous photo-sharing platform, has become an integral part of digital lives. Instagram's journey began with Kevin Systrom, a Stanford graduate who previously worked at Google. His initial creation, Burbn, was named after his affinity for whiskey and bourbon. Inspired by location-based platforms like Foursquare, Burbn allowed users to post check-ins along with photos—a novel concept at the time. However, it lacked the visual focus that would later define Instagram. Enter Mike Krieger, another Stanford graduate with experience in social media platforms. Systrom and Krieger joined forces, reworking Burbn into a streamlined app centered around mobile photography. They embraced minimalism, emphasizing images, comments, and the revolutionary *liking* feature. The duo opted for an iOS app, capitalizing on the iPhone 4's improved photographic capabilities.

In July 2010, Instagram's first photos graced the platform, and it officially launched on October 6, 2010. Remarkably, it garnered 25,000 users on its very first day, setting the stage for what would become a global phenomenon.

Rapid Growth and Acquisition

Instagram's ascent was meteoric. Within three months, it boasted one million users—a feat that left the tech world astounded.

In April 2012, the game-changing moment arrived: Facebook Inc. acquired Instagram for approximately $1 billion in cash and stock. This strategic move solidified Instagram's position as a social media power-house making it one of the world's largest social networks.

Under Facebook's ownership, Instagram continued to innovate and expand its features, introducing video sharing in June 2013 and launching the Explore tab to discover new content and accounts. The platform's user base expanded rapidly beyond the United States, with international users playing an increasingly significant role in shaping Instagram's cultural impact.

Monetization and Diversification (2015 to 2018)

As Instagram's user base surpassed 500 million MAU in June 2016, the platform shifted its focus toward monetization and revenue generation. Sponsored content, influencer marketing, and native advertising became integral components of Instagram's business model, offering brands and businesses unprecedented access to highly engaged audiences.

The introduction of features such as Instagram Stories in August 2016, direct messaging, and shopping capabilities further enhanced the platform's appeal and utility for both users and advertisers. By June 2018, Instagram's user base had skyrocketed to **one billion**. The app's visual appeal, user-friendly interface, and addictive features fueled its exponential growth.

Integration of New Features and IGTV (2018 to 2022)

Instagram continued to evolve and innovate, introducing new features and functionalities to enhance user engagement and diversify its offerings. IGTV, launched in June 2018, provided users with a platform for long-form vertical video content, competing directly with platforms like You-Tube and Snapchat. The platform also prioritized initiatives to promote authenticity, well-being, and community safety, implementing measures to combat cyberbullying, harmful content, and misinformation.

IGTV, short for Instagram TV, was a standalone video application by Instagram for Android and iOS smartphones. It allowed for longer videos compared to Instagram feeds. IGTV was available as a stand-alone app, though basic functionality was also available within the Instagram app and website.

On 1 March 2022, Instagram's parent company, Meta, announced the shutdown of IGTV, due to their focus on Instagram Reels.

As Instagram navigates the dynamic landscape of social media and digital culture, its influence continues to resonate across industries, from fashion and beauty to travel, food, and entertainment. The platform's emphasis on visual storytelling, creativity, and community engagement has made it a preferred destination for individuals, brands, and content creators alike.

With ongoing investments in AR, e-commerce, and video content, Instagram is poised to remain a dominant force in the social media landscape, shaping trends, conversations, and cultural movements for years to come.

Some of the benefits of using Instagram

1. **Visual storytelling**: Instagram is a powerful platform for visual storytelling. Users can share their experiences, adventures, and daily moments through captivating photos and videos. Whether it is a scenic landscape, a delicious meal, or a candid snapshot, Instagram allows users to express themselves creatively.

2. **Connectivity**: Instagram fosters connections among people worldwide. Users can follow friends, family, celebrities, and brands, staying updated on their lives, interests, and activities. The platform bridges geographical gaps and brings people closer together.

3. **Business promotion**: for businesses, Instagram offers a dynamic marketing channel. Brands can showcase their products, services, and company culture. Features like Instagram Shopping and sponsored posts enable direct interaction with potential customers.

4. **Influencer culture**: Instagram has given rise to influencers—individuals who build substantial followings based on their expertise, lifestyle, or niche. Influencers collaborate with brands, promote products, and shape trends, creating a symbiotic relationship.

5. **Creativity and inspiration**: the platform inspires creativity. Users explore diverse content, from art and fashion to travel and fitness. Instagram's filters, *Stories*, and *Reels* encourage experimentation, allowing users to express themselves uniquely.

Instagram Stories and Reels

Instagram Stories and Reels are two prominent features within the Instagram platform, both serving as powerful tools for users to share engaging content with their followers.

Instagram Stories

Instagram Stories are short-lived, ephemeral posts that disappear after 24 hours. They appear at the top of a user's feed in a horizontal bar and are represented by profile icons. Users can post a combination of photos, videos, text, stickers, and interactive elements such as polls, questions, and countdowns to their Stories. These posts allow for creative expression and spontaneity, often capturing moments from everyday life candidly and authentically. Users can also apply various filters, effects, and AR features to enhance their Stories. Additionally, Instagram offers features like Highlights, which allow users to save their Stories beyond 24 hours, and Stories Archive, which automatically saves all posted Stories for future reference.

Instagram Reels

Instagram Reels, introduced in August 2020, are short-form video clips of up to 60 seconds in length. They are displayed in a dedicated Reels tab on a user's profile and are also featured in the Explore feed, making them highly discoverable by a broader audience. Reels are designed for creative expression and storytelling, enabling users to showcase their talents, skills, and creativity through various editing tools such as audio tracks, effects, text overlays, and AR filters. Users can create Reels by recording video clips directly within the Instagram app or by uploading prerecorded videos from their device's gallery. Similar to Stories, Reels offers a wide range of editing options to personalize content and engage viewers. Additionally, Instagram provides a music library and audio effects to enhance Reels with popular songs and sound bites.

Both Instagram Stories and Reels offer unique opportunities for users to connect with their audience, express themselves creatively, and explore trending content within the platform's vibrant community. While Stories focuses on ephemeral moments and real-time updates, Reels emphasize short-form video content and creative expression, contributing to the diverse and dynamic nature of Instagram's multimedia ecosystem.

Controversies Surrounding Instagram

Despite its immense popularity, Instagram has faced several controversies over the years. Some of the most notable ones include:

1. Privacy concerns:
   - **Data collection**: Instagram collects extensive user data, including location, interests, and browsing habits. Critics argue that this compromises user privacy.
   - **Third-party apps**: unauthorized third-party apps have exploited Instagram's application programming interface (API), leading to data leaks and privacy breaches.
2. Mental health impact:
   - **Image pressure**: Instagram's focus on curated, idealized images can lead to feelings of inadequacy and low self-esteem among users.
   - **Comparison culture**: constant exposure to others' seemingly perfect lives can contribute to anxiety and depression.

3. Cyberbullying and harassment:
   - **Trolling and hate speech**: Instagram battles cyberbullying, but offensive comments and hate speech persist.
   - **Anonymity**: anonymity allows users to harass others without consequences.
4. Algorithmic bias:
   - **Content prioritization**: Instagram's algorithm favors certain content, potentially reinforcing existing biases and excluding marginalized voices.
   - **Shadowbanning**: users have reported being *shadowbanned*, where their content is hidden without clear reasons.
5. Fake news and misinformation:
   - **Spread of false information**: Instagram struggles to combat the spread of fake news, conspiracy theories, and misinformation.
   - **Inadequate fact-checking**: unlike platforms like Facebook, Instagram lacks robust fact-checking mechanisms.
6. Content moderation challenges:
   - **Nudity and violence**: striking a balance between artistic expression and inappropriate content remains a challenge.
   - **Inconsistent policies**: Instagram's content guidelines sometimes lead to uneven enforcement.
7. Influencer marketing and authenticity:
   - **Sponsored posts**: the rise of influencers has blurred the line between genuine content and paid promotions.
   - **Authenticity crisis**: users question whether influencers' lives are authentic or staged.
8. Ownership and monopoly:
   - **Facebook acquisition**: Instagram's acquisition by Facebook raised antitrust concerns.
   - **Dominance**: Facebook's control over Instagram and WhatsApp creates a social media monopoly.

What Might Trigger the Decline of Instagram?

Predicting the exact factors that could lead to the decline or transformation of Instagram is speculative, and outcomes may be influenced by various elements. However, potential triggers for the end of Instagram could include:

1. **Changing user preferences:** if users shift toward platforms offering novel features or addressing emerging trends that Instagram fails to adapt to.
2. **Privacy concerns:** increased concerns about user privacy, data security, or mishandling of information could erode user trust and impact Instagram's popularity.
3. **Competition:** growing competition from emerging platforms with unique offerings might attract users away from Instagram.
4. **Technological advances:** rapid technological changes that introduce new communication mediums or ways of sharing content could alter user preferences.
5. **Regulatory challenges:** stringent regulations or legal issues related to privacy, antitrust, or other matters may affect Instagram's operations.
6. **Monetization challenges:** if Instagram faces difficulties in maintaining a profitable and sustainable business model, it could impact its long-term viability.

Instagram's Future Outlook

Instagram, a social media platform with over 1.2 billion MAU, has been a significant player in the digital world. Its future seems promising, considering its user growth and revenue stream predictions.

User Growth

Instagram's user base is expected to grow at 6.5 percent in 2024, before slowing to 4.7 percent in 2025. This deceleration follows a similar pattern impacting other major social media platforms. By 2025, it has been forecast that there will be 1.44 billion MAU of the social media platform. This indicates a steady growth in Instagram's user base, which is a positive sign for its future.

The platform's popularity is not just limited to Instagram alone. A large number of users use it alongside other social media platforms such as Facebook (80.8 percent), YouTube (77.4 percent), and TikTok (52.8 percent). This suggests that Instagram is an integral part of a cross-platform marketing strategy, further solidifying its position in the social media landscape.

Revenue Streams

Instagram's revenue has been on a steady rise. In 2023, Instagram was projected to generate an estimated $23 billion in revenue in the United States alone. This revenue is set to increase to $29 billion in 2025. Boosted by more e-commerce and video ads, Instagram's ad revenue reached more than $26 billion in the United States, up 40 percent from 2020. By 2023, the photo app could account for 61 percent of Meta's ad revenue.

Conclusion

Given these predictions, it looks like Instagram is poised for continued growth in both its user base and revenue streams. The platform's ability to adapt and innovate, coupled with its strong cross-platform presence, suggests a bright future. However, as with any tech company, Instagram must continue to evolve and adapt to changing user behaviors and market trends

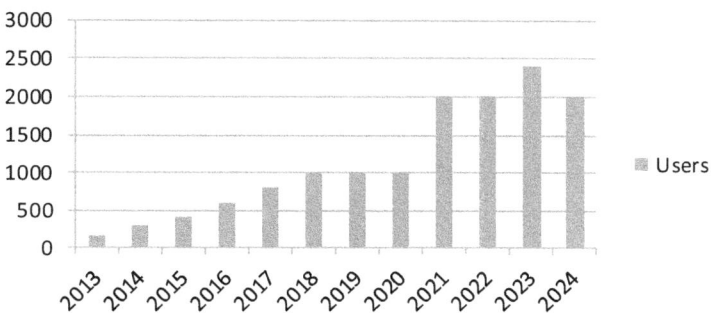

Instagram users (in millions)

to maintain its growth trajectory. It will be interesting to see how Instagram navigates these challenges and opportunities in the coming years.

Instagram endnote references[‡‡]

[‡] These URLs present an overview of Instagram, important statistics about its user base and engagement, tips and tricks for using Instagram features effectively, guides on leveraging Instagram for business marketing and branding, as well as best practices for businesses utilizing the platform. They provide a comprehensive understanding of Instagram's capabilities and usage.

Title: "Instagram—Wikipedia," https://en.wikipedia.org/wiki/Instagram; Title: "37 Instagram Stats That Matter to Marketers in 2023," https://blog.hoot-suite.com/instagram-statistics/; Title: "Instagram Tips and Tricks: How to Get the Most Out of the App," www.cnet.com/tech/mobile/instagram-tips-and-tricks/; Title: "How to Use Instagram for Business: 12 Tips and Strategies," https://www.businessinsider.com/guides/tech/instagram; Title: "How to Use Instagram for Business: A Complete Guide for Beginners," www.socialmediaexaminer.com/how-to-use-instagram-for-business/. Data Sources as of July 2024 https://sproutsocial.com/insights/instagram-stats/; www.oberlo.com/statistics/instagram-user-growth; www.statista.com/statistics/183585/instagram-number-of-global-users/; https://fastercapital.com/content/Instagram-business-model--Decoding-Instagram-s-Revenue-Streams--A-Business-Model-Analysis.html.

LinkedIn: A Digital Space for Professionals

LinkedIn logo

LinkedIn, a professional networking platform, has become an essential tool for individuals and businesses alike, facilitating connections, career advancement, and industry networking since its inception.

Founding and Development

LinkedIn was founded by Reid Hoffman, Allen Blue, Konstantin Guericke, Eric Ly, and Jean-Luc Vaillant in December 2002 and officially launched in May 2003.

LinkedIn has undergone significant growth and evolution, reflecting the changing landscape of professional networking and digital communication.

LinkedIn, one of the oldest social media platforms, has woven itself into the fabric of professional networking.

From Zero to Mega-Giant

- **Profile pages:** on May 5, 2003, LinkedIn officially launched, offering users profile pages akin to digital résumés. These pages allowed professionals to showcase their skills, education, and employment history.
- **Connections**: users formed connections by accepting invitations and building networks that spanned industries and continents.
- **Job postings**: in **2005**, LinkedIn introduced job listings, transforming it into a valuable resource for job seekers and recruiters.

- **Profitability**: after initial slow growth, LinkedIn turned profitable in **2007**. By then, it had over **15 million members**.
- **Global reach**: by **2011**, LinkedIn's membership surpassed **100** million, solidifying its status as a global professional network.

LinkedIn's Notable Milestones

- **LinkedIn premium**: in 2005, the platform introduced premium subscription services, granting users greater control over search features and access to additional perks. To this day, professionals and businesses leverage LinkedIn Premium.

- **Jobs feature:** 2009 witnessed the launch of LinkedIn's Jobs feature, becoming one of the platform's most popular attributes. Job seekers and employers alike found immense value in this tool.
- **Leadership transition**: in the same year, Jeff Weiner assumed the roles of CEO and president, steering LinkedIn toward becoming one of the world's largest online communities.

Microsoft's Acquisition

- In 2018, Microsoft acquired LinkedIn for a staggering $26 billion. Under Microsoft's guidance, LinkedIn's growth and profitability soared.
- According to Statista, by the end of 2023, around 750 million business people use LinkedIn, making it the largest professional social network in the world.

LinkedIn's Unique Niche

LinkedIn's key benefits include:

- **Professional networking:**
  - Connecting with peers: LinkedIn allows building a network of colleagues, industry experts, and potential

collaborators. These connections can lead to valuable opportunities, mentorship, and knowledge sharing.

o Expanding reach: LinkedIn facilitates connecting with professionals beyond their immediate circle, opening doors to new contacts and insights.

- **Career advancement:**
  o Job opportunities: LinkedIn is a powerful job search platform. One can explore job listings, follow companies, and receive personalized job recommendations based on one's profile.
  o Profile enhancement: a well-crafted LinkedIn profile acts as a digital résumé highlighting one's skills, experience, and achievements to attract recruiters and employers.
- **Industry insights and learning:**
  o Following influencers: LinkedIn facilitates staying updated on industry trends by following thought leaders, influencers, and organizations. Their posts and articles provide valuable insights.
  o LinkedIn learning: LinkedIn provides access to a vast library of online courses and tutorials to enhance skills and earn certifications.
- **Brand building and thought leadership:**
  o Publish content: one can share articles, blog posts, and updates related to one's field establishing oneself as an authority in one's domain.
  o Recommendations: LinkedIn users can receive endorsements and recommendations from colleagues. Positive feedback adds credibility to one's profile.
- **Business development and sales:**
  o Company pages: businesses can create company pages to showcase their products, services, and culture. It is an excellent platform for brand visibility.
  o Lead generation: LinkedIn can help identify potential clients, partners, and investors, engage in meaningful conversations, and build professional relationships.

- **Recruitment and talent acquisition:**
  - o Recruit top talent: employers and recruiters can find qualified candidates by posting job openings, searching profiles, and leveraging LinkedIn's recruitment tools.
  - o Employee referrals: LinkedIn can encourage employees to refer candidates which often yields high-quality hires.
- **Networking events and groups:**
  - o Join industry groups: LinkedIn enables sharing knowledge and networking with like-minded professionals.
  - o Events and webinars: one can attend virtual events, webinars, and conferences hosted on LinkedIn. These platforms make possible networking and learning.
- **Visibility and reputation management:**
  - o Search engine optimization: LinkedIn profiles often appear in search engine results. A well-optimized profile enhances one's online visibility.
  - o Professional brand: LinkedIn contributes to one's online reputation, maintaining a positive and professional presence.

LinkedIn Trends

LinkedIn is shaped by several key trends and developments in the professional networking and career development space.

Some aspects influencing its trajectory include:

1. **Expansion of features:**
   - LinkedIn continues to evolve beyond its traditional role as a professional networking platform. It has been integrating new features such as *LinkedIn Learning,* which offers online courses to enhance professional skills, and *LinkedIn Live,* which allows users to broadcast live video content. The platform may continue to expand its offerings to cater to the diverse needs of professionals, including job seekers, recruiters, freelancers, and entrepreneurs.

2. **Focus on personal branding:**
   - LinkedIn has become increasingly important for personal branding and career development. As professionals recognize the value of showcasing their skills, expertise, and achievements online, LinkedIn provides a platform for individuals to build and promote their personal brand. The future of LinkedIn may involve further enhancements to profile customization, content creation tools, and analytics to help users effectively establish and manage their professional identities.

3. **Remote work and digital networking:**
   - The shift toward remote work and digital networking, accelerated by the COVID-19 pandemic, has reinforced the importance of online platforms like LinkedIn for professional connections, job opportunities, and knowledge sharing. LinkedIn may continue to play a central role in facilitating virtual networking, remote recruitment processes, and online collaboration among professionals worldwide.

4. **AI and data-driven insights:**
   - LinkedIn leverages AI and data analytics to provide personalized recommendations, insights, and job opportunities to its users. This trend is likely to continue, with LinkedIn harnessing AI to improve the relevance of content, job matches, and networking suggestions based on individual preferences, behavior, and career goals.

5. **Integration with Microsoft ecosystem:**
   - Following its acquisition by Microsoft in 2016, LinkedIn has been integrated with Microsoft's suite of productivity tools, such as Outlook, Office 365, and Teams. This integration allows for seamless connectivity between professional networking and productivity workflows. The future of LinkedIn may involve deeper integration with Microsoft's ecosystem, providing users with enhanced collaboration, communication, and productivity capabilities.

6. **Global expansion and market penetration:**
   - LinkedIn has been expanding its presence in emerging markets and diversifying its user base beyond traditional professional sectors. This trend is expected to continue, with LinkedIn focusing on user acquisition, localization efforts, and partnerships to penetrate new markets and tap into the growing demand for professional networking and career development services globally.

LinkedIn's Potential Challenges

While LinkedIn has experienced significant growth and success, several potential negative future outlooks could impact its trajectory:

- Saturation and decline in user engagement: as social media platforms continue to proliferate and diversify, LinkedIn may face challenges in maintaining user engagement and attracting new users. Saturation in the professional networking market could lead to stagnation or decline in user growth, particularly if competitors offer more innovative features or appeal to niche audiences.
- Privacy and data security concerns: like many tech companies, LinkedIn faces ongoing scrutiny over privacy practices and data security. Instances of data breaches, privacy violations, or misuse of user data could damage trust and reputation, leading to user attrition and regulatory penalties.
- Competition from emerging platforms: emerging technologies and platforms could disrupt LinkedIn's dominance in the professional networking space. New entrants or innovative startups may offer alternative solutions for networking, job searching, or professional development, posing a threat to LinkedIn's market share.
- Shifts in workforce dynamics: changes in workforce dynamics, such as the rise of remote work, the gig economy, or automation, could impact LinkedIn's relevance and utility. If LinkedIn fails to adapt to evolving trends and preferences

in the labor market, it may struggle to remain a vital tool for professionals and recruiters.

- Monetization challenges: LinkedIn relies heavily on advertising, premium subscriptions, and recruitment services for revenue. Economic downturns or changes in advertising preferences could affect its revenue streams. Additionally, if users perceive the platform's paid features as overpriced or lacking value, they may seek alternative platforms or reduce spending on LinkedIn services.
- Regulatory and legal risks: increased regulatory scrutiny or changes in legislation related to data privacy, antitrust, or labor practices could pose challenges to LinkedIn's operations and business model. Compliance costs, legal disputes, or regulatory fines could impact profitability and growth prospects.
- Cultural or reputational issues: LinkedIn's corporate culture, leadership decisions, or public relations controversies could influence its long-term viability. Negative perceptions of the company's values, workplace culture, or ethical standards may deter users, employees, or business partners.

What Might Trigger the Decline of LinkedIn?

1. **Changing professional networking trends:** if there is a shift in how professionals prefer to network or if new platforms emerge with more innovative approaches to professional connections.
2. **Privacy and security concerns:** escalating concerns about data privacy or security breaches could erode user trust and impact LinkedIn's reputation.
3. **Competition:** increased competition from emerging platforms specifically designed for professional networking or offering unique features may draw users away from LinkedIn.
4. **Technological advancements:** rapid technological changes that introduce more efficient or engaging ways for professionals to connect and share information could influence user preferences.

5. **Monetization challenges:** if LinkedIn faces difficulties in maintaining a profitable business model or encounters challenges in effectively monetizing its platform.
6. **Corporate changes:** leadership changes or shifts in corporate strategy may impact LinkedIn's ability to adapt to market dynamics.
7. **News outlets:** reputable business and technology news outlets, such as Forbes, Bloomberg, or TechCrunch, often cover developments in the tech industry, including changes in social media platforms. Regularly checking these sources can provide insights into any challenges LinkedIn may be facing.
8. **Official statements:** LinkedIn's official blog, press releases, and any statements from its parent company, Microsoft, can offer direct information on the platform's strategies and responses to challenges.
9. **Financial reports:** analyzing LinkedIn's financial reports, usually available on Microsoft's investor relations page, can provide insights into the platform's financial health and potential challenges.
10. **Industry analyses:** reports from market research firms and industry analyses can provide a broader perspective on professional networking trends, competition, and factors influencing LinkedIn's position.

LinkedIn's Future Outlook

LinkedIn, the world's largest professional networking platform, has established itself as a leading player in the professional social media space. With over 740 million members across 200 countries and territories, LinkedIn has carved out a unique niche in the social media landscape.

User Growth Predictions

LinkedIn's user base is expected to increase by 22.3 percent (approx. 171.9 million users) between 2024 and 2028. This growth is likely to be fueled by LinkedIn's focus on professionals and its ability to provide a platform for networking and connecting with potential clients, partners, and employers. The platform's decision to focus on professionals exclusively has allowed it to cater specifically to the needs and aspirations of career-oriented individuals.

Global Volume		
60.6M		
US		11.1M
IN		7.5M
UK		4.1M
ES		3.4M
FR		3.4M
BR		2.7M
Other		28.5M

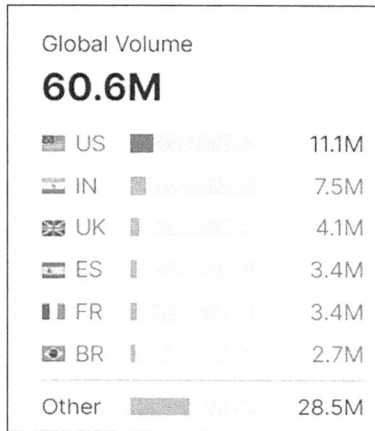

LinkedIn's global usage

Revenue Stream Predictions

LinkedIn's yearly revenue increased from $10.3 billion in the fiscal year 2021 to more than $13.8 billion in the fiscal year 20,224. By 2026, it is predicted that LinkedIn will generate yearly ad sales of almost $8 billion. Unlike platforms like Facebook or Instagram, which primarily rely on advertising as their main revenue source, LinkedIn has diversified its income streams to ensure long-term sustainability. A significant portion of LinkedIn's revenue comes from its premium subscriptions, which offer enhanced features and additional tools to users.

Future Outlook

Looking ahead, LinkedIn's business model is poised to continue evolving and adapting to the changing needs of professionals and businesses.

As technology advances and new opportunities emerge, LinkedIn is well-positioned to leverage its existing assets and build upon its revenue streams. The platform's ability to collect vast amounts of data on its users, including their job history, skills, interests, and professional connections, allows it to offer targeted advertising and recruitment services. This effectively matches employers with potential candidates and helps businesses reach their desired audience. In conclusion, the future of LinkedIn looks promising with steady user growth and increasing revenue streams. The platform's focus on professionals and its ability to adapt to changing market needs positions it well for continued success in the coming years. However, like any other social media platform, LinkedIn will need to continue innovating and adapting to stay relevant and competitive in the rapidly evolving digital landscape.

LinkedIn endnote references[§]

[§] These URLs cover an overview of LinkedIn, important statistics about its user base and professional usage, tips and tricks for optimizing your LinkedIn profile and presence, guides on leveraging LinkedIn for job searching and career growth, as well as best practices for businesses utilizing the platform for marketing, recruiting and networking. They provide a comprehensive understanding of LinkedIn's features and applications.

Title: "LinkedIn—Wikipedia," https://en.wikipedia.org/wiki/LinkedIn; Title: 37 "LinkedIn Statistics for 2023: Advertising, Demographics & More," https://blog.hubspot.com/marketing/linkedin-stats; Title: "LinkedIn Tips and Tricks You'll Wish You Knew Sooner," www.cnet.com/tech/services-and-software/linkedin-tips-and-tricks/; Title: "How to Use LinkedIn to Find a Job, Get Hired, and Market Yourself," www.businessinsider.com/guides/tech/linkedin; Title: "How to Use LinkedIn for Business: A Step-by-Step Guide," www.socialmediaexaminer.com/how-to-use-linkedin-for-business/; www.untaylored.com/post/the-business-model-and-revenue-streams-of-linkedin-explained; https://kinsta.com/blog/linkedin-statistics/. Data Sources as of July 2024 (1) "LinkedIn Usage and Revenue Statistics (2024) - Business of Apps," www.businessofapps.com/data/linkedin-statistics/. (2) "The Business Model and Revenue Streams of LinkedIn Explained," www.untaylored.com/post/the-business-model-and-revenue-streams-of-linkedin-explained. (3) "LinkedIn Statistics and Trends for 2024 - Sprouts," https://sprouts.ai/blog/linkedin-statistics-and-trends-for-2024/. (4) "Number of LinkedIn Users in 2024: User Demographics, Growth, and ...," https://financesonline.com/number-of-linkedin-users/. (5) "Global Social Network Users Growth 2027 | Statista," www.statista.com/statistics/270919/worldwide-social-network-user-growth/. (6) "Chart: LinkedIn's Impressive Revenue Growth | Statista," www.statista.com/chart/524/revenue-growth-of-linkedin/. (7) "LinkedIn User Rate to Grow Faster Than Expected Through 2023 - MarTech," https://martech.org/linkedin-user-rate-to-grow-faster-than-expected-through-2023/. (8) "Top Social Media Statistics and Trends of 2024—Forbes," www.forbes.com/advisor/business/social-media-statistics/.

Pinterest: A Visual Inspiration Hub

Pinterest logo

Pinterest is a social media platform that allows users to share and discover content through virtual pin boards called boards. It was launched in March 2010 by Ben Silbermann, Paul Sciarra, and Evan Sharp. Users can curate and organize content known as pins to reflect their interests and inspirations.

Pinterest has evolved from a niche photo-sharing platform to a global destination for inspiration, ideas, and discovery across various interests and industries.

Founding and Development

The development of Pinterest began in December 2009. The earliest versions of Pinterest were pretty rudimentary. Pinterest originated from Ben Silbermann's desire to create a platform that would allow users to discover and share visual inspiration and ideas.

Launched in March 2010, Pinterest's early years were characterized by its emphasis on curation, organization, and visual storytelling. Nine months after the launch, the website had about 10,000 users.

Early Years (2010 to 2012)

The platform's intuitive interface and emphasis on high-quality imagery quickly attracted users, particularly those interested in fashion, home decor, cooking, and DIY projects.

By December 2011, Pinterest had gained widespread attention and surpassed 10 million MAU.

Expansion and Monetization (2012 to 2015)

As Pinterest's user base continued to grow, the platform focused on expanding its features and monetization strategies.

The introduction of *Rich Pins* in 2012 allowed businesses to enhance their pins with additional information such as product details, pricing, and availability, laying the foundation for e-commerce integration on the platform. Pinterest also introduced advertising solutions such as Promoted Pins in 2014, enabling businesses to reach targeted audiences and drive engagement with sponsored content.

Diversification and International Expansion (2016 to 2019)

In subsequent years, Pinterest diversified its offerings and expanded its presence globally, catering to diverse interests and demographics. The launch of Pinterest Lens in 2017 introduced visual search capabilities, allowing users to discover ideas and products by capturing images with their smartphone cameras. Pinterest also prioritized international expansion, launching localized versions of the platform in various countries and regions to cater to non-English-speaking users and cultural nuances.

Innovation and Growth (2020 to Present)

Pinterest has continued to innovate and evolve its platform to meet the evolving needs and preferences of its users. The introduction of features such as Story Pins, Idea Pins, and Pinterest TV has transformed the platform into a multimedia destination for creators to share their stories, tutorials, and inspiration in immersive formats. Pinterest has also invested in content moderation and safety measures to ensure a positive and inclusive user experience, implementing policies to combat misinformation, harmful content, and cyberbullying.

Features

Pinterest offers several key unique features. Pins are the core unit of content on Pinterest. They consist of images or videos that users save to their boards. Boards are collections of related pins that users create to organize and save content. Pinterest's visual discovery feature lets users explore and discover content based on their interests. With robust search capabilities, they can find specific topics and browse through categories.

Future Outlook and Continued Expansion

As Pinterest looks toward the future, its commitment to creativity, inspiration, and discovery remains unwavering. The platform's vast library of user-generated and curated content, combined with its visual search capabilities and personalized recommendations, positions it as a leading destination for individuals seeking inspiration and ideas across various interests and lifestyles.

With ongoing investments in technology, content discovery, and community engagement, Pinterest is poised to continue shaping the way people discover, organize, and share ideas for years to come.

Impact

Pinterest has a significant impact on the digital ad market.

In September 2022, Pinterest reported 445 million MAU. However, Pinterest's Q2 2022 Shareholder Report shows that the platform's average MAUs in the United States and Canada fell to 92 million, a decrease of 8 percent year over year (YoY) compared to 100 million in the same period of the previous year. Overall global MAUs declined 5 percent, with a 4 percent drop in European MAUs, and a 3 percent decline in the rest of the world, compared to the same period of the previous year.

What Might Trigger the Decline of Pinterest?

Potential triggers for the decline of Pinterest:

1. **Changing user preferences:** if users shift toward platforms offering newer and more appealing features, drawing them away from Pinterest.
2. **Monetization challenges:** if Pinterest faces difficulties in sustaining its revenue model or encounters challenges in effectively monetizing its platform.

3. **Competition:** increased competition from emerging platforms with unique features or a more engaging user experience may impact Pinterest's user base.

4. **Privacy concerns:** escalating concerns about user privacy or data security could erode trust and affect user engagement.

5. **Content moderation issues:** if Pinterest encounters challenges in content moderation or faces controversies related to the nature of the content shared on the platform.

6. **Technological shifts:** rapid advancements in visual content-sharing technologies or the rise of new platforms offering unique ways to discover and save ideas.

7. **News outlets:** reputable technology and business news outlets, such as TechCrunch, Forbes, or Reuters, often cover developments in the tech industry, including changes in popular platforms like Pinterest.

8. **Official statements:** statements from Pinterest's official blog or any communications from its parent company can provide insights into the platform's strategies and responses to challenges.

9. **Financial reports:** analyzing the financial reports of Pinterest or its parent company, usually available on its investor relations page, can give you insights into the platform's financial health and potential challenges.

10. **Industry analyses:** reports from market research firms and industry analyses can provide a broader perspective on visual content-sharing trends, competition, and factors influencing Pinterest's position.

Pinterest's Future Outlook

The future of Pinterest, a popular social media platform, appears promising when considering its user growth and revenue stream predictions.

User Growth

Pinterest's user base is projected to grow consistently between 2024 and 2028, with an estimated increase of 5.1 million users (+ 5.25 percent) in the United States alone. This growth trajectory suggests that Pinterest will continue to attract new users, potentially reaching a peak of 102.2 million users by 2028. This growth is likely driven by the platform's unique value proposition as a visual discovery engine, where users can find inspiration and ideas for various interests and projects.

Revenue Stream

Pinterest's revenue has been growing at a steady pace. In Q4 2023, the company reported a 12 percent YOY growth, with revenue reaching $981 million. The total revenue for 2023 increased by 9 percent YOY to $3,055 million. This growth trend is expected to continue into Q1 2024, with revenue predicted to be in the range of $690 million to $705 million, representing a 15 to 17 percent growth YOY.

Future Outlook

Pinterest's future seems bright, given its consistent user growth and robust revenue streams. The platform's unique focus on visual discovery and personal inspiration sets it apart from other social media networks, making it an attractive platform for users seeking creative ideas and businesses looking to reach these engaged users.

However, the social media landscape is highly competitive and constantly evolving. Pinterest will need to continue innovating and adapting to user needs and market trends to maintain its growth trajectory. The company's trend forecasts, such as *Pinterest Predicts*, demonstrate its commitment to understanding and anticipating user interests, which could play a crucial role in its future success.

In conclusion, based on current user growth and revenue stream predictions, Pinterest is well-positioned for continued growth and success in the coming years. However, the company's ability to sustain this

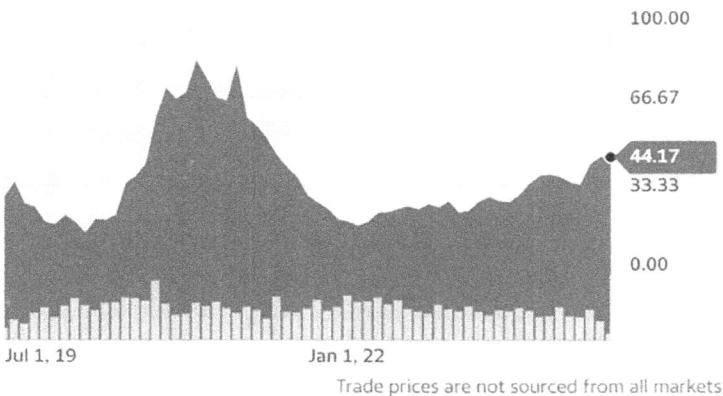

100.00

66.67

44.17

33.33

0.00

Jul 1, 19   Jan 1, 22

Trade prices are not sourced from all markets

Pinterest Inc. five-year stock price fluctuation

momentum will depend on its capacity to innovate, adapt, and continue delivering value to its users and advertisers.

Predictions are based on current trends and analysis, but the future remains speculative.

Pinterest endnote references[¶]

[¶] These URLs cover an overview of Pinterest, important statistics on its user base and usage, tips and tricks for using Pinterest features effectively, guides on leveraging Pinterest for business marketing and branding, as well as best practices for businesses utilizing the visual platform. They provide a comprehensive understanding of Pinterest's capabilities and applications.

Title: "Pinterest—Wikipedia," https://en.wikipedia.org/wiki/Pinterest; Title: "25 Powerful Pinterest Stats Marketers Need to Know in 2023," https://blog.hootsuite.com/pinterest-stats/ Title: "Pinterest Tips and Tricks: How to Use the Visual Discovery App," www.cnet.com/tech/services-and-software/pinterest-tips-and-tricks/; Title: "How to Use Pinterest for Business: A Complete Guide," www.socialmediaexaminer.com/how-to-use-pinterest-for-business/. Data Sources as of July 2024 (1) "U.S.: Pinterest Users 2019-2028 | Statista," www.statista.com/forecasts/1146884/pinterest-users-in-the-united-states. (2) "Pinterest—Pinterest Announces Fourth Quarter and Full Year 2023 ...," https://investor.pinterestinc.com/press-releases/press-releases-details/2024/Pinterest-Announces-Fourth-Quarter-and-Full-Year-2023-Results-Delivers-Record-High-Users-and-Robust-Margin-Expansion/default.aspx. (3) "Pinterest Predicts: 2023 Trend Forecast | Pinterest Business," https://business.pinterest.com/en-in/pinterest-predicts/2023/. (4) "Pinterest Predicts: Our 2024 Trend Forecast,"" https://business.pinterest.com/pinterest-predicts/. (5) "Pinterest Announces Fourth Quarter and Full Year 2022 Results," https://investor.pinterestinc.com/press-releases/press-releases-details/2023/Pinterest-Announces-Fourth-Quarter-and-Full-Year-2022-Results/default.aspx. (6) "Pinterest—Pinterest Announces First Quarter 2022 Results," https://investor.pinterestinc.com/press-releases/press-releases-details/2022/Pinterest-Announces-First-Quarter-2022-Results/default.aspx. (7) "Pinterest—Pinterest Announces Second Quarter 2021 Results," https://investor.pinterestinc.com/press-releases/press-releases-details/2021/Pinterest-Announces-Second-Quarter-2021-Results/default.aspx. (8) "U.S. Pinterest user growth 2022 | Statista," www.statista.com/statistics/426528/pinterest-us-user-growth/. (9) "Pinterest Shares New Insights into Trends Gaining Momentum on the ...," www.socialmediatoday.com/news/pinterest-shares-new-insights-into-trends-gaining-momentum-on-the-platform/606945/.

Reddit: A Community Knowledge Exchange

Logo used since 2023

Reddit logo

Founded by University of Virginia roommates Steve Huffman, Alexis Ohanian, and Aaron Swartz in June 2005, Reddit has evolved from a simple forum to a diverse ecosystem of communities, known as subreddits, covering virtually every topic imaginable.

Reddit, a vast online community and social news aggregation platform, has become a cornerstone of Internet culture, fostering discussions, sharing content, and connecting people across the globe since its inception.

Registered members submit content to the site such as links, text posts, and images, which are then voted up or down by other members.

Founding and Early Years (2005 to 2007)

Reddit was created with the vision of providing users with a platform to share links, discuss topics, and engage with like-minded individuals in an open and democratic environment. Reddit's early years were characterized by its minimalist design, user-driven content, and emphasis on community interaction.

The platform's voting system, which allows users to up-vote or down-vote posts and comments, played a crucial role in determining the visibility and prominence of content, fostering a culture of user empowerment and moderation.

Expansion and Acquisition (2007 to 2012)

As Reddit's user base grew, the platform expanded its features and functionalities to accommodate the increasing diversity of interests and communities.

The introduction of subreddits in 2008 allowed users to create and curate specialized communities around specific topics, ranging from technology and gaming to politics and art.

In October 2006, Reddit was acquired by Condé Nast Publications, marking a significant milestone in its journey and providing the resources and support to fuel its growth and development.

Community-Driven Growth (2012 to 2015)

In the following years, Reddit experienced exponential growth, driven by its passionate and engaged user base. The platform's influence extended beyond internet culture into mainstream media, politics, and entertainment, with notable events such as the *Ask Me Anything* series attracting high-profile figures and celebrities. Reddit's role in facilitating discussions and organizing grassroots movements, such as the SOPA/PIPA protests in 2012**, underscored its significance as a platform for activism and social change.

Content Moderation and Challenges (2015 to 2019)

As Reddit's user base continued to expand, the platform grappled with challenges related to content moderation, community management, and harassment. The emergence of toxic and abusive behavior within certain communities prompted Reddit to implement stricter policies and guidelines to combat harassment, hate speech, and misinformation. These efforts, while necessary to maintain a safe and welcoming

---

** The SOPA/PIPA protests in 2012 were a series of coordinated protests against two proposed laws in the United States Congress—the Stop Online Piracy Act (SOPA) and the PROTECT IP Act (PIPA).

environment, also sparked debates around free speech and censorship on the platform.

Features

Reddit combines web content, social news, a forum, and a social network into one platform. Registered members can contribute to the site with content such as images, text, videos, and links. All content on the site can be voted up or down by other members.

Reddit offers a variety of tools and services to developers, including a dedicated Developer Platform for running apps on the Reddit platform, a Data API for developers accessing and using content on Reddit, an Ads API for advertisers accessing information about their campaigns on Reddit, and Reddit Embeds for embedding content from Reddit on apps. Reddit has continually developed new methods for Reddit users, affectionately dubbed Redditors, to engage on the site.

Recent Developments and Future Outlook

In recent years, Reddit has focused on enhancing its user experience, introducing features such as Reddit Premium, awards, and a redesigned interface to improve navigation and engagement. The platform has also invested in content discovery and recommendation algorithms to surface relevant and personalized content for users.

Looking ahead, Reddit continues to evolve and innovate, reaffirming its commitment to fostering communities, facilitating discussions, and empowering users to shape the future of the platform.

Corporate Policy Changes and User Protests

- In June 2023, Reddit experienced a massive revolt by its volunteer moderators. The trigger was Reddit's decision to charge for access to its API. This change affected outside companies and users who relied on the API for their own products and services.

- In response, over 8,000 subreddits (forums within Reddit) collectively went offline for days. This protest highlighted the passionate user base of Reddit, which values the platform's ethos of democratized content sharing and policing.
- The aftermath of this protest led to some reforms, but it also left Reddit denizens skeptical about the company's actions.

Quality of Posts and User Behavior

- Some users have noticed a decline in the quality of posts. Factors contributing to this include:
  - Migrations from platforms like Facebook and Instagram may have diluted the content quality.
  - Toxicity in comment sections due to arguments between users with varying levels of expertise.
  - Down vote feature, which can exacerbate suppression of dissenting opinions on mainstream subreddits like r/politics.

Adaptation and Uncertainty

- Reddit's corporate parent has made changes based on user demands, but the impact remains mixed. Users are curious about how Reddit's new normal will evolve.
- While some lament the changes, others continue to engage with the platform, waiting to see how it adapts to the evolving landscape.

Impact

Reddit has had a significant impact on society and culture. It has been the site of some of the internet's most significant events and movements. Reddit's users can detect trends and news before anyone else, and then comment on them, often with extraordinary wit or illuminating know-how. As of October 2023, Reddit was the 18th most-visited website in the world.

What Might Trigger the Decline of Reddit?

The **decline of Reddit** has been a topic of discussion, and several factors have been suggested by users and researchers.

1. **Content moderation issues:** if Reddit struggles to effectively moderate its content and combat issues such as misinformation, hate speech, and harassment, it could lead to a decline in user trust and engagement. Negative experiences with content moderation may drive users away from the platform in search of safer and more welcoming alternatives.
2. **Monetization challenges:** Reddit's advertising-based revenue model may face challenges if it fails to attract advertisers or generate sufficient revenue without compromising user experience. Advertiser dissatisfaction or shifts in advertising trends could impact Reddit's financial viability and long-term sustainability.
3. **Competition:** intense competition from other social media platforms, community forums, or content aggregation sites could lead to a decline in Reddit's user base if it fails to differentiate itself or innovate sufficiently to retain users' attention and engagement.
4. **Regulatory pressures:** changes in regulations related to online content, user privacy, or data protection could pose challenges to Reddit's operations and user engagement. Compliance with regulatory requirements or legal disputes may impact Reddit's ability to operate effectively in certain jurisdictions.

5. **Community fragmentation:** if Reddit's diverse communities (subreddits) become increasingly fragmented or polarized, it could lead to a decline in overall user engagement and cohesion. Disputes between moderators, divisive content, or toxic behavior within communities may drive users away from the platform.

6. **Technological shifts:** rapid advancements in technology, such as the emergence of new social media platforms, changes in internet infrastructure, or shifts in user preferences toward different types of content consumption, could impact Reddit's relevance and user adoption over time.

7. **User experience issues:** persistent issues with site performance, usability, or mobile experience could lead to user frustration and dissatisfaction, ultimately driving users to seek alternative platforms that offer a better overall experience.

8. **Leadership changes:** significant changes in leadership, management decisions, or strategic direction that are not well-received by users or stakeholders could lead to a decline in Reddit's popularity and user trust.

9. **Cultural shifts:** changes in societal attitudes, cultural trends, or generational preferences may impact Reddit's user demographics and user behavior, leading to shifts in user engagement and overall platform dynamics.

Future Outlook: Reddit—A User-Driven Powerhouse

Reddit, the popular social news aggregation and discussion website, has gained significant attention in recent years for its unique business model and diverse revenue streams.

User Base

As of 2023, Reddit had a substantial user base, with site traffic up by 22.3 percent YOY from November 2022 to 2023. This growth is a testament to Reddit's appeal as a platform for news, entertainment, and niche interests. However, like many social media platforms, Reddit's user growth is expected to slow down in the coming years.

The challenge for Reddit lies in maintaining its user engagement and exploring untapped markets. Despite these challenges, Reddit's democratic nature, which allows the most popular content to rise to the top, creates a user-driven experience that fosters an engaged community and ensures a constant stream of fresh content[1].

Revenue Stream

In terms of revenue, Reddit has devised several streams to sustain its operations and future growth. One of Reddit's primary sources of revenue is advertising, offering various formats, including display ads, promoted posts, and sponsored links. With millions of active users, advertising on Reddit provides an excellent opportunity for businesses to reach their target demographics.

Another significant revenue stream for Reddit comes from its premium memberships, such as Reddit Gold. These memberships offer users enhanced features and benefits, such as an ad-free experience, exclusive access to premium subreddits, and the ability to create custom award icons. This model not only generates direct revenue but also increases ecosystem engagement.

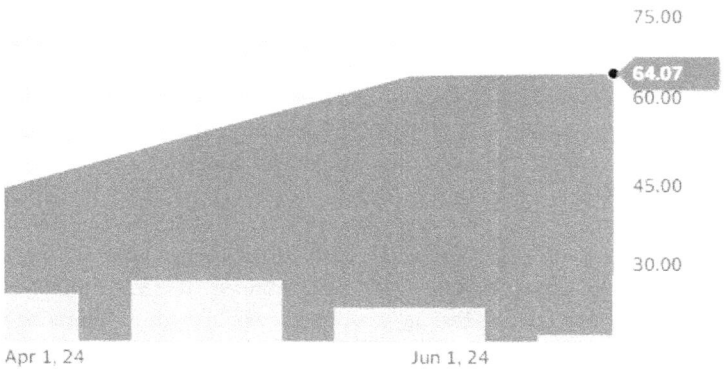

Reddit: five-year stock price fluctuation

Conclusion

Looking ahead, Reddit's future appears promising, backed by robust user growth and diversified revenue streams. The platform's ability to adapt to changing market dynamics, coupled with its strategic efforts to diversify its revenue streams, will likely ensure its continued dominance in the social media landscape. However, it will be crucial for Reddit to continue innovating and adapting to maintain its growth trajectory and meet the evolving needs of its users.

Reddit endnote references[††]

[††] These URLs cover an overview of Reddit, tips and tricks for using the platform effectively, important statistics about Reddit's user base and engagement, a beginner's guide to understanding and navigating Reddit, as well as best practices for businesses looking to leverage Reddit for marketing purposes. They provide a comprehensive look at Reddit's features, communities, and potential applications.

Title: "Reddit—Wikipedia," https://en.wikipedia.org/wiki/Reddit; Title: "Reddit Tips, Tricks and Best Practices for 2023," www.cnet.com/tech/services-and-software/reddit-tips-tricks-and-hacks/; Title: "25 Reddit Statistics Marketers Need to Know in 2023," https://blog.hubspot.com/marketing/reddit-stats; Title: "How to Use Reddit: A Beginner's Guide to the Popular Forum Site," www.businessinsider.com/guides/tech/reddit; Title: "How to Use Reddit for Business: A Marketer's Guide," www.socialmediaexaminer.com/how-to-use-reddit-for-business/. Data Sources as of July 2024 (1) "The Business Model and Revenue Streams of Reddit Explained," www.untaylored.com/post/the-business-model-and-revenue-streams-of-reddit-explained. (2) "Predictions for Social Media in 2023 and Beyond? : r/socialmedia—Reddit," www.reddit.com/r/socialmedia/comments/zy6ytk/predictions_for_social_media_in_2023_and_beyond/. (3) "3 Social Media Predictions for 2024:r/marketing—Reddit," www.reddit.com/r/marketing/comments/18vea09/3_social_media_predictions_for_2024/. (4) "How Accurate Are SocialBlade Channel Growth Predictions? : r ... - Reddit," www.reddit.com/r/PartneredYoutube/comments/gwmrzy/how_accurate_are_socialblade_channel_growth/. (5) "Instagram Growth Strategy for 2024 (+15K in 3 months)—Reddit," www.reddit.com/r/InstagramMarketing/comments/1ad3x0o/framework_instagram_growth_strategy_for_2024_15k/. (6) undefined. www.reddit.com/r/NewTubers/comments/iozwa9/how_accurate_have_social_blade_future_projections/.

Snapchat: An Ephemeral Expression Platform

Snapchat logo

Source: https://icons8.com/icons/set/snapchat-public.

Snapchat is a multimedia app that can be used on smartphones running Android or iOS. It allows users to send pictures or videos, named Snaps, to friends. These Snaps vanish after they have been viewed. The platform also offers a Chat function, similar to some instant messaging services. Snapchat has captured the attention of users worldwide since its inception in 2011.

Snapchat has evolved from a simple photo-sharing app to a multifaceted platform for communication, content creation, and community engagement.

Founding and Early Years (2011 to 2013)

Founded by Evan Spiegel, Bobby Murphy, and Reggie Brown while they were students at Stanford University, Snapchat was launched in September 2011 under the original name *Picaboo* with the concept of allowing users to send photos that would disappear after a short period. The app was later renamed Snapchat, reflecting its focus on ephemeral messaging. Its unique feature of disappearing photos, coupled with the ability to overlay text and drawings on images, quickly attracted a young and tech-savvy user base. Despite initial skepticism from investors and industry observers, Snapchat gained traction among teenagers and young adults, paving the way for its rapid growth and expansion.

Reportedly, Brown came up with the idea of a social media app that enabled users to post photos and videos that disappeared from the site after a few moments. The company was later renamed Snap Inc.

Snapchat was initially focused on private, person-to-person photo sharing, but it can now be used for a range of tasks, including sending videos, live video chatting, messaging, creating caricature-like Bitmoji avatars, and sharing a chronological *story* that is broadcasted to choose followers.

Innovations and Growth (2014 to 2016)

Snapchat's early success prompted the introduction of new features and functionalities aimed at enhancing user engagement and monetization.

The launch of *Stories* in October 2013 revolutionized the app by allowing users to create and share collections of photos and videos that would disappear after 24 hours. This feature proved immensely popular and became a cornerstone of Snapchat's platform, inspiring similar features on rival platforms such as Instagram and Facebook. The introduction of *Lenses*, *Geofilters*, and *Discover*, further diversified Snapchat's offerings, catering to a wide range of user interests and preferences.

Snapchat has introduced many innovative features over the years. Some of the key features include the ability to add filters and AR-based lenses to Snaps and show your live location on a world map.

Snapchat also allows users to store media in a private area. Other features include the ability to express themselves, connect with other teens locally and across long distances, and learn how other teens cope with challenging life situations and mental health conditions.

IPO and Expansion (2017 to 2019)

Snapchat went public in March 2017 with its highly anticipated IPO, valuing the company at over $24 billion. The IPO marked a significant milestone for Snapchat, providing the company with the financial resources to fuel its growth and expansion efforts. Despite facing competition from larger tech giants such as Facebook and Instagram, Snapchat continued to innovate and differentiate itself through features like AR lenses, original content partnerships, and the redesign of its app interface. The company also expanded its user base beyond its core demographic of young users, targeting older demographics and international markets.

Challenges and Adaptations (2020 to Present)

In recent years, Snapchat has faced challenges related to user growth, monetization, and competition from rival platforms. The COVID-19 pandemic posed unique challenges as user behavior shifted and advertisers reduced spending on digital platforms. However, Snapchat responded by doubling down on innovation, introducing features like Spotlight, a platform for user-generated content, and expanding its e-commerce capabilities through partnerships with brands and retailers. The company also focused on improving its advertising tools and analytics to attract and retain advertisers.

Snapchat's Positive Outlook

Snapchat has been on an impressive trajectory, and its future outlook appears promising.

- Growth:
  - As of 2024, Snapchat boasts a substantial user base, and its global reach continues to expand. Snapchat is expected to have 431 million DAUs‡‡ in 2024, marking a 4.10 percent increase from the previous year. By 2025, the app's user base is projected to reach 467 million DAUs.
- Demographics:
  - India leads the pack with the largest Snapchat audience, boasting 144 million users.
  - Around 51 percent of Snapchat users are female, while 48.2 percent are male.
  - The United States follows closely with 108 million users.
  - France ranks third with 24.7 million Snapchat users.
  - In Europe, 92 million users engage with Snapchat daily.
  - Snapchat reaches over 75 percent of the millennial and Gen Z population in the United States.
  - Users aged 18 to 24 form the largest share of Snapchat's advertising audience.

---

‡‡ DAU definition: A common metric for software companies, DAUs meaning daily active users is a measurement not of the gross user count but an attempt to describe the active user count.

- o In all, 75 percent of 13 to 34-year-olds in 20 countries actively use Snapchat.
- o Overall, 65 percent of U.S. internet users aged 15 to 29 are on Snapchat.
- Financial statistics:
  - o In 2022, Snapchat's revenue increased by 12 percent to $4.6 billion compared to the prior year. Q4 2022 revenue reached $1,300 million.
  - o Net loss was $288 million, including restructuring charges.
  - o Snapchat+ is a $3.99/month subscription service offering exclusive features.
- Fun facts:
  - o The app processes over four billion snaps (photos and videos) daily.
  - o There are 35 million+ businesses listed on Snap Maps.
  - o Total time spent watching Spotlight content grew over 100 percent YOY.
  - o Its popularity with Gen Z consumers makes it an attractive advertising platform for companies.
  - o The expansion of its self-serve advertising platform, higher-value ads like Commercials, and new AR-based ads in its lenses and games are expected to drive revenue growth.
- Differentiation and features:
  - o Snapchat's unique features, such as AR lenses, in-app games, and the Discover tab, set it apart from competitors like Instagram.
  - o Its popularity among teen users and its growing library of engaging content contribute to its sustained growth.

Snapchat's Potential Challenges

Some potential challenges and negative aspects that could impact Snapchat's future outlook include:

- **Competition from rivals:** Snapchat faces intense competition from platforms like Instagram, TikTok, and Facebook.

These competitors often replicate Snapchat's features, diluting its uniqueness. Instagram's Stories feature, for instance, has significantly impacted Snapchat's growth by attracting users away from the original ephemeral content concept.

- **Monetization challenges:** While Snapchat has made strides in monetization through advertising, it still lags behind giants like Facebook and Google. The platform needs to strike a balance between user experience and ad revenue. Overloading users with ads could drive them away

- **User retention and aging demographics:** Snapchat's core user base is younger (Gen Z and millennials). As these users age, the platform must adapt to retain them. Attracting older demographics remains a challenge. If Snapchat fails to diversify its user base, it could face stagnation.

- **Privacy concerns and data security:** Privacy scandals and data breaches can erode user trust. Snapchat must continually enhance its security measures. Striking the right balance between data collection for personalization and user privacy is crucial.

- **Innovation fatigue:** Keeping users engaged requires consistent innovation. If Snapchat fails to introduce compelling new features, it risks losing relevance. The platform must stay ahead of trends and adapt swiftly to changing user preferences.

- **Financial sustainability:** Despite revenue growth, Snapchat's profitability remains a concern. It needs to manage costs effectively and diversify revenue streams. Dependence on advertising revenue makes it vulnerable to market fluctuations.

- **Platform addiction and mental health impact:** Social media addiction and its impact on mental health are growing concerns. Snapchat must address these issues responsibly. Balancing engagement with user well-being is a delicate task.

What Might Trigger the Decline of Snapchat?

Potential triggers for the decline of Snapchat:

- Changing user preferences: if users shift toward platforms offering newer and more appealing features, drawing them away from Snapchat.
- Monetization challenges: if Snapchat faces difficulties in sustaining its revenue model or encounters challenges in effectively monetizing its platform.
- Competition: increased competition from emerging platforms with unique features or a more engaging user experience may impact Snapchat's user base.
- Privacy concerns: escalating concerns about user privacy or data security could erode trust and affect user engagement.
- Adverse content issues: if Snapchat encounters challenges in content moderation or faces controversies related to the nature of the content shared on the platform.
- Technological shifts: rapid advancements in communication technologies that offer new ways of sharing content or interacting with friends could influence user preferences.
- News outlets: reputable technology and business news outlets, such as TechCrunch, Forbes, or Reuters, often cover developments in the tech industry, including changes in popular platforms like Snapchat.
- Official statements: statements from Snapchat's official blog or any communications from its parent company, Snap Inc., can provide insights into the platform's strategies and responses to challenges.
- Financial reports: analyzing Snap Inc.'s financial reports, usually available on their investor relations page, can give insights into Snapchat's financial health and potential challenges.
- Industry analyses: reports from market research firms and industry analyses can provide a broader perspective on social media trends, competition, and factors influencing Snapchat's position.

The Future of Snapchat: A Perspective

Snapchat, a popular social media platform, has shown promising trends in both user growth and revenue streams. The future of Snapchat appears to be bright, with projections indicating a steady upward trend in user growth and revenue.

User Growth

Snapchat's user base is projected to grow steadily between 2023 and 2027, with a cumulative increase of 87.5 million users, or a 14.94 percent growth. This growth is not limited to a specific region or demographic. Snapchat is expected to have 734.8 million MAU worldwide in 2024. The number of Snapchat users in France alone is forecast to increase by 2.4 million users (+9.04 percent) between 2023 and 2027.

Moreover, Snapchat's appeal to various age groups, regions, and user preferences is expected to diversify. Technological advancements like AR and AI are expected to play a significant role in attracting and retaining users across various age groups.

Revenue Streams

Snapchat's revenue streams have also shown promising growth. In 2023, Snapchat's revenue was $4,606 million, compared to $4,602 million in 2022. The fourth quarter of 2023 alone saw a revenue increase of 5 percent YOY to $1,361 million.

Looking ahead, Snap Inc. expects the company to generate 50 percent revenue growth over the next several years. This growth rate is claimed to be independent of user base growth, suggesting that Snapchat's revenue streams are robust and diversified.

Conclusion

In conclusion, Snapchat's future looks promising based on its user growth and revenue stream predictions. The platform's ability to attract a diverse user base and generate robust revenue growth positions it well for future success.

However, as with any prediction, these trends are subject to change and should be monitored closely. As Snapchat continues to innovate and adapt to changing market conditions, it will be interesting to see how these predictions hold up.

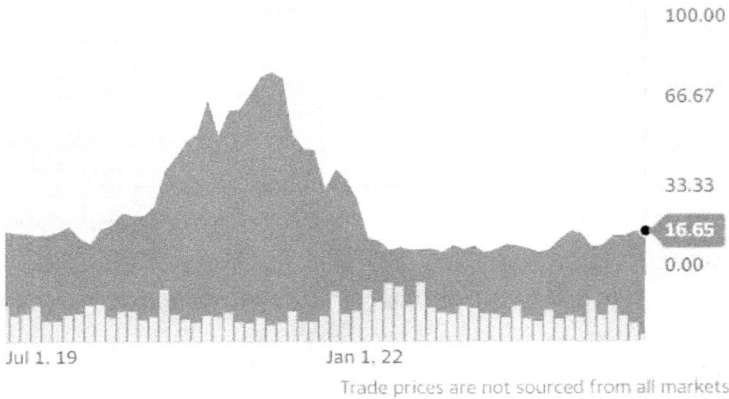

Snapchat five-year stock price fluctuation

Snapchat endnote references[§§]

[§§] These URLs cover an overview of Snapchat, important statistics on its user base and usage, tips and tricks for using Snapchat features effectively, guides on leveraging Snapchat for business marketing and influencer collaborations, as well as instructions on finding and sharing your personal Snapchat URL. They provide a comprehensive look at understanding and utilizing Snapchat.

Title: "Snapchat—Wikipedia," https://en.wikipedia.org/wiki/Snapchat; Title: "27 Snapchat Stats Marketers Need to Know in 2023," https://blog.hootsuite.com/snapchat-statistics/; Title: "Snapchat Tips and Tricks: Best Hidden Features for 2023," www.cnet.com/tech/mobile/snapchat-tips-tricks/; Title: "How to Use Snapchat: A Guide for Brands and Influencers," www.businessinsider.com/guides/tech/snapchat; Title: "How to Find and Share Your Custom Snapchat URL," www.cnet.com/tech/services-and-software/how-to-find-share-your-custom-snapchat-url/. Data Sources as of July 2024 https://marketsplash.com/snapchat-statistics/; www.emarketer.com/insights/snapchat-user-statistics/; www.knowskit.com/snapchat-user-demographics-evolution; https://investor.snap.com/news/news-details/2024/Snap-Inc.-Announces-Fourth-Quarter-and-Full-Year-2023-Financial-Results/default.aspx.

Telegram: A Versatile Communication Nexus

Telegram logo

Telegram, founded by Pavel Durov and his brother Nikolai Durov, was launched in 2013 as a cloud-based messaging app focused on providing users with privacy, speed, and security features. Pavel Durov, known for creating the popular Russian social network VKontakte (VK), envisioned Telegram as a platform where users could communicate freely without fear of surveillance or data breaches.

Founding and Early Years (2013 to 2016)

- Telegram gained popularity quickly, particularly among users who were concerned about privacy and security due to its end-to-end encryption feature.
- The app attracted users globally, especially in countries with strict censorship laws or government surveillance, where users sought secure communication channels.
- Telegram introduced features such as secret chats, self-destructing messages, and cloud-based storage for messages and media files, further enhancing its appeal to privacy-conscious users.
- Despite facing occasional controversies and criticism for being used by extremist groups or for facilitating illegal activities due to its encrypted nature, Telegram continued to grow its user base.

Mid-2010s (2016 to 2019)

- Telegram continued innovating its platform, introducing features like Telegram Channels, which allowed users to broadcast messages to large audiences, and Telegram Bots, which enabled automated interactions and services within the app.

- The app saw increased adoption by businesses, media organizations, and public figures for communication, broadcasting updates, and engaging with followers.
- Telegram also expanded its offerings with the introduction of Telegram Groups, allowing users to create and join communities based on shared interests, topics, or geographical locations.
- Despite facing occasional service disruptions because of government bans or technical issues, Telegram maintained its commitment to user privacy and security, positioning itself as a leading secure messaging platform.

Recent Years (2020 to Present)

Telegram continued to evolve its platform, introducing features such as **Voice Chats**, allowing users to participate in live audio conversations within groups and channels, and **Payments**, enabling users to make purchases and transactions directly within the app.

- **December 2023 (first update):**
  - Customize channel appearance: channels gained the ability to customize their appearance with unique backgrounds or emoji statuses as they leveled up.
  - Posts in stories: messages in channels could be reposted to stories, and stories showed more statistics.
  - Customize channel appearance: channels could include real-world prizes in giveaways.
- **December 2023 (second update):**
  - **Upgraded calls**: voice and video calls received improved interfaces, increased performance, and better battery efficiency.
  - **Epic bot update:** bots became more powerful, able to react to messages, manage reactions, quotes, links, and send replies to other chats.

- **January 2024:**
  - Saved Messages 2.0: users could sort saved messages by chat and tag them with emoji.
  - One-time voice messages: recordings could be set to automatically delete after playing once.
  - Read time in private chats: messages in one-on-one chats displayed the exact time they were opened by the recipient.
- **February 2024:**
  - Stories for groups: groups could post stories, change appearance, and unlock features using boosts from members.
  - Voice-to-text for groups: voice transcription was introduced for group chats.

Challenges

Telegram faced increased scrutiny from regulators and governments in some countries, particularly regarding its encryption policies and its role in facilitating communication among protest movements and dissenting voices.

These are just a few examples of countries where Telegram has encountered increased scrutiny and regulatory challenges from governments:

- **Russia**: Telegram faced significant pressure and legal challenges from the Russian government, leading to the blocking of the platform multiple times due to concerns over its encryption protocols and its use by extremist groups.
- **Iran:** the Iranian government has also targeted Telegram, citing concerns over its use by protesters and its encryption features, leading to intermittent bans and restrictions on the platform.
- **China**: Telegram has been subject to censorship and intermittent blocking by the Chinese government, primarily due to concerns over its role in facilitating uncensored communication and its popularity among activists and dissidents.

- **Indonesia:** Telegram faced scrutiny and temporary blocks in Indonesia due to concerns over the spread of extremist content and terrorist propaganda on the platform.
- **Brazil:** in Brazil, Telegram has faced scrutiny over its handling of misinformation and illegal activities, leading to government investigations and requests for user data.

What Might Trigger the Decline of Telegram?

Telegram, the Dubai-based messaging app, has garnered 400 million users and positioned itself as a rebellious alternative to platforms like WhatsApp. However, there are several reasons why its decline might be on the horizon:

1. **Privacy concerns:** if Telegram faces significant privacy breaches or fails to maintain its reputation as a secure messaging platform, users may lose trust in the service and seek alternative messaging apps.
2. **Competition:** intense competition from other messaging platforms offering similar features, such as WhatsApp, Signal, and Discord, could lead to a decline in Telegram's user base if it fails to differentiate itself or innovate sufficiently.
3. **Regulatory challenges:** changes in regulations regarding data privacy, encryption, or messaging services in various countries could pose challenges to Telegram's operations and user engagement, potentially leading to a decline in its popularity.
4. **Monetization issues:** if Telegram struggles to effectively monetize its platform or implement sustainable revenue streams without compromising user experience or privacy, it may face financial difficulties that could impact its long-term viability.
5. **Technological shifts:** rapid advancements in technology, such as the emergence of new communication protocols or disruptive innovations in messaging services, could render Telegram's features outdated or less appealing to users over time.
6. **User migration:** if key demographics or user segments shift to other messaging platforms for various reasons, such as better features,

stronger security, or wider adoption among their social circles, Telegram could experience a decline in its user base.

7. **Leadership changes:** significant changes in leadership, management decisions, or strategic direction that are not well-received by users or stakeholders could lead to dissatisfaction and a subsequent decline in Telegram's popularity.

8. **External events:** unforeseen external events, such as security incidents, legal disputes, or economic downturns, could negatively impact Telegram's reputation, user engagement, and overall growth trajectory.

9. **Failure to innovate:** if Telegram fails to innovate and adapt to changing user preferences, technological trends, or market dynamics, it risks becoming stagnant and losing relevance in the highly competitive messaging app landscape.

10. **Lack of default end-to-end encryption:** unlike WhatsApp and Signal, Telegram chats are not automatically end-to-end encrypted. While you can activate the *secret chat* option for individual contacts, group chats, and channels remain unencrypted by default. This raises concerns about privacy and security.

11. **Access to contacts and metadata**: Telegram has access to your contacts and metadata. Although it claims to support free speech, it does not explicitly oppose censorship. This balance between privacy and potential misuse remains a point of contention.

12. **Founder's rhetoric:** Pavel Durov, Telegram's founder, champions privacy as a fundamental right and portrays the rivalry between Telegram and WhatsApp as a battle of good versus evil. However, the company's actual practices do not always align with this rhetoric.

13. **Competition from established platforms:** while Telegram positions itself against big tech, it faces stiff competition from established giants like Facebook, WhatsApp, and Instagram. The majority of internet users are still entrenched in the Facebook ecosystem, making it challenging for Telegram to break through.

14. **User behavior and trends:** user preferences and trends can significantly impact an app's success. If users shift away from Telegram due to concerns about privacy, security, or other factors, its decline could accelerate.

The Future of Telegram: A Glimpse Into User Growth and Revenue Streams

Telegram has been making significant strides in the social media landscape. As of 2023, it boasted 700 million MAU, with projections indicating a user base of one billion by 2024. This impressive growth, representing a 40 percent increase since the beginning of 2021, underscores Telegram's appeal and its potential for future expansion.

User Growth

The app's daily active users also paint a promising picture, with 55.2 million users engaging with the platform. This represents a remarkable 30 percent increase since November 2020. Such statistics place Telegram among the top five downloaded apps globally, further emphasizing its growing popularity.

Revenue Predictions

In terms of revenue, Telegram has shown a promising trajectory. As of 2023, it generated $68.8 million, a significant increase from $9.4 million in 2021. This revenue growth can be attributed to the company's monetization efforts, which include Telegram Premium and the Telegram Ad platform.

Looking ahead, Telegram's revenue model is poised for further innovation. The company recently introduced a reward system that allows channel owners with substantial subscribers to earn 50 percent of the revenue from ads shown in their channels. This initiative, which pays out in Toncoin, Telegram's native cryptocurrency, represents a novel approach to revenue generation and user engagement.

Moreover, Telegram's exploration of blockchain technology and a decentralized economy sets the stage for a new era of messaging apps where users have more control over their data and digital assets. This could potentially attract a new user base interested in blockchain and cryptocurrency, further boosting Telegram's growth.

However, it is important to note that Telegram's open network architecture, while attracting many loyal users due to its strong privacy protections, has also enabled some illicit activities. This presents a challenge for Telegram to strengthen protections without closing the platform.

Conclusion

In conclusion, Telegram's impressive user growth and innovative revenue streams paint a promising future for the social network. However, the company will need to navigate challenges related to its open network architecture to ensure its continued success. With its forward-thinking strategies and commitment to user privacy, Telegram is well-positioned to continue its upward trajectory in the social media landscape. Moreover, it is essential for Telegram to continually address these potential challenges, prioritize user privacy and security, innovate its features, and remain responsive to evolving market conditions to sustain its growth and relevance over time. While Telegram has carved out a niche, its future depends on how it addresses these challenges and adapts to evolving user needs.

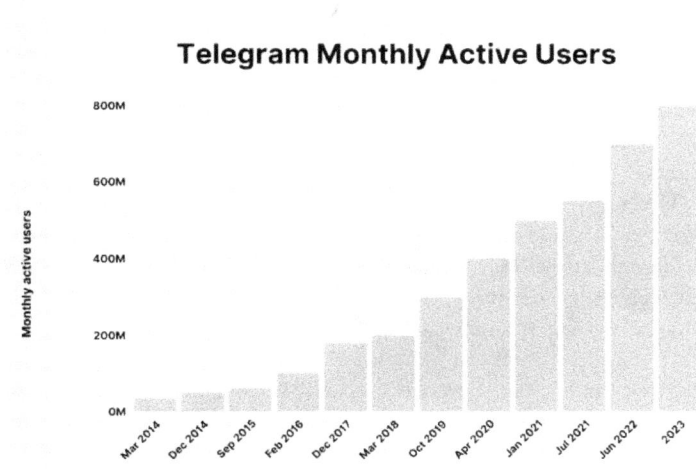

Telegram monthly active users

*Telegram endnote references*⁹⁹

¶¶ These URLs present an overview of Telegram, tips and tricks for using its features effectively, a guide on how to use the secure messaging app, documentation on Telegram's deep linking capabilities and API, as well as an official FAQ addressing common questions about the platform. Together, they provide a comprehensive look at understanding and utilizing Telegram's messaging services.

Title: "Telegram (software)—Wikipedia," https://en.wikipedia.org/wiki/Telegram_(software); Title: "Telegram Tips and Tricks: Better Messaging on Any Device," www.cnet.com/tech/services-and-software/telegram-tips-tricks/; Title: "How to Use Telegram, the Secure Messaging App: A Guide," www.businessinsider.com/guides/tech/telegram; Title: "Deep Links—Telegram APIs" https://core.telegram.org/api/links; Title: "Telegram FAQ," https://telegram.org/faq https://avada.io/articles/telegram-statistics/, www.demandsage.com/telegram-statistics/, https://whop.com/blog/telegram-statistics/.

TikTok: A Short-Form Creativity Platform

TikTok logo

TikTok, a platform for short-form mobile videos, is a strong YouTube competitor, especially among younger demographics.

TikTok offers a variety of features that enhance the user experience. Users can create and share videos, use filters and effects, add stickers and emojis, and incorporate music into their videos. The platform also has a Duet feature that allows users to create videos alongside another user's video. Furthermore, TikTok's algorithm recommends content based on users' viewing habits, making it easy for users to discover new content.

Founding and Early Development (2016 to 2018)

- TikTok, originally known as Douyin in China, is a video-sharing app that allows users to create and share short-form videos on any topic. It was launched in September 2016 by ByteDance, a Chinese tech company founded by Zhang Yiming and Liang Rubo. The platform has evolved from its predecessor, Musical.ly, to become a popular social media platform with features like filters, stickers, voiceovers, and background music.
- In September 2017, ByteDance expanded its reach beyond China with the launch of TikTok, targeting international markets and catering to a global audience. The platform's intuitive interface, algorithmic feed, and emphasis on user-generated content fueled its rapid growth and adoption. In 2018, ByteDance acquired Musical.ly and merged it with TikTok, leading to a significant increase in TikTok's user base.

The app gained significant popularity in China and Thailand, attracting 100 million users within a year.

Global Expansion and Popularity Surge (2018 to 2019)

- TikTok's global expansion gained momentum in 2018 as the app gained traction among teenagers and young adults in markets outside of China, including the United States, India, and Europe. The platform's virality was propelled by a combination of factors, including its addictive *For You* feed, which uses machine learning algorithms to personalize content recommendations based on user preferences and engagement patterns.
- TikTok's emphasis on creativity, authenticity, and relatability resonated with users, leading to the proliferation of viral challenges, memes, and trends.

TikTok Revenue Generation

- Advertising: TikTok offers paid advertisements for brands to promote their products and services. Brands can use TikTok For Business to enhance their marketing solutions through features such as in-feed videos, brand takeovers, hashtag challenges, and branded effects.
- In-app purchases: users can make in-app purchases, such as buying virtual coins to give as gifts during live performances.
- TikTok for business: this platform allows brands to engage with audiences and promote their products or services.
- Creator commissions: TikTok uses its Creator Fund to encourage popular *TikTokers* to keep creating engaging content. As a creator, once you have at least 10,000 followers and at least 100,000 video views over the last 30 days, you have the potential to start earning money.
- Branded hashtag challenges and branded effects: brands can create their own hashtag challenge and pay TikTok so their tag shows up on people's discovery pages. TikTok also offers

users branded custom stickers, augmented-reality filters, and lenses to add to their videos.

- TikTok shopping: creators can use TikTok Shop to reach a wider audience and promote their brands and products.
- TikTok ads: with TikTok's Ads Manager, brands can reach new audiences by getting their brand in front of the right viewers.
- Music royalties: TikTok also pays music royalties for the songs used in the videos.

Challenges and Regulatory Scrutiny (2019 to 2020)

TikTok faced challenges and controversies as its user base expanded and its influence grew. Concerns about privacy, data security, and content moderation prompted regulatory scrutiny and investigations by governments around the world, particularly in the United States, EU, United Kingdom, Australia, Canada, and India.

In June 2020, India banned TikTok and several other Chinese apps citing national security concerns, dealing a significant blow to TikTok's global user base and revenue.

Resilience and Adaptation (2020 to Present)

Despite facing setbacks, TikTok has demonstrated resilience and adaptability, leveraging its strengths in content creation, community engagement, and viral marketing to sustain its growth and relevance. The platform has introduced new features and initiatives to enhance user experience and address concerns about privacy and safety, including increased transparency around content moderation policies and partnerships with industry organizations to promote digital literacy and online safety.

What Might Trigger the Decline of TikTok?

Potential triggers for the decline of TikTok:

1. Emergence of competing platforms: if new platforms with innovative features or better content discovery mechanisms emerge, draw users away from TikTok.

2. Privacy concerns: escalating concerns about user data privacy or security breaches could erode trust and impact TikTok's popularity.

3. Monetization challenges: TikTok faces difficulties in maintaining a sustainable and profitable business model, including issues with advertising revenue or creator monetization.

4. Content moderation issues: challenges in effectively moderating content or controversies related to the nature of content shared on the platform.

5. Legal and regulatory challenges: ongoing or intensified legal challenges, regulatory issues, or bans in key markets could impact TikTok's operations.

6. Changing user demographics: TikTok struggles to adapt to shifting user demographics or preferences, leading to a decline in its user base.

7. News outlets: reputable technology and business news outlets, such as TechCrunch, The Verge, or Reuters, often cover developments in the tech industry, including changes in popular platforms like TikTok.

8. Official statements: statements from TikTok's official blog or any communications from its parent company, ByteDance, can provide insights into the platform's strategies and responses to challenges.

9. Financial reports: analyzing ByteDance's financial reports, usually available on their investor relations page, can give you insights into TikTok's financial health and potential challenges.

10. Industry analyses: reports from market research firms and industry analyses can provide a broader perspective on short-form video consumption trends, competition, and factors influencing TikTok's position.

To stay informed on TikTok's current status and potential challenges, consider consulting reputable news sources, technology analyses from platforms like TechCrunch or The Verge, and any official statements or reports released by TikTok or its parent company, ByteDance.

TikTok's Three Biggest U.S. Concerns

TikTok as a *Data Collector*?

- TikTok gathers a significant amount of data, with critics often alleging that it collects an *excessive* amount. While TikTok maintains that its data collection practices align with industry standards, skeptics frequently raise concerns about the app's extensive data harvesting.
- A cyber-security report released in July 2022 by researchers at Internet 2.0, an Australian cyber-security firm, is commonly cited as supporting evidence. According to the report, an analysis of the app's source code revealed that TikTok engages in what is deemed "excessive data harvesting." This includes collecting information such as user location, device specifications, and installed applications.
- However, a study conducted by Citizen Lab found that, when compared to other popular social media platforms, TikTok's data collection practices are similar in nature and primarily aimed at tracking user behavior.
- Additionally, a report by the Georgia Institute of Technology from the previous year asserted that the majority of other social media and mobile applications engage in similar data collection practices.

TikTok as a *Spying* App?
- Concerns have been raised that TikTok could potentially serve as a tool for the Chinese government to conduct surveillance on its users.
- TikTok has adamantly asserted its independence and stated that it has not shared user data with the Chinese government, nor would it comply with such requests if they were made. While this assertion may reassure some, many individuals recognize that sharing personal data with social networks is often an implicit part of using their services. These platforms typically collect user data to facilitate targeted advertising on

their platforms or to sell to third-party advertisers seeking to reach users across the internet.

- What distinguishes TikTok from other mainstream apps is its ownership by the Beijing-based tech giant ByteDance, rather than a U.S.-founded company like Facebook, Instagram, Snapchat, and YouTube. While these other platforms also collect substantial amounts of user data, critics are particularly wary of TikTok's Chinese ownership.

- For years, there has been a belief by U.S. lawmakers and others worldwide that data collected by these platforms would not be misused in ways that could compromise national security. However, concerns were escalated by Donald Trump's 2020 executive order, which alleged that TikTok's data collection practices could potentially enable China to conduct espionage and surveillance activities targeting federal employees and contractors.

- Although evidence supporting these concerns remains largely theoretical, apprehensions are fueled by a vague provision in China's National Intelligence Law passed in 2017. Article seven of this law mandates that Chinese organizations and citizens must "support, assist, and cooperate" with the country's intelligence efforts. This provision is frequently cited by those suspicious of TikTok and other Chinese companies.

- However, researchers from the Georgia Institute of Technology argue that this provision is often taken out of context and note that the law includes safeguards protecting the rights of users and private companies.

- Since 2020, TikTok executives have sought to reassure users that Chinese staff cannot access the data of non-Chinese users. However, in 2022, ByteDance admitted that several of its Beijing-based employees did access the data of at least two journalists in the United States and United Kingdom to monitor their locations and verify whether they were meeting with suspected leakers.

- TikTok has emphasized that user data has never been stored in China and has made efforts to build data centers in Texas for U.S. user data and in Europe for data from its citizens.

- In the EU, the company has taken additional steps beyond those of other social networks by enlisting an independent cybersecurity company to oversee data usage at its European sites. TikTok states that "the data of our European users is safeguarded in a specially designed protective environment and can only be accessed by approved employees subject to strict independent oversight and verification."

TikTok, as a *Brainwashing* Tool?

- In November 2022, Christopher Wray, the director of the Federal Bureau of Investigation, informed U.S. lawmakers that "The Chinese government could potentially manipulate the recommendation algorithm, which could be exploited for influence operations." This assertion has been reiterated on numerous occasions.
- These concerns are exacerbated by the practices observed on TikTok's sister app, Douyin, which is exclusively available in China and is subject to heavy censorship. Douyin is reportedly designed to promote educational and wholesome content to its young user base.
- In China, all social networks undergo extensive censorship, with a team of internet regulators tasked with deleting content critical of the government or inciting political unrest.
- During TikTok's early rise in popularity, there were notable instances of content censorship on the platform. For example, a user in the United States had her account suspended for discussing the treatment of Muslims in Xinjiang by the Beijing government. Following significant public outcry, TikTok issued an apology and reinstated the account.
- However, since then, instances of censorship on TikTok have been limited, with most issues revolving around controversial moderation decisions common to all social media platforms.
- A comparison conducted by researchers at Citizen Lab between TikTok and Douyin concluded that TikTok does not engage in the same level of political censorship. In 2021, they stated, "The platform does not overtly enforce post censorship."

- Similarly, analysts from the Georgia Institute of Technology investigated topics such as the independence of Taiwan or jokes about Chinese Premier Xi Jinping. Their findings indicated that videos covering these topics can easily be found on TikTok and are often widely shared.
- The prevailing narrative suggests that concerns surrounding TikTok largely remain theoretical, centered on potential risks rather than concrete evidence of misuse.
- Critics argue that TikTok could serve as a "Trojan horse," appearing benign but potentially wielding significant influence during periods of conflict, for instance.
- While India banned TikTok in 2020, along with dozens of other Chinese platforms, a similar ban in the United States would have significant ramifications for the platform, as U.S. allies often follow suit with such decisions. This was evident when the United States successfully lobbied to prevent Chinese telecom giant Huawei from participating in 5G infrastructure projects, citing similar theoretical risks.

These risks primarily flow in one direction. China has long blocked access to U.S. apps for its citizens, mitigating concerns about potential foreign influence.

The Promising Future of TikTok

TikTok, a social media platform that has revolutionized short-form video content, continues to demonstrate remarkable growth and potential. The platform's user base and revenue streams are expanding at an impressive rate, suggesting a promising future.

User Growth

TikTok's user growth has been nothing short of phenomenal. As of 2024, TikTok has over one billion MAU. This rapid growth is even more impressive when considering that it took Facebook and Instagram almost a decade to reach a similar user base. Looking ahead, industry analysts expect TikTok's user growth rate to continue, albeit at a decelerating pace. In 2024, experts have forecast an annual increase of 9.3 percent, and by

2025, TikTok's growth rate is set to slow to 7 percent. Despite the slow-down, the total number of TikTok users is predicted to reach a staggering 2.6 billion daily users by 2025.

Revenue Streams

TikTok's revenue streams, particularly its ad revenue, are also on an upward trajectory. Starting at $3.88 billion in 2021, the revenue is expected to rise to $22 billion by 2025, representing an average annual growth rate of 61.7 percent over the five years. TikTok generated an estimated $16.1 billion in revenue in 2023, a 67 percent increase year-on-year. The platform has also been exploring new revenue streams, such as social commerce. In 2023, there were an estimated 33.3 million social media shoppers on TikTok, up 40.5 percent from 2022.

Future Outlook

Given these trends, the future of TikTok appears bright. The platform's ability to attract and retain users, coupled with its growing revenue streams, suggests that it will continue to be a major player in the social media landscape. However, the platform's future growth will likely depend on its ability to innovate and adapt to changing user preferences

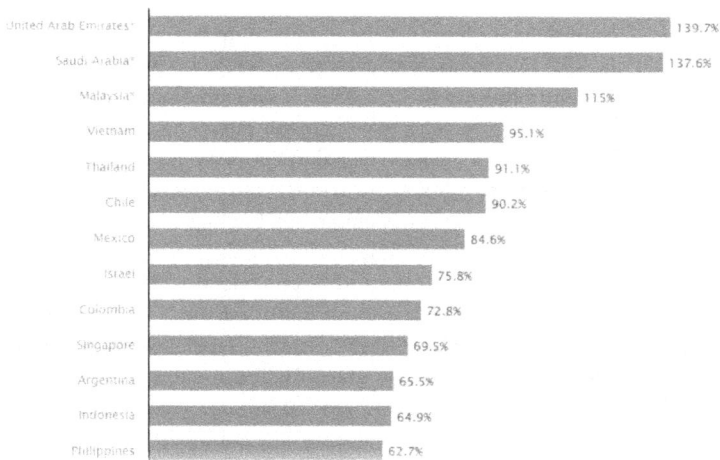

Country	Penetration
United Arab Emirates	139.7%
Saudi Arabia	137.6%
Malaysia	115%
Vietnam	95.1%
Thailand	91.1%
Chile	90.2%
Mexico	84.6%
Israel	75.8%
Colombia	72.8%
Singapore	69.5%
Argentina	65.5%
Indonesia	64.9%
Philippines	62.7%

TikTok penetration in selected countries and territories as of April 2024

and market conditions. As the platform matures, it will need to find new ways to engage users and monetize content. Nevertheless, given its track record of rapid growth and innovation, TikTok seems well-positioned to meet these challenges and continue its upward trajectory.

In conclusion, based on its user growth and revenue stream predictions, TikTok is poised for continued success in the future. Its innovative approach to short-form video content, combined with its expanding user base and revenue streams, makes it a formidable force in the social media landscape.

Tiktok endnote references***

*** These URLs present an overview of TikTok, tips and tricks for using the app's features effectively, important statistics about TikTok's user base and engagement, guides on leveraging TikTok for business marketing and branding, as well as information on affiliate marketing opportunities on the platform. Together, they provide a comprehensive understanding of TikTok's capabilities and usage.

Title: "TikTok—Wikipedia," https://en.wikipedia.org/wiki/TikTok; Title: "TikTok Tips and Tricks: How to Get the Most Out of the Video App," www.cnet.com/tech/services-and-software/tiktok-tips-tricks/; Title: "37 TikTok Stats That Matter to Marketers in 2023," https://blog.hootsuite.com/tiktok-stats/; Title: "How to Use TikTok: A Guide for Brands and Businesses," www.businessinsider.com/guides/tech/tiktok; Title: "TikTok Affiliate Marketing: A Guide for Brands and Creators," www.shopify.com/blog/tiktok-affiliate-marketing. Data Sources as of July 2024 (1) "TikTok Statistics You Need to Know in 2024—Backlinko," https://backlinko.com/tiktok-users. (2) "TikTok Growth Rate (2021–2025)—Oberlo," www.oberlo.com/statistics/tiktok-growth-rate. (3) "The Future of TikTok Growth: Total TikTok Users Predicted to Reach 2.6 ...," https://techstart-ups.com/2022/07/15/future-tiktok-growth-total-tiktok-users-predicted-reach-2-6-billion-daily-users-2025-new-study-found/. (4) "In-depth Analysis of TikTok's Growing Ad Revenue (2021–2025)," www.spocket.co/statistics/tiktok-ad-revenue-analysis. (5) "TikTok Revenue and Usage Statistics (2024– Business of Apps," www.businessofapps.com/data/tik-tok-statistics/. (6) "TikTok Shop Statistics (2024): Revenue, Growth & Trends," https://capitaloneshopping.com/research/tiktok-shopping-statistics. (7) "Track TikTok Analytics, Future Predictions, & TikTok Usage Graphs ..." https://socialblade.com/tiktok/. (8) "TikTok Growth Rate (2021–2025) —Oberlo," https://bing.com/search?q=TikTok+user+growth+predictions. (9) "TikTok to Rank as the Third Largest Social Network, 2022 Forecast Notes," https://techcrunch.com/2021/12/20/tiktok-to-rank-as-the-third-largest-social-network-2022-forecast-notes/. (10) "100+ TikTok Statistics for 2024 - whop.com," https://whop.com/blog/tiktok-statistics/.

Viber: A Unified Communication Hub

Viber logo

Viber, a messaging and calling app, was founded in 2010 by Talmon Marco and Igor Magazinik, both former Israeli soldiers. These visionary minds aimed to create a seamless communication platform that combined voice calling and messaging.

The company's initial goal was to provide a secure communication platform for military personnel, but it quickly pivoted to target the consumer market.

Founding and Early Days (2010)

- The company was funded by individual investors, described by Marco as "friends and family," who invested **$20** million.
- Viber's unique selling point was its spontaneity—unlike scheduled Skype calls, Viber allowed instant, impromptu conversations.

Monetization and Growth

- Initially, Viber did not generate revenue. However, in 2013, it introduced Viber Out for voice calling and the Viber graphical messaging *sticker market* as monetization strategies.
- By May 2013, Viber had 120 employees.
- In July 2013, Viber's support system faced a defacement by the Syrian Electronic Army, but no sensitive user information was compromised.

Acquisition by Rakuten (2014)

- On February 13, 2014, Japanese multinational company Rakuten acquired Viber Media for a whopping $900 million.
- The sale earned the Shabtai family (Benny, Gilad, and Ofer) approximately $500 million from their 55.2 percent stake in the company.
- Since then, Viber has been known as Rakuten Viber and continues to thrive as a global communication platform.

Key Features and User Base

- Viber is available across platforms, including **Google Android, iOS, Microsoft Windows, Apple macOS, and Linux**.
- Users register and identify themselves through their **cellular telephone numbers**, although desktop access does not require mobile connectivity.
- Beyond instant messaging, Viber allows users to exchange media like images and videos. It also offers a paid international calling service called **Viber Out**.
- As of 2018, Viber boasts over a billion registered users worldwide.

Current State

- Viber's user-friendly interface and diverse features have made it a go-to platform for both individuals and businesses.
- The company is headquartered in Cyprus and has offices in London, Manila, Moscow, Paris, San Francisco, Singapore, and Tokyo.

What Might Trigger the Decline of Viber?

Viber, once a prominent messaging platform, has experienced a notable shift in its fortunes over the years. Some factors that might have contributed to its decline include:

1. **Competition:** intense competition from other messaging platforms offering similar features, such as WhatsApp, Telegram, Signal, and Facebook Messenger, could lead to a decline in Viber's user base if it fails to differentiate itself or innovate sufficiently to attract and retain users.

2. **Feature stagnation:** if Viber fails to innovate and introduce new features or improvements to its platform, it risks becoming stagnant and losing relevance among users who seek advanced messaging functionalities and experiences.

3. **Monetization challenges:** Viber's revenue model relies heavily on advertising and premium features. If Viber struggles to effectively monetize its platform or generate sufficient revenue without compromising user experience, it may face financial difficulties that could impact its long-term viability.

4. **Privacy concerns:** if Viber faces significant privacy breaches or fails to maintain its reputation as a secure messaging platform, users may lose trust in the service and seek alternative messaging apps that prioritize user privacy and data security.

5. **Technological shifts:** rapid advancements in technology, such as the emergence of new communication protocols or disruptive innovations in messaging services, could render Viber's features outdated or less appealing to users over time.

6. **User migration:** if key demographics or user segments shift to other messaging platforms for various reasons, such as better features, stronger security, or wider adoption among their social circles, Viber could experience a decline in its user base.

7. **Regulatory challenges:** changes in regulations regarding data privacy, encryption, or messaging services in various countries could pose challenges to Viber's operations and user engagement, potentially leading to a decline in its popularity.

8. **External events:** unforeseen external events, such as security incidents, legal disputes, or economic downturns, could negatively impact Viber's reputation, user engagement, and overall growth trajectory.

9. **User experience issues:** persistent issues with app performance, usability, or customer support could lead to user frustration and dissatisfaction, ultimately driving users to switch to alternative messaging platforms that offer a better overall experience.

Viber's Vibrant Future: A Forecast of Growth and Revenue Generation

User Growth

Viber has shown promising signs of growth and revenue generation. Founded in 2010, Viber has steadily expanded its user base, reaching 1.3 billion users worldwide by 2022. This figure represents approximately 16.25 percent of the global population, a testament to Viber's widespread adoption.

The platform's popularity is particularly pronounced in Southeast Asia, Eastern Europe, and other parts of Asia. This regional popularity, coupled with its availability in 193 countries, provides a solid foundation for future growth. Viber's user engagement is also noteworthy, with users interacting on the app for an average of eight minutes per interaction.

Revenue Stream

Viber's revenue stream, primarily driven by its parent company Rakuten Inc., generated about $1.73 billion in the fiscal year 2021. This impressive figure is bolstered by the platform's business accounts, which delivered approximately 7.5 billion messages in 2021. As of 2021, Viber Business had revenue of $196.4 million, indicating a significant contribution to the overall revenue.

The future of Viber appears bright, given these promising trends in user growth and revenue generation. The platform's robust user base, combined with its strong revenue streams, positions it well for future expansion and profitability. However, as with any social networking platform, Viber's future success will depend on its ability to innovate, retain its user base, and continue to generate revenue in an increasingly competitive market.

Conclusion

In conclusion, based on current user growth and revenue stream predictions, Viber is poised for a vibrant future. Its strong foothold in key regions, coupled with its impressive revenue figures, suggests a promising trajectory for this social networking platform. However, continued innovation and user engagement will be crucial to maintaining this momentum in the years to come.

Viber remains a popular messaging and calling app, known for its user-friendly interface, diverse features, and commitment to user privacy and security. Its evolution reflects a continued focus on providing users with innovative communication tools and services to stay connected with friends, family, and communities across the globe. Viber's journey—from its spontaneous beginnings to its acquisition by Rakuten—reflects its commitment to revolutionizing global communication.

Viber must continuously address these potential challenges, prioritize user privacy and security, innovate its features and services, and remain responsive to evolving market conditions to sustain its growth and relevance over time.

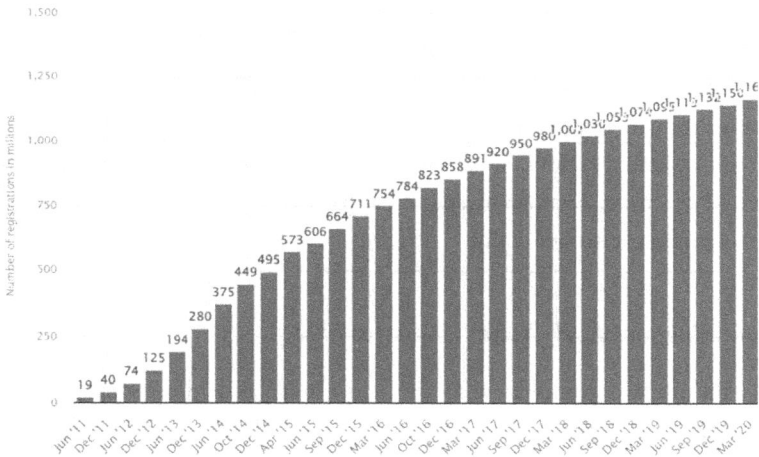

Number of unique Viber user IDs from June 2011 to March 2020 (in millions)

Viber endnote references[†††]

[†††] These URLs present an overview of Viber, the app's features effectively, important statistics about Viber's user base and engagement, as well as information on marketing opportunities on the platform. Together, they provide a comprehensive understanding of Viber's capabilities and usage.

Title: "Viber Review—How Good Is Viber for Paid Calling?," www.lifewire .com/viber-out-review-3426597; Title: "Rakuten Viber Messenger," https:// apps.apple.com/us/app/rakuten-viber-messenger/id382617920?mt=8;   Title: "Download Viber for Mac," https://filehippo.com/mac/download_viber-for-mac/; Title: "Viber App Review," www.lifewire.com/viber-app-review-3426625; Title: "Wikipedia Viber," https://en.wikipedia.org/wiki/Viber; Title: "Viber App Facts," https://facts.net/tech-and-sciences/12-facts-you-must-know-about-viber-application/ Data Sources as of July 2024 https://usesignhouse.com/blog/viber-stats/, https://financesonline.com/viber-statistics/, https://marketsplash.com/viber-statistics/, https://techreport.com/statistics/software-web/viber-statistics/.

WhatsApp: A Communication Revolution

WhatsApp logo

WhatsApp, a messaging platform renowned for its simplicity, reliability, and widespread adoption, has transformed the way people communicate across the globe since its inception. Founded by Jan Koum and Brian Acton in January 2009, WhatsApp has grown from a humble start-up to one of the most popular messaging apps worldwide, facilitating billions of messages exchanged daily.

Founding and Early Years (2009 to 2012)

WhatsApp was founded with the mission of providing a simple and affordable messaging solution for users around the world. WhatsApp initially targeted the iPhone market, offering a messaging app that leveraged the device's internet connectivity to send messages instead of traditional SMS. The app's focus on simplicity, privacy, and ad-free experience resonated with users, leading to rapid adoption and organic growth. By February 2013, WhatsApp had surpassed 200 million active users, cementing its status as a leading messaging platform.

Acquisition by Facebook and Global Expansion (2012 to 2014)

In February 2014, Facebook announced its acquisition of WhatsApp for $19 billion, marking one of the largest technology acquisitions in history. The acquisition provided WhatsApp with the resources and support to accelerate its global expansion and enhance its features and infrastructure. WhatsApp continued to prioritize user privacy and security, implementing end-to-end encryption to ensure that messages remained private and secure from third-party intrusion. The platform also expanded its reach beyond smartphones, introducing support for desktop and web-based messaging.

Introduction of Voice Calling and Video Calling (2015 to 2018)

In subsequent years, WhatsApp introduced new features to enhance its communication capabilities, including voice calling and video calling. The launch of voice calling in March 2015 allowed users to make free voice calls to other WhatsApp users over the internet, challenging traditional phone carriers and communication services. WhatsApp further expanded its offerings with the introduction of video calling in November 2016, enabling users to engage in face-to-face conversations with friends and family members regardless of geographical distance.

Focus on Business Solutions and Monetization (2018 to Present)

In recent years, WhatsApp has shifted its focus toward providing business solutions and exploring monetization opportunities. The introduction of WhatsApp Business in January 2018 offered businesses a platform to communicate with customers, provide customer support, and send promotional messages professionally and securely. WhatsApp also announced plans to monetize the platform through business messaging services, allowing businesses to reach potential customers through targeted advertising and promotional campaigns.

Future Outlook and Continued Innovation

As WhatsApp continues to evolve, its commitment to simplicity, privacy, and user experience remains at the forefront. The platform's ubiquity and global reach position it as a vital tool for communication, collaboration, and connection in an increasingly interconnected world. With ongoing investments in technology, features, and business solutions, WhatsApp is poised to remain a dominant force in the messaging landscape for years to come.

What Might Trigger the Decline of WhatsApp?

Potential triggers for the decline of WhatsApp:

1. **Security concerns:** escalating concerns about user data privacy or security breaches could erode trust and impact WhatsApp's popularity.
2. **Emergence of competing platforms:** if new messaging platforms with better features or enhanced security measures gain popularity, drawing users away from WhatsApp.
3. **Monetization challenges:** if WhatsApp faces difficulties in sustaining its revenue model or encounters challenges in effectively monetizing its platform.
4. **Regulatory changes:** stringent regulations or legal challenges related to privacy, antitrust, or other matters could impact WhatsApp's operations.
5. **Changing communication trends:** if there is a significant shift in how users prefer to communicate, favoring platforms with different communication mediums.
6. **Technical issues:** frequent technical glitches, outages, or service disruptions could affect user experience and lead to a decline in user satisfaction.
7. **News outlets:** reputable technology and business news outlets, such as TechCrunch, The Verge, or Reuters, often cover developments in the tech industry, including changes in popular messaging platforms like WhatsApp.
8. **Official statements:** statements from WhatsApp's official blog or any communications from its parent company, Meta, can provide insights into the platform's strategies and responses to challenges.
9. **Financial reports:** analyzing Meta's financial reports, usually available on their investor relations page, can give insights into WhatsApp's financial health and potential challenges.
10. **Industry analyses:** reports from market research firms and industry analyses can provide a broader perspective on messaging app trends, competition, and factors influencing WhatsApp's position.

WhatsApp: A Beacon of Growth and Revenue in the Digital Age

User Growth

WhatsApp has been a game-changer in the realm of digital communication. With its user-friendly interface and robust features, it has amassed a staggering user base of approximately two billion MAU as of 2023. The platform's growth trajectory is impressive, with projections indicating that it could reach almost three billion unique active users worldwide by June 2024. This represents a 7 percent increase compared to June 2023, demonstrating the app's enduring appeal and its potential for further expansion.

Revenue Model

WhatsApp's revenue model has evolved significantly since its inception. Initially, it operated on a subscription model, charging users a nominal fee for its services. However, following its acquisition by Facebook (now Meta) in 2014, the platform pivoted toward a more lucrative revenue model. The introduction of WhatsApp Business marked a significant milestone, providing users with the capability to create business profiles. These unlocked features such as business profiles, links to websites or Facebook pages, automatic responses, and seamless integration with the WhatsApp Business API. This API, a crucial tool, facilitates smooth integration into various systems for enhanced customer engagement.

WhatsApp Business charges companies for messages, particularly those engaging in over a thousand conversations. This has become a major revenue source for the platform. In 2022, WhatsApp reportedly generated over $906 million, and Forbes estimates that the company could generate $5 to $15 billion in the coming years.

However, while these figures are promising, they also present challenges. As WhatsApp continues to grow, it will need to navigate issues related to data privacy and security, particularly given its commitment to end-to-end encryption. Furthermore, as it expands its revenue streams, it will need to ensure that it maintains its user-friendly interface and does not compromise the user experience with intrusive advertising or complex features.

Conclusion

In conclusion, the future of WhatsApp looks bright, with robust user growth and promising revenue stream predictions. However, the platform will need to balance its commercial interests with its commitment to user privacy and experience. As it stands, WhatsApp is well-positioned to continue its trajectory of success in the digital age.

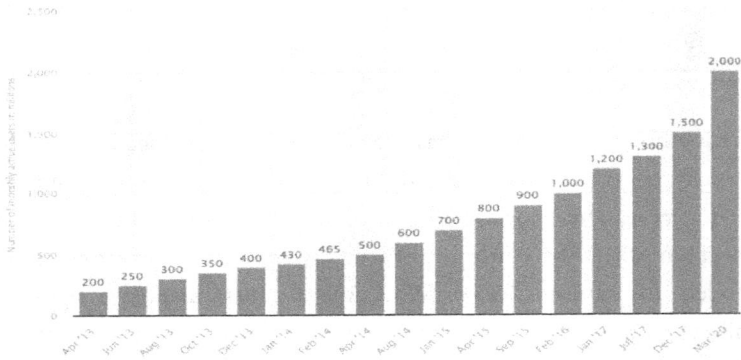

Details: Worldwide; WhatsApp; Facebook; April 2013 to March 2020   © Statista

Number of monthly active WhatsApp users worldwide from April 2013 to March 2020 (in millions)

Whatsapp endnote references‡‡‡

---

‡‡‡ These URLs cover an overview of WhatsApp, tips and tricks for using its features effectively, important statistics about WhatsApp's user base and usage, a beginner's guide to using the app, as well as a guide on leveraging WhatsApp for business marketing and communications. Together, they provide a comprehensive understanding of WhatsApp's capabilities and applications.

Title: "WhatsApp—Wikipedia," https://en.wikipedia.org/wiki/WhatsApp; Title: "WhatsApp Tips and Tricks to Help You Chat Like a Pro," www.cnet.com/tech/services-and-software/whatsapp-tips-tricks/; Title: "27 WhatsApp Statistics Marketers Need to Know in 2023," https://blog.hootsuite.com/whatsapp-statistics/; Title: "How to Use WhatsApp: A Guide for Beginners and Power Users," www.businessinsider.com/guides/tech/whatsapp; Title: "How to Use WhatsApp for Business: A Guide for Marketers," www.businessinsider.com/guides/tech/what-is-whatsapp-guide. Data Sources as of July 2024 (1) "WhatsApp - Statistics & Facts | Statista," www.statista.com/topics/2018/whatsapp/. (2) "WhatsApp User Statistics 2024: How Many People Use WhatsApp?—Backlinko," https://backlinko.com/whatsapp-users. (3) "27+ WhatsApp User Statistics that Prove WhatsApp Business is the Future ...," https://learn.rasayel.io/en/blog/whatsapp-user-statistics/. (4) "WhatsApp Global Unique Users 2024 | Statista," www.statista.com/statistics/1306022/whatsapp-global-unique-users/. (5) "WhatsApp Revenue Model (Business Model): How Does WhatsApp Make Money ...," www.whispy.io/whatsapp-revenue-model/. (6) "How Does WhatsApp Make Money? - Investopedia," www.investopedia.com/articles/personal-finance/040915/how-whatsapp-makes-money.asp. (7) "How Does WhatsApp Make Money? WhatsApp 2023 Revenue Models Explained," https://icoverage.io/B-Finance/WhatsApp-Revenue. (8) "WhatsApp Is Becoming a Key Driver of Mobile Messaging Growth," www.emarketer.com/content/whatsapp-is-becoming-a-key-driver-of-mobile-messaging-growth. (9) "How Does WhatsApp Make Money? WhatsApp 2023 Revenue Models Explained," https://bing.com/search?q=WhatsApp+revenue+stream+predictions. (10) "How WhatsApp Makes Money?—Revenue Streams of WhatsApp—The Brand Hopper," https://thebrandhopper.com/2023/06/05/how-whatsapp-makes-money-revenue-streams-of-whatsapp/.

X (Twitter): A Platform for Real-Time Communication

X logo

Twitter, a microblogging and social networking platform, has emerged as a powerful tool for real-time communication, news dissemination, and social interaction since its inception.

Founded by Jack Dorsey, Noah Glass, Biz Stone, and Evan Williams in March 2006, Twitter has undergone significant growth and transformation, shaping the way people share information, express opinions, and connect with others globally.

The Evolution of Twitter

In the digital dawn of 2006, a spark ignited within the mind of Jack Dorsey, one of Twitter's cofounders. His vision? A novel SMS-based communication platform that would allow friends to share their status updates. Imagine texting but with a twist—a global twist. This embryo of an idea was christened twttr.

At the same time, the podcasting company Odeo was navigating choppy waters. Apple's release of its own podcasting platform threatened Odeo's existence. Amidst this turmoil, Jack Dorsey pitched his SMS-based concept to Odeo's cofounder, Evan Williams. Evan, along with cofounder Biz Stone, gave Jack the green light to dive deeper into this aquatic experiment. And so, Twitter was born—initially as twttr, a name stripped of vowels in the trendy style of the dot-com era.

On March 21, 2006, at precisely 9:50 p.m., Jack Dorsey sent forth the inaugural tweet into the digital ether: "Just setting up my twttr [sic]." Little did he know that this seemingly innocuous message would ripple across the world, shaping the future of communication.

But Twitter's journey was not all smooth sailing. As the platform evolved, team members incurred hefty SMS charges on their personal phone bills. Meanwhile, Odeo faced its own tempest—a business model capsized by Apple's podcasting platform. In a daring move, Jack Dorsey, Biz Stone, Evan Williams, and other Odeo staff orchestrated a buyback, reclaiming their fledgling creation. The rights to Twitter now rested in their hands, but controversy swirled around the details of this transaction. Notably absent from the new venture was Noah Glass, a key player in Twitter's early days.

Founding and Early Years (2006 to 2008)

Twitter originated as an internal project within the podcasting company Odeo, where Jack Dorsey proposed the idea of an SMS-based communication platform.

The service, initially named *twttr*, was launched publicly in July 2006. Twitter's defining feature was its 140-character limit per tweet, a restriction inspired by the character limits of SMS messages at the time. Twitter initially gained traction among tech-savvy users and early adopters who embraced its simplicity and immediacy. The platform's use of hashtags, mentions, and retweets facilitated conversations and content discovery, fostering a sense of community and interconnectedness among users. The platform gained traction during notable events such as the South by Southwest Interactive conference in 2007, where its utility for real-time updates became evident.

Rapid Growth and Mainstream Adoption (2009 to 2012)

Twitter's user base expanded rapidly in the late 2000s and early 2010s, fueled by celebrity endorsements, media coverage, and word-of-mouth marketing. Twitter's user base experienced exponential growth during this period, fueled by celebrity endorsements, media coverage, and its integration with popular culture and events. High-profile users, including politicians, celebrities, and journalists, embraced Twitter as a platform for direct communication with their audiences. The introduction of features such as hashtags, retweets, and trending topics further enhanced user engagement and content discoverability. Twitter's role as a catalyst for social movements and political activism became increasingly pronounced, as evidenced by its role in the Arab Spring protests in 2011.

The platform became a go-to destination for breaking news, live events, and cultural phenomena, with hashtags such as #BlackLives-Matter, #MeToo, and #ArabSpring amplifying social movements and activism. Twitter's influence extended beyond individuals to businesses, brands, and public figures, who leveraged the platform for marketing, customer engagement, and public relations.

Monetization and Maturation (2013 to 2016)

Twitter shifted its focus toward monetization strategies to sustain its growth and relevance in the competitive social media landscape. Advertising initiatives, promoted tweets, and sponsored content became integral components of Twitter's revenue model. To monetize its platform and generate revenue, Twitter introduced advertising solutions such as Promoted Tweets, Trends, and Accounts, allowing businesses to reach targeted audiences and amplify their messages.

The acquisition of **Vine** in October 2012 marked Twitter's foray into short-form video content, enabling users to create and share looping six-second videos within the Twitter ecosystem. Twitter also invested in product enhancements, redesigns, and acquisitions to improve user experience and retention, including the launch of features such as Twitter Cards, Moments, and Periscope.

The company went public in November 2013 with its highly anticipated IPO, valuing the company at over $31 billion. However, despite its widespread popularity, Twitter faced challenges in retaining users and monetizing its platform effectively, leading to fluctuations in its stock price and concerns among investors.

Stagnation and Reinvention (2017 to 2023)

Twitter has grappled with issues such as user harassment, misinformation, and platform abuse, prompting efforts to enhance content moderation and community safety measures. The company introduced new features and product enhancements, including longer character limits, multimedia capabilities, and the introduction of fleets (temporary tweets).

As Twitter matured, debates raged over its character limit. Was 140 characters enough? In 2017, the platform doubled the limit to 280 characters, sparking both delight and consternation. However, innovation thrived within constraints. Users crafted micro-stories, threaded conversations, and poetic haikus—all within the confines of a tweet. Twitter became a canvas for creativity, a place where brevity birthed brilliance.

In 2021, Twitter introduced Spaces, a feature for hosting live audio conversations, as part of its broader efforts to compete with emerging social media platforms and capitalize on the growing popularity of audio-based content. The company has implemented measures to address these issues, including stricter enforcement of community guidelines, algorithmic changes to prioritize relevant content, and partnerships with third-party organizations to combat misinformation and disinformation. Twitter has also explored new revenue streams and business opportunities, such as subscription-based services and e-commerce integrations, to diversify its revenue sources and drive growth.

X (Formerly Twitter)

In 2022, Musk acquired Twitter, infusing it with his audacious vision. The platform shed its old skin, rebranding as X.

As X navigates the evolving landscape of social media and digital communication, its focus remains on innovation, user engagement, and fostering meaningful conversations.

Positive Outlook for X

Some insights into factors that might influence its future outlook:

1. **User growth:** Twitter's future success may depend on its ability to attract and retain users. Expanding its user base globally, especially in emerging markets, could contribute to its positive outlook.
2. **Monetization strategies:** Twitter's revenue generation methods, such as advertising and subscription services, will play a crucial role

in its future profitability. Innovations in these areas could enhance its financial performance.

3. **Product development:** introducing new features and improving existing ones to enhance user experience and engagement could be key to Twitter's growth. This includes initiatives related to content moderation, personalization, and platform security.

4. **Competitive landscape:** monitoring and adapting to changes in the social media landscape and responding effectively to competition from platforms like Facebook, Instagram, and emerging players will be important for Twitter's future success.

5. **Regulatory environment:** compliance with regulations related to user privacy, data protection, and content moderation will be critical for Twitter's operations. Adapting to evolving regulatory frameworks worldwide will be essential for its long-term viability.

6. **Technological innovation:** embracing advancements in technology, such as AI, machine learning, and blockchain, could enable Twitter to enhance its platform's functionality and security, potentially driving future growth.

These factors, among others, can collectively shape Twitter's future prospects. However, it's important to conduct a thorough analysis and consider various perspectives before forming any investment or strategic decisions related to the company.

Negative Outlook for X

Twitter, after Elon Musk's acquisition, faces a fascinating array of potential scenarios, including:

- Bankruptcy:
  - Twitter's financial future hinges significantly on advertisers, as the bulk of its revenue comes from ads.
  - If many sponsors pause or reduce their spending, it could spell trouble for the platform.
  - The loss of substantial revenues might make it challenging to maintain basic services or update the platform.

- o Reports suggest that Twitter requires over a billion dollars annually just to cover its debt service, and any threat to loan repayment or workforce security could endanger the business.
- Little content moderation and extremism:
  - o Elon Musk, a free speech advocate, has encouraged a wider range of voices on Twitter.
  - o He has brought back controversial figures like Donald Trump, Kathy Griffin, Babylon Bee, and Jordan Peterson to the platform.
  - o While this commitment to free speech is commendable, it may lead to greater toxicity and extremism on social media sites.
  - o A possible emphasis on content moderation could exacerbate these issues.
- Technical challenges:
  - o Twitter could face serious technical problems that impact user experience, stability, or security.
  - o Ensuring robust infrastructure and addressing technical glitches will be crucial for its survival.
- Innovation and survival:
  - o Smaller staff that focus on adding innovative new products could help Twitter weather the initial turbulence.
  - o By introducing fresh features and services, Twitter might attract users and advertisers, ensuring its longevity.

What Might Trigger the Decline of X (Twitter)?

Anticipating the precise factors leading to the decline of Twitter involves speculation, but potential triggers could include:

- **User migration:** if a significant portion of Twitter's user base migrates to other platforms offering better features or aligning with evolving preferences.

- **Monetization challenges:** if Twitter struggles to maintain a profitable business model or faces difficulties in monetizing its platform effectively.
- **Content moderation issues:** escalating concerns or controversies related to content moderation, fake news, or hate speech could impact user trust and engagement.
- **Competition:** increased competition from emerging platforms that provide unique features or a more compelling user experience may draw users away from Twitter.
- **Technological shifts:** rapid advancements in communication technologies that offer new ways of sharing information could influence user preferences.
- **Leadership changes:** shifts in leadership or corporate strategy may impact Twitter's direction and ability to adapt to market changes.
- **News outlets:** reputable technology and business news outlets such as TechCrunch, The Verge, or Reuters often cover developments in social media platforms. Regularly checking their articles can provide insights into any challenges Twitter may be facing.
- **Official statements:** following Twitter's official blog and press releases, as well as any statements from its leadership, can offer a direct source of information on the company's strategies and responses to challenges.
- **Financial reports:** examining Twitter's financial reports, usually available on their investor relations page, can give you insights into the company's financial health and potential challenges.
- **Industry analyses:** reports from market research firms and industry analyses can provide a broader perspective on social media trends, competition, and potential factors influencing Twitter's position.
- **Ownership change and rebranding:** since Elon Musk bought Twitter in October 2022 and rebranded it as X, it has lost approximately 13 percent of its app's daily active users. The rebranding only accelerated the decline.

- **Algorithm and policy changes:** under Musk's stewardship, X's main news feed algorithm has changed, privileging certain types of content over others. This has led to a degradation of X's key use case of delivering in-the-moment updates on key news events.
- **Loss of users and engagement:** visits to the company's website are down 14 percent compared to last September, far outstripping the 3.7 percent decline industrywide over the same period.
- **Legal and regulatory challenges:** X is the subject of multiple regulatory investigations by the U.S. Federal Trade Commission, Securities and Exchange Commission, and EU officials that could potentially lead to penalties.

These factors, among others, could contribute to a potential decline in X's user base and influence. X's future remains uncertain. Its fate will likely be shaped by a delicate balance between free speech, financial stability, and technical resilience. The platform's continued user growth and influence underscore its significance in the social media landscape.

Twitter's Future: A Tale of User Growth and Revenue Streams

Twitter, the microblogging giant, has been a significant player in the social media landscape for over a decade. However, the future of Twitter is a topic of intense debate, with varying predictions about its user growth and revenue streams.

User Growth

Starting with user growth, Twitter's user base has seen some fluctuations. As of 2021, Twitter had approximately 330 million MAU. However, projections for the future are not as optimistic. From 2021 to 2025, the average annual growth rate of Twitter users is expected to be –1 percent. A study in December 2022 revealed that Twitter's user base is projected to decline in the upcoming two years, with a decrease of nearly four percent in 2023 and five percent in 2024. Despite this, Twitter is projecting at least 315 million magnetizable daily active users in Q4 2023, indicating a potential for growth in magnetizable users.

Revenue Streams

Turning to revenue streams, Twitter has shown promising signs. In Q1 2022, Twitter reported adjusted earnings of 90 cents per share, a 462.5 percent YOY increase, and revenues increased 16 percent YOY to $1.20 billion. Advertising revenues, a significant part of Twitter's income, increased 23 percent YOY to $1.11 billion. However, subscription and other revenue reached $94 million, down 31 percent YOY.

Twitter's 2021 revenue was $5.08 billion, a 37 percent increase YOY. The company has set ambitious goals for the future, aiming for $7.5 billion or more in revenue in 2023. This goal is backed by Twitter's increased focus on performance ads and the small and medium business opportunities.

Conclusion

In conclusion, while Twitter faces challenges in user growth, its robust revenue streams and strategic focus on magnetizable users and performance ads present opportunities for future growth. However, the social media landscape is rapidly evolving, and Twitter's ability to adapt and innovate will be crucial in determining its future success.

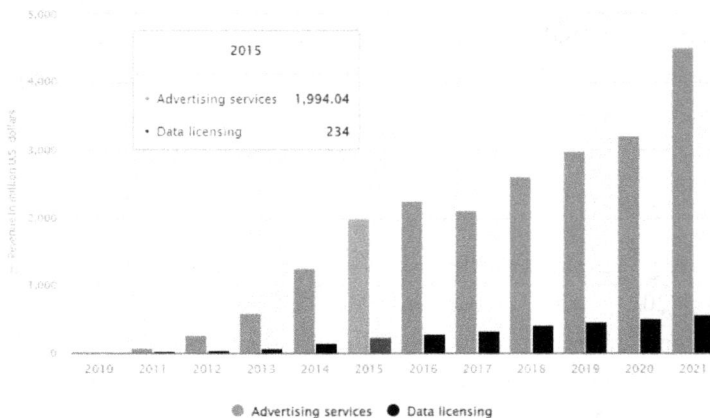

Annual revenue of X (formerly Twitter) from 2010 to 2021, by segment (in million U.S. dollars)

The platform continues to innovate and evolve its features, policies, and products to meet the evolving needs of its diverse user base. With ongoing investments in technology, machine learning, and content moderation, X could remain a vital platform for news, information, and social interaction for years to come.

Predicting the future of such a large and complex platform is inherently uncertain.

X (Twitter) endnote references[§§§]

[§§§] These URLs cover Wikipedia's overview of Twitter, statistics on its user base and engagement metrics, tips and tricks for using Twitter effectively for personal or business purposes, guides on leveraging Twitter for branding and marketing, as well as best practices for businesses utilizing the platform. They provide a comprehensive look at understanding and making the most of Twitter (now X).

Title: "Twitter—Wikipedia," https://en.wikipedia.org/wiki/Twitter; Title: "37 Twitter Statistics All Marketers Need to Know in 2023," https://blog.hubspot.com/marketing/twitter-stats; Title: "Twitter Tips, Tricks and Best Practices for 2023," www.cnet.com/tech/services-and-software/twitter-tips-tricks-and-hacks/; Title: "How to Use Twitter to Grow Your Personal Brand or Business," www.businessinsider.com/guides/tech/twitter; Title: "How to Use Twitter for Business: A Beginner's Guide," www.socialmediaexaminer.com/how-to-use-twitter-for-business/. Data Sources as of July 2024 (1) "Number of Twitter Users 2024: Demographics, Breakdowns & Predictions," https://financesonline.com/number-of-twitter-users/. (2) "Twitter User Growth (2021–2025)—Oberlo," www.oberlo.com/statistics/twitter-user-growth. (3) "Twitter: Annual Growth Rate Worldwide 2024 | Statista," www.statista.com/statistics/303723/twitters-annual-growth-rate-worldwide/. (4) "Twitter Targets 315M Daily Users by 2023, Expects to Double Revenue," https://variety.com/2021/digital/news/twitter-2023-projection-315-million-daily-users-doubling-revenue-1234915120/. (5) "Twitter (TWTR) Q1 Earnings Beat Estimates, Ad Revenues Rise—Yahoo Finance," https://finance.yahoo.com/news/twitter-twtr-q1-earnings-beat-172705310.html. (6) "Twitter Announces Fourth Quarter and Fiscal Year 2021 Results—PR Newswire," www.prnewswire.com/news-releases/twitter-announces-fourth-quarter-and-fiscal-year-2021-results-301479494.html. (7) "Track Twitter Analytics, Future Predictions, & Twitter Usage Graphs ...," https://socialblade.com/twitter/. (8) "Twitter Posts Fastest Revenue Growth Since 2014 in Pandemic Rebound," www.cnbc.com/2021/07/22/twitter-twtr-earnings-q2-2021.html. (9) "Twitter Announces Second Quarter 2021 Results—PR Newswire," www.prnewswire.com/news-releases/twitter-announces-second-quarter-2021-results-301339855.html. (10) "Twitter Q2: 206M Daily Users Amid Decline in U.S., Beats ... - Variety," https://variety.com/2021/digital/news/twitter-q2-2021-earnings-1235025920/.

YouTube: A Video Content Universe

YouTube logo

YouTube is an American online video-sharing platform owned by Google. YouTube allows users to upload videos, view them, rate them with likes and dislikes, share them, add videos to playlists, report, make comments on videos, and subscribe to other users.

Founding and Development

Founded by Steve Chen, Chad Hurley, and Jawed Karim in February 2005, YouTube has evolved from a small startup in a garage to a global platform with billions of users, shaping entertainment, education, and communication on a massive scale.

The idea of YouTube was born when the founders realized the difficulty of finding and sharing videos online. Initially, they thought of creating a video dating website called "Tune In, Hook Up," where people would upload videos of themselves to find dates. However, this idea did not take off, and they pivoted to a platform where users could upload, share, and view videos.

Early Years (2005 to 2007)

YouTube was born out of the founders' frustration with sharing video clips easily online. They envisioned a platform where users could upload, share, and discover videos effortlessly. The site officially went live in February 2005, allowing users to upload videos up to 10 minutes in length. YouTube's simplicity and focus on user-generated content quickly gained traction, attracting millions of users worldwide. In November 2006,

Google acquired YouTube for $1.65 billion, recognizing its potential as a dominant force in online video.

Growth and Monetization (2007 to 2012)

Under Google's ownership, YouTube experienced explosive growth and introduced various monetization strategies to support its operations. The launch of the YouTube Partner Program in 2007 allowed content creators to earn revenue through advertising displayed alongside their videos. This incentivized the creation of high-quality content and fostered the rise of YouTube celebrities and influencers. The platform also invested in infrastructure to support the growing demand for video streaming, including the introduction of HD video playback and live streaming capabilities.

Diversification and Original Content (2012 to 2016)

In response to competition and changing user preferences, YouTube diversified its content offerings and ventured into original programming. The creation of the YouTube Originals program in 2012 aimed to produce exclusive, premium content featuring collaborations with prominent creators, celebrities, and media companies. YouTube also expanded its reach to mobile devices with the launch of mobile apps for iOS and Android, catering to the growing number of users accessing the platform on smartphones and tablets.

Expansion Into Live Streaming and Virtual Reality (2016 to Present)

The launch of YouTube Live in 2016 allowed content creators to stream live video content in real-time, enabling interactive experiences such as live chats and audience participation. YouTube also invested in VR with the introduction of YouTube VR, a VR app offering immersive 360° video experiences. These advancements have expanded YouTube's content library to include VR documentaries, concerts, and gaming content.

Features

YouTube offers a variety of features that enhance the user experience. Users can upload videos, create playlists, comment on videos, and subscribe to other users' channels. It also provides live streaming capabilities, allowing users to broadcast live content. YouTube has also introduced features like Super Chat and Channel Memberships, which allow creators to monetize their content. Moreover, it offers features like Autoplay, Closed Captions, and Text Overlay for accessibility.

Impact

YouTube has had a significant impact on society, culture, and the economy. It has transformed the way people consume media, shifting the focus from traditional television and cinema to online video content. YouTube's creative ecosystem contributed over $35 billion to the U.S. GDP in 2022. It has also played a crucial role in shaping popular culture and trends, providing a platform for individuals to express their creativity and share their talents with the world.

Future Outlook and Continued Innovation

As YouTube continues to evolve, its commitment to innovation, diversity, and user engagement remains paramount. The platform's vast library of user-generated and professionally produced content, combined with its global reach and influence, positions it as a dominant force in online video for years to come. With ongoing investments in technology, content creation tools, and user experience enhancements, YouTube is poised to shape the future of digital entertainment and communication on a global scale.

What Might Trigger the Decline of YouTube?

Potential triggers for the decline of YouTube:

1. **Emergence of competing platforms:** if new platforms with innovative features or better content discovery mechanisms emerge, draw users away from YouTube.

2. **Adverse content issues:** escalating concerns about inappropriate or harmful content on the platform, coupled with challenges in effective content moderation, could impact user trust and engagement.

3. **Monetization challenges:** YouTube faces difficulties in maintaining a sustainable and profitable business model, including issues with advertising revenue or creator monetization.

4. **Technological shifts:** rapid advancements in streaming technologies or the rise of new mediums for content consumption could influence user preferences.

5. **Copyright and legal issues:** ongoing or intensified legal challenges related to copyright infringement or other legal matters could impact YouTube's operations.

6. **Changes in user behavior:** shifts in how users prefer to consume and engage with content, especially if preferences align with features not offered by YouTube.

7. **News outlets:** reputable technology and business news outlets, such as TechCrunch, The Verge, or Reuters, often cover developments in the tech industry, including changes in popular platforms like YouTube.

8. **Official statements:** statements and blog posts from YouTube's official blog or any communications from its parent company, Google, can provide insights into the platform's strategies and responses to challenges.

9. **Financial reports:** analyzing Google's financial reports, available on its investor relations page, can give insights into YouTube's financial health and potential challenges.

10. **Industry analyses:** reports from market research firms and industry analyses can provide a broader perspective on online video consumption trends, competition, and factors influencing YouTube's position.

YouTube: A Rising Star in the Digital Universe

YouTube, the world's largest video-sharing platform, has been experiencing a significant surge in both user growth and revenue streams.

User Projection

As of 2024, YouTube boasts over 2.7 billion active users worldwide. This number is projected to continuously increase, reaching an estimated 1.2 billion users by 2029. Such a massive user base is a testament to YouTube's global appeal and its ability to cater to diverse content preferences. The platform's user growth is not just impressive in numbers but also in diversity. For instance, Indian YouTube users make up 30.8 percent of total YouTube traffic. This indicates YouTube's successful penetration into various global markets, further solidifying its position as a truly international platform.

Revenue Growth

In terms of revenue, YouTube has shown remarkable growth. During the first quarter of 2023, YouTube generated revenue of $22.31 billion. The estimated revenue of YouTube in the United States alone is projected to reach 22 billion by 2025. Advertising remains the primary source of YouTube's revenue, with global advertising revenue crossing 8.1 billion U.S. dollars in the first quarter of 2024.

Moreover, YouTube's value has skyrocketed since Google's acquisition in 2006 for $1.65 billion. As of 2024, YouTube could be worth $400 billion— that is more than Disney and Comcast combined. This exponential increase in value underscores YouTube's successful monetization strategies and its significant impact on the digital advertising landscape.

Furthermore, YouTube's introduction of features such as Shorts, Live streaming, Chapters, Premieres, and the Community Tab continues to attract more content creators and consumers[7]. These features not only enhance user engagement but also provide creators with more avenues to generate revenue.

Conclusion

In conclusion, YouTube's future looks promising, with robust user growth and revenue stream predictions. Its ability to innovate and adapt to changing user preferences and market trends positions it well for continued success in the digital universe. However, like any other social network,

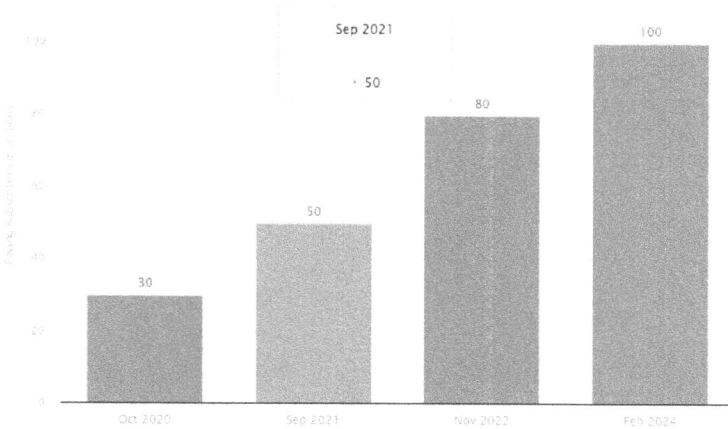

Details: Worldwide; YouTube; 2020 to 2024; YouTube Music and YouTube Premium subscribers

Paying YouTube Music and YouTube Premium subscribers worldwide from 2020 to 2024 (in millions)

YouTube must continue to evolve and address challenges such as content moderation and data privacy to sustain its growth trajectory. However, like any other platform, it has its challenges, including issues related to copyright, misinformation, and content moderation.

YouTube endnote references[¶¶¶]

[¶¶¶] These URLs cover an overview of YouTube, guides on how to use the platform effectively, provide interesting statistics and facts about YouTube's popularity and scale, as well as tips and tricks for getting the most out of YouTube as a user or content creator.

Title: "YouTube—Wikipedia," www.cnet.com/tech/services-and-software/youtube-video-site-how-to-use/; Title: "YouTube: How to Use the Insanely Popular Video," https://blog.hubspot.com/marketing/youtube-stats; Title: "37 Mind-Blowing YouTube Facts, Figures and Statistics," www.businessinsider.com/guides/tech/youtube; Title: "The Best YouTube Tips and Tricks for Power Users," www.tomsguide.com/round-up/best-youtube-tips.

CHAPTER 4

Emerging Trends and New Contenders

Some emerging trends and new contenders in the realm of social networking reflect evolving user preferences, concerns about privacy and authenticity, and the desire for alternatives to existing mainstream social media platforms. As users continue to seek out platforms that prioritize user control, data privacy, and meaningful interactions, these new contenders are likely to play an increasingly important role in shaping the future of social networking.

We explore hereafter some of the most familiar ones: Clubhouse, Mastodon, Vero, Parler, Goodreads, Nextdoor, Quora, Ravelry, Steemit, Diaspora, and MeWe.

Clubhouse: Audio-Only Networking and Its Prospects

Clubhouse logo

Founding and Development

Clubhouse (https://clubhouse.com/) has rapidly gained attention as a unique player in the social networking landscape, offering an audio-only platform for real-time conversations and networking.

Launched in 2020 by Paul Davison and Rohan Seth, Clubhouse allows users to join virtual rooms where they can participate in discussions, listen to speakers, and engage with others on a wide range of topics.

Features

The appeal of Clubhouse lies in its simplicity and focus on live audio interactions. By removing the visual element inherent in traditional social media platforms, Clubhouse fosters a more intimate and immersive experience, allowing users to connect with others based solely on voice and conversation. This format is particularly well suited for fostering genuine connections, facilitating meaningful discussions, and overcoming barriers such as language or accessibility.

Moreover, Clubhouse's exclusivity and invitation-only model have contributed to its allure and rapid growth. By initially limiting access to a select group of users and leveraging the concept of scarcity, Clubhouse generated curiosity and demand, leading to a surge in popularity and attracting high-profile users and influencers.

Additionally, Clubhouse's real-time nature enables spontaneous conversations and serendipitous connections, akin to attending live events or conferences. This real-time aspect adds an element of excitement and unpredictability to the platform, distinguishing it from asynchronous forms of communication prevalent on other social media platforms.

Challenges

However, Clubhouse also faces challenges and uncertainties as it seeks to capitalize on its early success and sustain long-term growth. Competition in the audio social networking space is intensifying, with established players like Twitter and Facebook launching their own audio features and platforms. Moreover, questions remain about the platform's ability to monetize and retain users over time, particularly as the novelty wears off and users' attention becomes increasingly fragmented.

Furthermore, Clubhouse has faced criticism and controversy regarding issues such as content moderation, privacy, and accessibility. As the platform scales and attracts a more diverse user base, addressing these concerns will be crucial to maintaining user trust and fostering a safe and inclusive community.

Overall, Clubhouse represents a compelling addition to the social networking landscape, offering a novel and immersive platform for audio-based interactions and networking. While challenges and uncertainties remain, its early success underscores the potential for audio-based communication to reshape how we connect, engage, and collaborate in the digital age.

Prospects and Opportunities

Niche communities: the Clubhouse offers unique opportunities for community building. Its platform fosters an environment where users can dive deep into niche topics, leading to the formation of tight-knit communities centered around shared interests, professions, or hobbies.

Thought leadership: experts, influencers, and thought leaders host rooms, sharing insights, knowledge, and experiences. Users can learn directly from industry leaders and engage in meaningful conversations.

Networking: clubhouse provides a space for professional networking. Users can connect with like-minded individuals, potential collaborators, and mentors.

Creativity and entertainment: musicians, comedians, and artists use Clubhouse to showcase their talents. Live performances, stand-up comedy, and interactive storytelling add an element of creativity and entertainment.

Inclusivity: audio interactions break down barriers related to language, appearance, and accessibility. Users can participate without worrying about visual representation.

Clubhouse: A Sonic Boom in Social Media or a Fading Echo?

The Clubhouse social network, an audio-based platform that has been likened to live podcasting, has seen a meteoric rise since its inception in 2020. The platform's user base surged from 600,000 in December 2020 to 10 million weekly active users (WAU). This growth trajectory is impressive, especially considering the platform was initially invite-only and exclusive to iOS users[2].

User Growth

Clubhouse's user growth has defied the slowing growth patterns across maturing social platforms. It hit 1 million users just nine months from launch and added 14 million WAU in 2024. This rapid pace even outpaced TikTok's early ascent, signaling the mainstream appeal of social audio formats.

Based on past growth trajectories, most analysts predict 25 to 30 million weekly active Clubhouse users by the end of 2023. With expanded language support and the launch of the Android app, user numbers are expected to exceed 50 million by 2024. This access to the full global smartphone market could potentially catapult Clubhouse to new heights.

Revenue Generation

However, despite its impressive user growth, Clubhouse's revenue generation remains a concern. As of now, Clubhouse does not generate any meaningful revenue. It has rolled out donations to some creators, but it does not take any cut from these donations. The lack of revenue generation may hurt Clubhouse's future prospects of obtaining funding, due to a shift in how investors perceive tech start-up value.

Moreover, Clubhouse faces stiff competition from other social media giants like Twitter, LinkedIn, and Spotify, who have all launched successful live audio apps. Twitter Spaces, in particular, appears to be gaining steam, leveraging its already large user base of celebrities, journalists, and other media types.

Conclusion

In conclusion, while Clubhouse's user growth predictions paint a promising picture, its future will largely depend on its ability to monetize effectively and fend off competition. The platform needs to innovate and diversify its revenue streams to ensure its sustainability in the long run. Only time will tell if Clubhouse will continue to be a sonic boom in the social media landscape or fade into an echo.

Clubhouse endnote references*

_____

* These URLs present an overview of the Clubhouse App, provide interesting statistics and facts about the App, and tips and tricks for getting the most out of it.

Title: "Here's What You Need to Know About Clubhouse, the Audio Social App," https://mashable.com/article/what-is-clubhouse-app; Title: "Clubhouse vs Twitter Spaces (How Other Audio Platforms Match Up)," https://blog.emb.global/user-experiences-of-clubhouse-vs-twitter-spaces/; Title: "Is Clubhouse Making Networking Too Exclusive?," www.welcometothejungle.com/en/articles/clubhouse-networking-app; Title: "Leveraging Clubhouse: New Strategies for Audio-Only Social Networking," https://crescitaly.com/blog/leveraging-clubhouse-new-strategies-for-audio-only-social-networking; Title: "Clubhouse (app)—Wikipedia," https://en.wikipedia.org/wiki/Clubhouse_(app). Data sources as of July 2024: (1) "Clubhouse By the Numbers: Stats and Trends to Know in 2024," www.marketingscoop.com/small-business/clubhouse-statistics/; (2) "Clubhouse Statistics: Revenue, Users and More (2023)," https://influencermarketinghub.com/clubhouse-stats/; (3) "40+ Clubhouse Statistics: Usage, Demographics and Growth—MarketSplash," https://marketsplash.com/clubhouse-statistics/; (4) "Clubhouse Revenue and Usage Statistics (2024)—Business of Apps," www.businessofapps.com/data/clubhouse-statistics/; (5) "2024 Clubhouse User Statistics—Trends & Data (Full List)," www.thinkimpact.com/clubhouse-statistics/; (6) "The Explosive Growth of Clubhouse in 2022: Key Statistics," https://expertbeacon.com/clubhouse-statistics/; (7) "en.wikipedia.org," https://en.wikipedia.org/wiki/Clubhouse_(app).

Mastodon: A Decentralized Social Network

Mastodon logo

Mastodon (https://mastodon.social/explore) is a decentralized, open-source social networking platform, launched in 2016. It was created by Eugen Rochko, a software developer from Germany. The platform was designed to provide a more authentic and user-controlled social media experience.

Founding and Development

Mastodon was announced on Hacker News in October 2016. The project is maintained by Mastodon gGmbH, a German nonprofit organization. Mastodon's development is crowdfunded, and the platform does not support advertisements. The platform gained significant adoption in 2022 following the acquisition of Twitter by Elon Musk.

Impact

Mastodon has seen a significant surge in popularity following Elon Musk's takeover of Twitter. Almost half a million new users joined the service in a matter of days. The platform has been particularly popular among users who are wary of the control that a single company can have over a social media platform.

Business Model

Mastodon is a nonprofit, meaning that its goal is to benefit the public, rather than shareholders. The platform is funded through crowdfunding and does not support advertisements. Mastodon's income is separate from the personal income of its founder, Eugen Rochko. **Mastodon**, the decentralized social media platform, offers a refreshing departure from the norm.

Features

Mastodon offers a variety of features that enhance the user experience. Users can post short-form status messages, known as toots, for others to see. On a standard Mastodon instance, these messages can include up to 500 text-based characters, which is greater than Twitter's 280-character limit. Some instances support even longer messages.

Mastodon servers run social networking software that is capable of communicating using W3C's ActivityPub standard[†]. A Mastodon user can therefore interact with users on any other server in the Fediverse[‡] that supports ActivityPub. Users join a specific Mastodon server, rather than a single centralized website or application. The servers are connected as nodes in a network, and each server can administer its own rules, account privileges, and whether to share messages to and from other servers.

Why Mastodon?

- Instant global communication: Mastodon's decentralized nature ensures that global communication is not monopolized by a single company.
- Open source: Mastodon is free and open-source, allowing users to modify and contribute to its development.
- Not for sale: your data and time belong to you. Mastodon will never serve ads or push profiles for you to see.

[†] ActivityPub is a decentralized social networking protocol that was standardized by the W3C (World Wide Web Consortium) in 2018.

[‡] The fediverse is a decentralized network of interconnected servers that allows people to interact with each other across different social media platforms. It is a portmanteau of *federation* and *universe*.

Decentralization and Independence

- Unlike traditional social networks, **Mastodon** operates on a **decentralized model**. Each server (or *instance*) is an independent entity, hosting its community of users.
- Users can choose an instance that aligns with their values or even host their own. This decentralization ensures that no single corporation controls the entire network[1].

Ad-Free Experience

- **Mastodon** prioritizes user experience over advertising revenue. No ads are cluttering your feed or invasive tracking of your data.
- The absence of ads allows for a more focused and authentic interaction with content and fellow users.

Community Building and Niche Interests

- Mastodon encourages the formation of **niche communities**. Users can find or create instances centered around specific interests, hobbies, or causes.
- Whether it is art, music, activism, or tech discussions, Mastodon provides a space for meaningful connections within these smaller circles.

User-Centric Moderation

- Each instance sets its own rules and regulations. Moderation decisions are made locally, not imposed by a central authority.
- Users can join instances with rules they agree with or even host their own instances with customized guidelines.

Rich Media Support

- Mastodon supports **audio, video, and picture posts**. It allows for **content warnings**, animated avatars, custom emojis, and more.
- Whether you are an artist, musician, or podcaster, Mastodon provides a canvas for creative expression.

Global Interoperability

- Built on open web protocols like **ActivityPub or** Mastodon can communicate with any other platform that implements these standards.
- With one Mastodon account, users gain access to a broader universe—the fediverse, where different decentralized platforms interact.

Mastodon: The Roaring Giant of Decentralized Social Media

Mastodon, an open-source, decentralized social network, has been steadily gaining traction as a significant player in the realm of online communication.

User Growth

As of 2024, Mastodon boasts over 2.5 million monthly active users, representing a staggering 600 percent year-over-year growth. This growth is particularly noteworthy given the platform's decentralized model, which allows users to set up their instances or join existing ones.

Analysts predict that if current trends continue, Mastodon could see 20 to 30 percent month-over-month user growth. This could potentially lead to Mastodon surpassing 10 million members within the next one to two years. Such a growth trajectory indicates a promising future for Mastodon, especially considering the platform's unique appeal in offering greater control, no algorithms, and a focus on privacy.

Revenue Generation

However, Mastodon's revenue generation model is quite different from traditional social media platforms. Instead of relying on advertising or venture capital funding, Mastodon primarily makes money through sponsorship, crowdfunding, and other value-added services. Direct sponsorship from individuals and businesses that support the platform's mission, Patreon support, and revenue from value-added services such as Fediverse subscriptions, Community fees, Cloud storage, and Elastic search fees, all contribute to Mastodon's revenue.

While this model aligns with Mastodon's ethos of decentralization and user control, it also presents challenges. The platform's ability to generate sufficient revenue to sustain its operations and fund future growth could be a critical factor in its long-term success.

Moreover, Mastodon's decentralized structure could enable the platform to expand into new markets and generate additional revenue streams. For instance, Mastodon could explore offering enterprise solutions for businesses or creating partnerships with other companies.

Conclusion

In conclusion, while Mastodon's user growth predictions are encouraging, its future will largely hinge on its ability to effectively monetize and sustain its operations. The platform's unique appeal and commitment to user control and privacy present exciting opportunities, but also significant challenges. Whether Mastodon will continue to roar in the social media landscape or fade into a distant trumpet remains to be seen.

Mastodon has positioned itself as a unique player in the social media space by focusing on providing an authentic and user-controlled experience. Its commitment to user privacy and its decentralized platform have attracted a diverse range of users. Despite facing initial technical challenges, Mastodon has managed to sustain its growth and continues to be a popular platform among social media users.

In summary, Mastodon's commitment to decentralization, privacy, and user empowerment positions it as a compelling alternative to mainstream social media. Its future depends on maintaining this delicate balance while continuing to attract users who value authenticity and independence.

Mastodon endnote references[§]

§ These URLs present an overview of the Mastodon App, provide interesting statistics and facts about the App, and tips and tricks for getting the most out of it. Title: "Mastodon (social network) - Wikipedia," https://en.wikipedia.org/wiki/Mastodon_(social_network); Title: "How to Use Mastodon | Android Central," www.androidcentral.com/apps-software/how-to-use-mastodon; Title: "Get an App for Mastodon – Mastodon," https://joinmastodon.org/apps; Title: "Mastodon – Apps on Google Play," https://play.google.com/web/store/apps/details?id=org.joinmastodon.android&hl=en_GB&gl=US; Title: "Mastodon on the App Store," https://apps.apple.com/us/app/mastodon/id1571998974. Data Sources as of July 2024 (1) "How Mastodon Makes Money: A Look Inside Their Business Model - Finty," https://finty.com/us/business-models/mastodon/; (2) "How Many People Use Mastodon in 2024? (New Stats)," www.marketingscoop.com/small-business/mastodon-users/; (3) "Mastodon's Growth: The Big Picture | Similarweb," www.similarweb.com/blog/insights/social-media-news/mastodon-growth/; (4) "How Mastodon Makes Money - Investopedia," www.investopedia.com/how-mastodon-makes-money-7482865; (5) "Decentralized Networks Growth Analysis: Instance Dynamics on Mastodon," https://link.springer.com/content/pdf/10.1007/978-3-031-53503-1_30; (6) "Mastodon Sees Another Surge in Active Users Following Twitter's ... - PCMag," www.pcmag.com/news/mastodon-sees-another-surge-in-active-users-following-twitters-rate-limiting; (7) en.wikipedia.org, https://en.wikipedia.org/wiki/Mastodon_(social_network).

Vero: The Authenticity-Oriented Alternative

Vero logo

Vero stands out as an intriguing player in the realm of social networking, positioning itself as an authenticity-oriented alternative amidst a landscape often characterized by curated personas[5] and algorithm-driven content.

Founding and Development

Founded in 2015 by Lebanese billionaire Ayman Hariri, Vero gained attention for its commitment to chronological timelines, ad-free experience, and chronological content presentation.

Features

At the core of Vero's appeal is its emphasis on fostering genuine connections and authentic interactions. The platform's chronological timeline feature ensures that users see content in the order it's posted, prioritizing real-time updates over algorithmically curated feeds. This approach resonates with individuals seeking more meaningful engagement and less manipulation by unseen algorithms.

Furthermore, Vero's ad-free model distinguishes it from many mainstream social media platforms that rely heavily on targeted advertising for revenue. By eschewing ads, Vero aims to create a more user-centric experience, free from the distractions and intrusions often associated with ad-supported platforms. This aligns with a growing sentiment among

---

[5] Curated personas provide a clear picture of the target user or buyer grounded in real research to guide product, marketing and business decisions.

users who are increasingly wary of the data-driven advertising model and its potential implications for privacy and user experience.

In addition to its commitment to authenticity and ad-free experience, Vero differentiates itself through its revenue model. While the platform offers a free tier, it also provides a subscription-based option, Vero True Social, which unlocks additional features and functionality for users willing to pay a nominal fee. This hybrid approach allows Vero to generate revenue without relying solely on advertising, potentially mitigating concerns over data monetization and ensuring alignment with user interests.

Challenges

However, Vero faces challenges in gaining traction and competing with established social media giants.

Breaking into a market dominated by platforms like Facebook, Instagram, and Twitter requires not only compelling features but also a critical mass of users and engagement. Additionally, maintaining authenticity and user trust is crucial, especially as the platform scales and faces inevitable pressures to monetize and evolve its business model.

Nevertheless, Vero's emphasis on authenticity and user-centric experience represents a noteworthy trend in the evolving landscape of social networking. As users seek alternatives that prioritize genuine connections, meaningful interactions, and user control, platforms like Vero have the opportunity to carve out a niche and offer compelling alternatives to the status quo.

Vero, the social media photo-sharing app that emerged in 2018, garnered both hype and long-term value.

Attention and Prospects

1. **Authenticity and control:**
   - Vero positions itself as a platform for those who love something enough to share it and want **control over their audience**. Unlike other platforms, Vero allows users to define who sees their content.
   - This emphasis on authenticity resonated with users who sought a more genuine social experience.

2. **Ad-free environment:**
   - Vero's commitment to an **ad-free experience** sets it apart. Users can engage without intrusive ads cluttering their feeds.
   - The absence of advertising enhances the user experience and aligns with the desire for uncluttered content.

3. **Photographers' haven:**
   - Photographers, in particular, found solace in Vero. It became a refuge for discovering other photographers and appreciating beautiful still images.
   - As Instagram shifted away from its original premise, Vero's focus on visual content appealed to photographers seeking a dedicated platform.

4. **Long-term appeal:**
   - Despite initial hype, Vero has maintained a loyal user base. Some photographers even claim they do not miss Instagram at all.
   - Its longevity suggests that there is a niche audience valuing authenticity and control over mass appeal.

5. **Challenges and considerations:**
   - **User base**: Vero's invite-only model initially created buzz but also limited its growth. Expanding while maintaining exclusivity is a challenge.

Monetization

   - The platform lacks clear monetization strategies. Balancing growth without compromising user experience remains crucial.

Competition

   - Established players like Instagram and emerging contenders are vying for attention. Vero must innovate to stay relevant.

The Future

- Vero's future hinges on maintaining its unique appeal. If it continues to foster meaningful connections and authentic sharing, it could carve a permanent niche.
- Whether it remains a well-kept secret or gains broader adoption depends on its ability to adapt and resonate with users.

Vero: A New Dawn in Social Networking

Vero, a social networking app that has been around since 2015, has recently gained significant momentum. The sudden rise of Vero is speculated to be a result of the ongoing backlash against algorithm-defined feeds, particularly on Instagram. Vero's layout is much like Instagram, with a focus on images, but it allows users to post a wider variety of content, including music, links, book and film recommendations, and other sharing options.

User Base

Vero's user base grew from less than one million to nearly three million in just a few days. This rapid growth indicates a strong appetite for an alternate social network, one that is free of ads and algorithms. However, other platforms that initially gained popularity for similar reasons, such as Ello and Snapchat, have struggled to maintain their user-centric ideals as they scaled.

Business Model

Vero's business model is unique in the social media landscape. Unlike traditional social platforms, Vero aims to monetize through a subscription-based model rather than ads. This promises a more enjoyable and user-centric environment. Vero plans to eventually charge users *a few dollars per year* to use the app. For now, they are using this as a growth device, stating that the first million users will never have to pay any fees.

However, the question remains: Can Vero sustain its growth and revenue model in the long run? While the subscription-based model is appealing to users who are tired of ad-driven platforms, it is yet to be seen whether users will be willing to pay for social media when there are free alternatives available. Furthermore, as Vero grows, it may face the same challenges as Snapchat and other platforms in maintaining its user-centric ideals.

Conclusion

In conclusion, while Vero's recent growth and unique business model are certainly noteworthy, it is still uncertain whether it represents a new dawn in social networking or just a passing trend. Its future will largely depend on its ability to retain users and generate revenue in a market dominated by free, ad-supported platforms.

Only time will tell if Vero can truly redefine what a social network can and should be.

Vero has positioned itself as a unique player in the social media space by focusing on providing an authentic and ad-free user experience. Its chronological feed and diverse content-sharing capabilities have attracted a wide range of users. Despite facing initial technical challenges, Vero has managed to sustain its growth and continues to be a popular platform among social media users.

In summary, Vero's authenticity-oriented approach and ad-free environment make it an intriguing alternative. Its journey reflects the delicate balance between niche appeal and widespread success in the ever-evolving social media landscape.

Vero endnote references**

** These URLs present an overview of the Vero Social Network.

Title: "Vero.co," https://vero.co/; Title: "Vero (app) - Wikipedia," https://en.wikipedia.org/wiki/Vero_(app); Title: "Vero: What to Know About the New App and Its CEO | TIME," www.entrepreneur.com/science-technology/every-thing-you-need-to-know-about-vero-the-social-media/309748; Title: "What is Vero?," https://neilpatel.com/blog/what-is-vero/; Title: "Vero-True Social," https://apps.apple.com/us/app/vero-true-social/id971055041. Data Sources as of July 2024 (1) "What Is Rising Social App Vero – and Should You Be on It?," www.socialmediatoday.com/news/what-is-rising-social-app-vero-and-should-you-be-on-it/518010/; (2) "Everything You Need to Know About Vero, the Social Media Platform Co ...," www.entrepreneur.com/science-technology/everything-you-need-to-know-about-vero-the-social-media/309748; (3) "Vero Statistics for 2024 | Latest User Counts and More," https://expandedramblings.com/index.php/vero-facts-statistics/, (4) "VERO — True Social," https://vero.co/, (5) "As Concerns Over Data Privacy Abound, Vero Is doing Social Media a ...," www.thestreet.com/social-media/as-concerns-over-data-privacy-abound-vero-is-doing-social-media-a-little-differently; (6) "VERO Forecast — Price Target — Prediction for 2025 — TradingView," www.tradingview.com/symbols/NASDAQ-VERO/forecast/.

Parler: A Controversial Rise and Fall

Parler logo

Parler's (https://parler.com/) trajectory exemplifies the intersection of technology, free speech, and societal norms in the digital age.

Founding and Development

Launched in 2018, Parler positioned itself as a social media platform advocating for unrestricted expression, particularly appealing to individuals disenchanted with perceived censorship on mainstream platforms. Its rise to prominence coincided with heightened concerns over content moderation and perceived biases on platforms like Twitter and Facebook.

Features

The platform gained significant attention in 2020, attracting a surge of users, particularly those espousing conservative viewpoints. However, Parler's stance on content moderation, or rather, its lack thereof, soon became a focal point of controversy. Critics argued that the platform had become a haven for hate speech, misinformation, and incitement to violence, particularly in the aftermath of the 2020 United States presidential election and the Capitol riot in January 2021.

This controversy culminated in a series of significant setbacks for Parler. In January 2021, following the Capitol riot, Apple and Google removed Parler from their app stores, citing concerns over its content moderation practices. Additionally, Amazon Web Services terminated its hosting services for Parler, effectively taking the platform offline. These actions underscored the challenges faced by platforms that prioritize unrestricted speech while grappling with the responsibility to mitigate harmful content.

Challenges

Parler's rise and fall highlight several emerging trends in the digital landscape. First, it underscores the growing polarization in online discourse and the challenges platforms face in balancing free expression with the need to combat harmful content. Second, it reflects the increasing scrutiny of technology companies' content moderation practices and their societal implications. Finally, it underscores the potential consequences for platforms that fail to effectively address concerns over misinformation, hate speech, and incitement to violence.

Parler's Path: A Forecast of Growth and Revenue

Parler has positioned itself as a champion of free speech. It has attracted a significant user base, particularly among those who feel their voices are suppressed on other platforms[5]. However, the future of Parler is not without challenges.

User Growth

Parler's user base saw exponential growth during 2020. At its peak, around the U.S. election period in November to January, Parler reported having 15 million total users and about 4 million active users. However, the platform's usage tends to spike during political activities and diminishes afterward. As of the end of November, Parler had about 1.62 million total visits, representing a drop of about 8.08 percent over the last six months.

The majority of Parler's visits are from U.S. residents, with other top visitors from the United Kingdom, Brazil, Spain, and Israel. Given the United Nation's population growth estimates and predicting Internet penetration rates based on historical trends, the total global social media users could potentially reach over 4.75 billion half a decade from now. This presents a potential growth opportunity for Parler if it can expand its user base globally.

Revenue Streams

Parler has been exploring various revenue streams. One of them is through a nonfungible token (NFT) marketplace it hosts called DeepRedSky, which features NFTs from Parler itself, as well as partners like The Babylon Bee[1]. Parler also generates revenue through merchandise.

However, the platform faces an uphill battle in generating ad revenue and boosting its engagement metrics amid rising competition and recent usage declines. The acquisition of Parler by Kanye West, now legally known as Ye, could potentially bring new opportunities and challenges for the platform.

Conclusion

In conclusion, while Parler has experienced significant growth and has explored various revenue streams, its future is uncertain. Its user growth is highly dependent on political activities, and it faces stiff competition in the social media market. Its success will likely depend on its ability to maintain its user base, expand globally, and diversify its revenue streams. Parler's controversial journey highlights the challenges faced by platforms that prioritize free speech while gSource: https://commonsrappling with the consequences of unfiltered content. Its fate serves as a cautionary tale for emerging contenders in the social media landscape.

Parler endnote references††

†† These URLs present an overview of the Parler Social Network.

Title: "Wikipedia: Parler," https://en.wikipedia.org/wiki/Parler; Title: "What Is Parler? Everything You Need to Know About the Conservative Social Network," https://mashable.com/article/what-is-parler-explainer; Title: "The Rise and Fall of Parler," https://blog.avast.com/the-rise-and-fall-of-parler-avast; Title: "The Rise, Fall, and Future of Parler," www.fastcompany.com/90594015/history-of-parler; Title: "Parler Has Now Been Booted by Amazon, Apple and Google," www.cnn.com/2021/01/09/tech/parler-suspended-apple-app-store/index.html.   Data Sources as of July 2024 (1) "Parler's First 13 Million Users | FSI - Stanford University," https://fsi.stanford.edu/news/sio-parler-contours; (2) "Parler - Wikipedia," https://en.wikipedia.org/wiki/Parler; (3) "Parler User Stats Analysis: How Many People Use Parler in 2022?," https://therobusttrader.com/parler-user-stats/; (4) "Number of Social Media Users in 2024: Demographics & Predictions," https://financesonline.com/number-of-social-media-users/; (5) "Key Facts About Parler | Pew Research Center," www.pewresearch.org/short-reads/2022/10/20/fast-facts-about-parler-as-kanye-west-reportedly-plans-acquisition-of-site/; (6) "Even With Ye, Parler Faces Headwinds in Crowded Social Media Market," www.spglobal.com/marketintelligence/en/news-insights/latest-news-headlines/even-with-ye-parler-faces-headwinds-in-crowded-social-media-market-72578469; (7) "Parler Company Profile 2024: Valuation, Funding & Investors - PitchBook," https://pitchbook.com/profiles/company/436822-12; (8) "What Is Parler? Everything You Need to Know About the ... - Mashable," https://mashable.com/article/what-is-parler-explainer; (9) en.wikipedia.org. https://en.wikipedia.org/wiki/Parler.

Goodreads: A Literary Universe Navigator

Goodreads logo

Geared toward book enthusiasts, providing a platform for readers to share book recommendations and reviews, Goodreads is a social cataloging website that allows individuals to search its database of books, annotations, quotes, and reviews. Users can sign up and register books to generate library catalogs and reading lists. They can also create their own groups of book suggestions, surveys, polls, blogs, and discussions.

Founding and Development

Goodreads was founded in December 2006 and launched in January 2007 by Otis Chandler and Elizabeth Khuri Chandler. The idea came about when Otis Chandler was browsing through his friend's bookshelf for ideas. He wanted to integrate this scanning experience and create a space where people could write reviews regarding the books that they read. Goodreads addressed what publishers call the *discoverability problem* by guiding consumers in the digital age to find books they might want to read.

Features

Goodreads offers several features that enhance the user experience. Users can create and share reviews, use tags to track each year's books, audiobooks, or read-aloud, as well as custom collections. The platform also has a "Want to Read" feature that allows users to add books to their reading list. Furthermore, Goodreads gives you the ability to virtually invite your friends into your living room to discuss the books on your shelves.

Impact

Goodreads arguably has an outsized impact on the publishing industry. Its members have produced 26 million book reviews and 300 million ratings over the past year. But for some authors, it has become a toxic work environment that can sink a book before it is even published. However, the platform can also be helpful to authors. The Goodreads author program allows any author with a book in the Amazon database to claim a profile and earn a badge verifying their identity.

Monetization

Goodreads generates revenue through several methods:

1. **Advertising**: Goodreads offers paid advertisements for authors or publishers to promote their books. They provide customized advertising solutions based on the client's budget.
2. **Book discovery packages**: Goodreads' business model revolves around offering "book discovery packages" that consists of "owned, earned, and paid media"
3. **Sponsored newsletters and new releases mailers**: Goodreads sends sponsored newsletters and new releases mailers to millions of users every month.
4. **Advertorial placements**: also known as the author spotlight, this is another way Goodreads generates revenue.
5. **Personal selection emails:** Goodreads can target an author's fans by showing a new release.
6. **Sponsored homepage polls**: Goodreads also earns revenue through sponsored homepage polls.
7. **Giveaways program**: Goodreads' giveaways is one of the popular features of the platform. Although international readers can almost always enter a giveaway, the service itself is only available for U.S. and Canadian authors who want to run print book giveaways.
8. **Affiliate links**: Goodreads also earns revenue through affiliate links.

Navigating the Future: A Forecast of Goodreads' Growth and Revenue Streams

Goodreads, since its inception in 2007, has been a dominant player in the online book community, providing a platform for users to track their reading history, discover new books, leave reviews, and interact with other readers. However, the landscape of social networking is rapidly evolving, and Goodreads' future will likely be shaped by its ability to adapt to these changes.

User Growth

In terms of user growth, Goodreads has maintained a significant lead due to its age and integration with Amazon's Kindle devices. As of 2022, Goodreads boasted over 140 million users. However, the emergence of competitors like StoryGraph, which offers new features and addresses issues found with existing book apps, poses a challenge to Goodreads' dominance.

Revenue Streams

Goodreads' revenue streams are also a critical factor in its future. The social networking market as a whole is projected to reach $129.60 billion in 2022, with an expected annual growth rate of 7.30 percent, resulting in a projected market volume of $189.50 billion by 2027. Goodreads, as a part of this market, could potentially tap into this growth. However, the methods of generating revenue for social networks are changing. Traditional advertising is replaced by more innovative methods.

For instance, one emerging revenue channel is the sale of anonymized conversations about vendors' products or services. Another is partnering with Internet providers to receive payment when a particular online community's information is downloaded. If Goodreads can successfully implement such strategies, it could diversify its revenue streams and ensure its financial sustainability. Issues such as *review bombing*, where fake users target authors and negatively impact their ratings, have been a concern. Addressing these issues will be crucial for Goodreads to maintain its user base and reputation.

Conclusion

In conclusion, while Goodreads has a strong foundation and a large user base, its future will depend on its ability to innovate, both in terms of user experience and revenue generation. By addressing current issues and exploring new revenue channels, Goodreads has the potential to remain a leading platform in the online book community.

Goodreads has become a hub for sharing and discovering content, fostering discussions, and connecting with communities that share similar interests. It has played a significant role in shaping internet culture and continues to be a major player in the social media space.

Goodreads endnote references‡‡

---

‡‡ These URLs present an overview of the Goodreads Social Network.

"Wikipedia: Goodreads," https://en.wikipedia.org/wiki/Goodreads; "Must-Have Apps for Book Lovers," www.makeuseof.com/tag/mobile-apps-book-lovers/; "Goodreads: A Social Network Site for Book Readers," www.academia.edu/53204596/ Goodreads_A_social_network_site_for_book_readers; "Goodreads Website," www.goodreads.com/. Data Sources as of July 2024 (1) "Goodreads vs. StoryGraph: Which is Better in 2024? - Reedsy," https://reedsy.com/discovery/blog/goodreads-vs-storygraph; (2) "Social Networking - Worldwide | Statista Market Forecast," www.statista.com/outlook/amo/app/social-networking/worldwide; (3) "The Social Network Business Plan: 18 Strategies That Wi... - Goodreads," www.goodreads .com/book/show/5129176-the-social-network-business-plan; (4) "Trendsin Social Network Analysis: Information Propagation, User ...," www.goodreads.com/book/ show/33893878-trends-in-social-network-analysis; (5) "How to Use Goodreads to Dramatically Grow Your Audience," https://jenndepaula.com/blog/how-to-use-goodreads-to-dramatically-grow-your-audience; (6) "Sociable: 34 Predictions for Social Media Marketing in 2024," www.marketingdive.com/news/ 34-predictions-social-media-marketing-2024/698021/.

Nextdoor: A Local Community Connected

Nextdoor logo

Introduction

Nextdoor is a private social network for neighborhoods. The platform allows neighbors within the same geographical area to share information and communicate.

Founding and Development

Nextdoor was co-founded by Nirav Tolia, Sarah Leary, Prakash Janakiraman, and David Wiesen in 2008. The concept and patents that Nextdoor is based on were invented by "FatDoor" CEO Raj Abhyanker in 2006. Early investors included Benchmark Capital, Shasta Ventures, and Rich Barton. As of February 2014, Nextdoor had 80 to 100 employees.

Features

Next door is a discussion-style platform where neighbors post updates, polls, and events, and ask for recommendations, as well as list items for sale. Posting a new discussion is easy. At the top of the home page of the Nextdoor website (hit the plus sign on mobile devices) is a text box. Before writing a post, select a category the post falls under, whether it is a recommendation, item for sale, safety concern, lost and found, or general update.

Impact

Nextdoor is where communities come together to greet newcomers, exchange recommendations, and read the latest local news. Where neighbors support local businesses and get updates from public agencies.

Where neighbors borrow tools and sell couches. It is how to get the most out of everything nearby.

Nextdoor primarily generates revenue through the following methods:

- **Advertising**: Nextdoor offers paid advertisements for businesses to promote their products and services. These advertisements are displayed as sponsored content on the platform.
- **Local Deals**: Businesses can pay a fixed fee to offer local deals to Nextdoor users.
- **Display Ads**: Nextdoor also earns revenue through display ads that are shown in the app.
- **Sponsored Posts:** Businesses can pay to have their posts sponsored, which increases their visibility on the platform.

Nextdoor: A Hyperlocal Powerhouse in the Making

Nextdoor, the hyperlocal social network, has been showing promising signs of growth and revenue potential. The platform's unique focus on fostering community interactions within neighborhoods has led to a steady increase in user engagement[12].

Active Users

Active user Average Revenue Per User (ARPU) increased by 58 percent year over year to $1.57. By the end of 2023, the platform had exceeded 88M Verified Neighbors, with a Q4 WAU count of 41.8M, marking a 5 percent increase year-over-year. This growth trajectory suggests a strong future for Nextdoor, especially considering the platform's unique position in the social media landscape

Revenue Streams

In Q2 2021, Nextdoor's revenue increased by 66 percent year over year to $45.8 million.

Nextdoor's revenue streams are primarily driven by sponsored posts, local deals, and neighborhood sponsorships. The platform's hyperlocal approach allows businesses to target specific neighborhoods with their advertisements, creating a highly relevant user experience. This strategy not only benefits local businesses but also contributes to Nextdoor's revenue growth.

Looking ahead, Nextdoor's revenue predictions are optimistic. In 2022, investors anticipated revenue of $260.0 million for the year. By the end of 2023, Nextdoor reported revenue of $218.3 million, a 3 percent increase year-over-year. These figures, coupled with the platform's user growth, suggest a positive outlook for Nextdoor's financial future. However, while Nextdoor's user growth and revenue streams are promising, the platform also reported a net loss in 2023. This indicates that while Nextdoor is growing, it is still in a phase of investment and expansion. The company's decision to increase its share repurchase program by $150 million further demonstrates its confidence in its long-term growth.

Conclusion

In conclusion, Nextdoor's unique hyperlocal approach, combined with its steady user growth and diverse revenue streams, positions it as a strong contender in the social media landscape. While challenges remain, the platform's recent performance and future predictions suggest a bright

Table 4.1 *Nextdoor availability by country (July 2024)*

Nextdoor is currently available in:
The United States
The Netherlands
Germany
France
Italy
Spain
Australia
Sweden
Denmark
Canada

Source: https://help.nextdoor.com/s/article/Where-is-Nextdoor-available?language=en_CA.

future. As Nextdoor continues to grow and adapt, it has the potential to redefine the way we connect with our local communities.

Nextdoor has become a hub for sharing and discovering content, fostering discussions, and connecting with communities that share similar interests. It has played a significant role in shaping Internet culture and continues to be a major player in the social media space.

Nextdoor endnote references[§§]

[§§] These URLs present an overview of the Nextdoor Social Network.

"Nextdoor—Wikipedia," https://en.wikipedia.org/wiki/Nextdoor; "How Does Nextdoor Make Money? - Nextdoor Help Center," https://help.nextdoor.com/s/article/how-does-nextdoor-make-money?language=en_US.

Data Sources as of July 2024 (1) "Nextdoor Provides Q2 Highlights Showing Strong Growth in Revenue and ...," https://about.nextdoor.com/press-releases/nextdoor-provides-q2-highlights-showing-strong-growth-in-revenue-and-engagement/; (2) "Nextdoor Reports Fourth Quarter and Full Year 2023 Results," https://about.nextdoor.com/financial-news/nextdoor-reports-fourth-quarter-and-full-year-2023-results/; (3) "How Does Nextdoor Make Money? Business Model of Nextdoor," www.soocial.com/how-does-nextdoor-make-money/; (4) "How Does Nextdoor Make Money? | Nextdoor Business Model 2024 - SEOAves," https://seoaves.com/how-does-nextdoor-make-money-nextdoor-business-model/; (5) "Nextdoor Beats Expectations in First Earnings Report Since Going Public ...," https://techcrunch.com/2022/03/01/nextdoor-beats-expectations-in-first-earnings-report-since-going-public-last-year/; (6) "The Next Big Social Network: Nextdoor - Axios," www.axios.com/2021/06/14/the-next-big-social-network-nextdoor; (7) "Why Nextdoor is Optimistic About AI-Fueled Growth Despite Declining ...," www.marketingxdigital.com/2023/08/10/why-nextdoor-is-optimistic-about-ai-fueled-growth-despite-declining-user-count/; (8) "Nextdoor Continues to Grow Users as Measured by Comscore," https://business.nextdoor.com/en-us/enterprise/blog/nextdoor-continues-to-grow-users-as-measured-by-comscore; (9) "Nextdoor Updates Full Year 2021 and 2022 Guidance," https://about.nextdoor.com/press-releases/nextdoor-updates-full-year-2021-and-2022-guidance/.

Quora: A Knowledge Exchange Network

Quora logo

Founding and Development

Quora is a social question-and-answer website and online knowledge market based in Mountain View, California. It was cofounded by former Facebook employees Adam D'Angelo and Charlie Cheever in June 2009. The platform was made available to the public on June 21, 2010: initially praised for its interface and quality of answers, Quora experienced rapid user base growth.

The development stage of Quora's platform took approximately nine months, and the portal gained traction as employees invited friends (who, in turn, invited friends of friends) to join the site.

In 2014, Quora joined the startup accelerator Y Combinator. The Q&A platform has raised hundreds of millions of dollars from investors including Peter Thiel, Tiger Global Management, Josh Hannah, Sam Altman, and others. Some estimates put the value of the company today at over $2 billion.

Features

- **Knowledge sharing:** Quora's mission is to share and grow the world's knowledge, connecting people who have it with those who need it.
- **User interaction:** users can ask questions, provide answers, upvote, downvote, and follow topics.
- **Social networking:** it includes elements like following other users, sharing answers, and creating a detailed profile.

- While primarily a question-and-answer platform, it has social networking elements where users can follow topics and engage in discussions.
- On Quora, users can ask and answer questions, and each question is assigned to a specific category.
- Users can proclaim themselves as experts in certain categories.
- The questions and answers posted on Quora can be rated negatively or positively by users. As of 2020, the website was visited by 300 million users a month.

Expansion

- **Multilingual support:** Quora expanded to support various languages, including Spanish, French, German, and Italian.
- **AI chatbot platform Poe:** recently secured $75 million in funding to further develop its AI chatbot platform, Poe.

Monetization

Quora primarily generates revenue through the following methods:

- **Advertising**: Quora sells ad space on its website and mobile app. Advertisements are strategically placed so that they appear as part of the content rather than acting as an overt marketing tool.
- **Quora+ subscriptions**: Quora charges fees for Quora+ subscriptions. These subscriptions provide users with additional features and benefits.
- **Quora Spaces subscriptions**: Quora takes a 5 percent commission on Quora Spaces subscriptions. Spaces are communities where people gather to talk about specific topics.
- **Commission from premium posts**: Quora collects a small commission from the money that subscribers pay to view premium posts.

Impact on the Marketplace

- **Marketing tool:** Quora is used by marketers to drive referral traffic and leads, as well as to establish brand authority.
- **SEO benefits:** answers on Quora can rank highly in search engine results, providing visibility.

Future Outlook: Quora: A Rising Star in the Social Network Sky

Quora, the popular question-and-answer platform, has been making significant strides in the digital landscape.

User Base

With over 400 million monthly active users, it has emerged as a powerhouse in online knowledge sharing. The user base has seen a 120 percent increase since 2016, indicating a strong growth trajectory.

The platform's user demographics are diverse and engaged, with a 43/57 female-to-male ratio. A significant portion of the users are well-educated and affluent, with 65 percent having a college degree and 54 percent reporting a household income >$100k. This demographic is particularly attractive to advertisers, suggesting a promising future for Quora's primary revenue stream: advertising.

Business Model

Quora's ad-based business model, coupled with its high engagement rate, has been a key factor in its success. The platform also generates revenue through Quora+ subscriptions and takes a 5 percent commission on Quora Spaces subscriptions. In 2023, Quora reported $20 million in revenue, a figure that is likely to grow given the platform's increasing popularity and expanding user base.

Moreover, Quora's SEO strategy has been successful in making the website a leading search engine result for a wide variety of topics. This, combined with the fact that users spend twice as much time on Quora than on LinkedIn, indicates a high level of user engagement and satisfaction.

However, like any other social network, Quora faces challenges. The platform must continue to innovate and improve its services to retain its user base and attract new users. It must also navigate the complex landscape of digital advertising, balancing the need for revenue with the user experience.

Conclusion

Quora continues to evolve, with a focus on enhancing user experience and expanding its AI capabilities. Its impact on the marketplace as a knowledge-sharing platform remains significant, and its future developments, especially in AI, are anticipated with interest.

- **Positive:** Quora's AI platform, particularly Poe, could dictate the company's future, with the potential for significant growth and creator monetization.
- **Negative:** there are no specific negative outlooks mentioned in the search results, but general challenges could include maintaining user engagement and managing content quality as the platform scales.

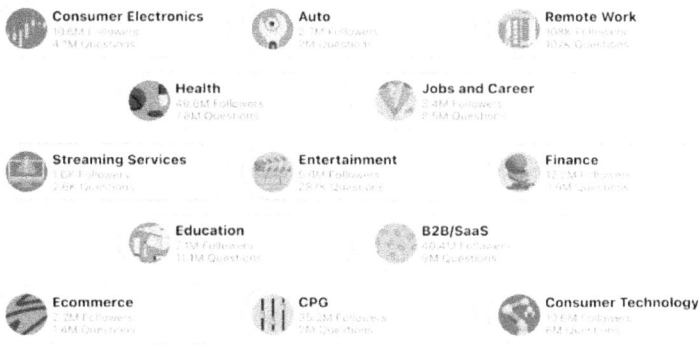

Quora users engage in discussions of 300,000 topics across 24 languages

In conclusion, given its strong user growth, successful revenue streams, and high user engagement, Quora seems well-positioned for continued success in the future. However, it will need to continue innovating and adapting to the ever-changing digital landscape to maintain its upward trajectory.

Quora endnote references[¶¶]

¶¶ These URLs present an overview of the Quora Social Network.

"How Quora Works and Makes Money - Investopedia," www.soocial.com/how-does-quora-make-money/#google_vignette; "How Does Quora Make Money? Business Model of Quora - Social," www.investopedia.com/articles/investing/041916/how-quora-works-and-makes-money.asp; "Quora Founders - Bing," https://en.wikipedia.org/wiki/Quora; "What is Quora? |Getting Started on the Question and Answer Portal," www.ionos.ca/digitalguide/online-marketing/web-analytics/what-is-quora/. Data Sources as of July 2024 (1) "25 Awesome Quora Statistics for 2024 (Insights and Trends)," https://persuasion-nation.com/quora-statistics/; (2) "Detailed Quora Statistics: All-Time Stats & Data (2024) - Demand Sage," www.demandsage.com/quora-statistics/; (3) "How Does Quora Make Money? Business Model of Quora," www.soocial.com/how-does-quora-make-money/; (4) "How Quora Works and Makes Money - Investopedia," www.investopedia.com/articles/investing/041916/how-quora-works-and-makes-money.asp; (5) "21+ Top Quora Statistics for 2024 (Users + Growth)," https://startupbonsai.com/quora-statistics/; (6) "How Does Quora Make Money? Analyzing Its Business Model - productmint," https://productmint.com/the-quora-business-model-how-does-quora-make-money/.

Ravelry: A Knitting and Crochet Community Hub

Ravelry logo

Geared toward the knitting and fiber arts community, Ravelry is a free social networking service providing a platform for sharing projects, patterns, and ideas.

The platform is designed as an organizational tool for a variety of fiber arts, including knitting, crocheting, spinning, and weaving.

Founding and Development

Cassidy and Jessica Forbes founded Ravelry with the idea of creating a web presence for all fiber artists. Ravelry provides a place for knitters, crocheters, designers, spinners, and dyers to keep track of their yarn, tools, and pattern information, and look to others for ideas and inspiration. The site was in beta through early 2010, and new features and enhancements are still added frequently.

Impact

Ravelry has been mentioned by Tim Bray as one of the world's more successful deployments of Ruby on Rails technologies.*** As of March 2020, Ravelry had almost nine million registered users and approximately one million monthly active users.

On Ravelry, users can post content related to a wide range of fiber arts. Some of the most popular categories on Ravelry include:

*** Ruby on Rails (RoR) is open-source full-stack framework software specifically to build different web applications. Ruby on Rails has two parts: Ruby—the general-purpose programming language that is super versatile. Rails—frameworks for creating websites, apps, and systems.

- **Sweaters**: sweaters are the most common type of knitting pattern in Ravelry.
- **Yarns**: 60.1 percent of all yarns listed on Ravelry are sheep's wool1. Red Heart Super Saver Solids Yarn is the most popular yarn in Ravelry.
- **Softies**: softies are the most common type of crochet pattern on Ravelry.
- **Accessories, home, and toys and hobbies**: these categories are popular among users who have used Red Heart Super Saver for their projects.

Popularity

Ravelry is a vibrant community and platform for fiber artists, offering a range of features and resources. The popularity of categories can vary over time and are influenced by the current trends and interests of the Ravelry community.

Ravelry has positioned itself as a unique player in the social media space by focusing on providing an authentic and user-controlled experience. Its commitment to user privacy and its decentralized platform have attracted a diverse range of users.

Despite facing initial technical challenges, Ravelry has managed to sustain its growth and continues to be a popular platform among social media users.

Features

Ravelry offers a variety of features that enhance the user experience. Users can keep track of their projects, stash, tools, and library, as well as plan what they want to make in the future and track their favorite things from all around the site. Ravelry patterns can be added to a logged-in user's *Favorites*, *Queue*, or *Projects* pages, indicating the user's interest in, stated desire to make, or progress into the pattern, respectively. A user can additionally record their fiber-related tools (*Needles & Hooks*) and available yarn (*Stash*) with which to complete these projects.

Ravelry also includes a searchable community-edited yarn and pattern database where users share information and project photos. The database was created by encouraging people to share their projects and information. The community-edited yarn and pattern database is something that has never existed before. If someone else has used a pattern or yarn, no matter how obscure, you can probably find information and project photos on Ravelry.

- Community and resource hub: a free website for knitters, crocheters, and fiber artists to share projects, ideas, and resources.
- **Pattern database:** a vast collection of patterns, with tools for managing personal projects and stashes.
- Social networking: forums, groups, and social features to connect with other fiber enthusiasts.

Growth

Ravelry has grown to be a key organizational tool for the fiber arts community, with a significant user base. The platform has expanded to support a diverse range of fiber arts beyond knitting and crocheting. Ravelry connects users worldwide, fostering a global community of fiber artists.

Monetization

- Advertising and merchandise: Ravelry generates revenue through advertising, merchandise sales, and pattern sales fees.
- Pattern sales: designers can sell patterns directly on Ravelry, contributing to the platform's income.
- Market expansion: Ravelry has significantly expanded the market for independent knitwear designers and yarn dyers.
- Visibility for small businesses: the platform provides visibility for small, fiber-related businesses through advertising and pattern sales.

Future Outlook

- **Positive:** continued growth in user base and patterns, with potential for further expansion in features and global reach.

- **Negative:** challenges may include maintaining relevance in a rapidly evolving digital landscape and ensuring a sustainable revenue model.

A Vibrant Social Network With a Promising Future

User Base

Ravelry, a social network dedicated to knitters, crocheters, and other fiber artists, has shown significant growth and potential in recent years. As of January 2023, Ravelry boasts a user base of 11 million, a substantial increase from the 9 million registered users it had in March 2020. This growth trend suggests a promising future for the platform. The site's monthly visits have also been impressive, with around 1.1 million visits each month. This high level of engagement is a testament to the platform's ability to attract and retain users, which is a crucial factor for the sustainability of any social network.

Revenue Model

Ravelry's revenue model is unique and appears to be effective. The platform is free for independent designers to list patterns for sale, which encourages a constant influx of new content. This model not only benefits the designers who gain visibility and potential income but also the users who have access to a wide variety of patterns.

The platform's demographics reveal a predominantly American user base, with 61.6 percent of users hailing from the United States. However, there is also a significant presence of users from other countries, indicating the platform's global reach and potential for further international expansion.

In terms of content, sweaters are the most common type of knitting pattern on Ravelry, suggesting a strong interest in this particular type of project among users. This could guide future content strategies for the platform, as well as for designers seeking to reach a larger audience.

However, with growth comes challenges. The market has exploded with new yarn dyers and knitwear designers, making it harder for individual businesses to stand out. Ravelry will need to continue innovating and providing tools for these small businesses to differentiate themselves and succeed on the platform.

Conclusion

In conclusion, Ravelry's user growth and unique revenue model suggest a bright future for this niche social network. However, the platform will need to navigate the challenges that come with this growth, particularly in terms of supporting its small business users. With its dedicated and engaged user base, Ravelry is well-positioned to continue thriving in the years to come.

Ravelry's commitment to fostering a creative and collaborative environment for fiber artists has made it a cornerstone of the fiber arts community. Its future will likely be shaped by its ability to innovate and adapt to the needs of its users.

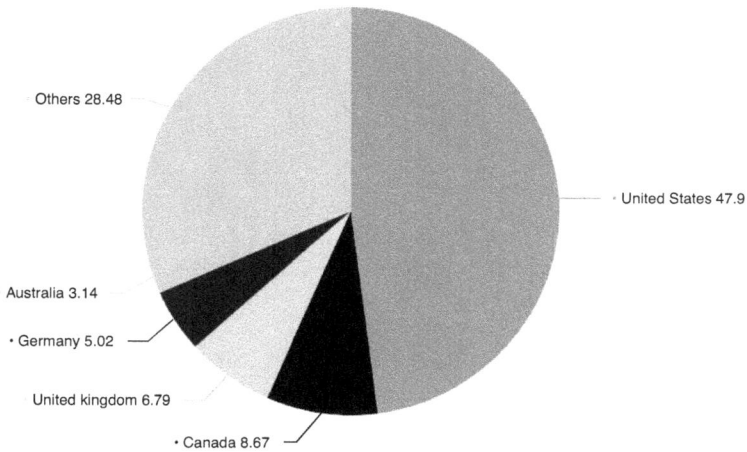

Share of visits to the crafts website ravelry.com worldwide as of May 2024, by country

Ravelry endnote references[†††]

[†††] These URLs present an overview of the Ravelry Social Network.

"Ravelry—Wikipedia," https://en.wikipedia.org/wiki/Ravelry; "How to Use Ravelry (Easy Tutorial) | Darn Good Yarn," www.darngoodyarn.com/blogs/darn-good-blog/how-to-use-ravelry-easy-tutorial?_ab=0&_fd=0&_sc=1. Data Sources as of July 2024 (1) "Ravelry Reveals! 79+ Statistics, Insights, Trends, Stats For 2023," https://knitlikegranny.com/ravelry-stats/; (2) "Ravelry at 10: How the Knitting Social Network has Inspired, Impacted ...," https://craftindustryalliance.org/raverly-at-10-how-the-knitting-social-network-has-inspired-and-impacted-yarntrepreneurs/; (3) "2022 Community Stats - Unraveled," https://blog.ravelry.com/2022-community-stats/; (4) "Ravelry Company Profile 2024: Valuation, Funding & Investors - PitchBook," https://pitchbook.com/profiles/company/182029-69; (5) undefined, www.ravelry.com/contact; (6) undefined, www.ravelry.com/; (7) undefined, www.linkedin.com/company/ravelry/; (8) Getty Images, www.gettyimages.com/detail/news-photo/in-this-photo-illustration-the-ravelry-logo-is-seen-news-photo/1152688020

Steemit: A Blockchain Content Platform

Steemit logo

Steemit is built on blockchain technology[‡‡‡] and users are rewarded with cryptocurrency for creating and curating content.

Steemit is a blockchain-based blogging and social media platform that was launched on March 24, 2016. It was cofounded by Ned Scott, who previously worked for Gellert Global Group, a family-owned private equity group, and Daniel Larimer, the founder of Bitshares.

Founding and Development

Steemit was the first application built upon the Steem blockchain. The platform was designed to reward users with a cryptocurrency, more specifically STEEM, for publishing and curating content (i.e., posts), and also for their comments. The company is owned by Steemit Inc., a privately held company based in New York City with a headquarters in Virginia.

Steemit was announced on Hacker News in October 2016 by Eugen Rochko. The project is maintained by Mastodon gGmbH, a German nonprofit organization.[§§§] Steemit's development is crowdfunded, and the platform does not support advertisements.

[‡‡‡] Blockchain is a decentralized, distributed digital ledger that records transactions across many computers in a network. It is designed to securely, transparently, and immutably record data without the need for a central authority

[§§§] The gGmbH is a nonprofit company with limited liability under German law. In German this is gemeinnützige Gesellschaft mit beschränkter Haftung— gGmbH for short. Here gemeinnützig (nonprofit) means that the company's purpose is to benefit the common good.

Steemit's audience is diverse. As of the latest data, the platform had over 1.2 million registered users. The largest age group of visitors is 25- to 34-year-olds. In terms of gender distribution, about two-thirds (65.52%) of Steemit users are male.

Features

Steemit offers a variety of features that enhance the user experience. Users can post short-form status messages, known as *toots*, for others to see. On a standard Steemit instance, these messages can include up to 500 text-based characters, which is greater than Twitter's 280-character limit. Some instances support even longer messages.

Steemit servers run social networking software that is capable of communicating using W3C's ActivityPub standard similar to Mastodon. A Steemit user can therefore interact with users on any other server in the Fediverse that supports ActivityPub. Users join a specific Steemit server, rather than a single centralized website or application. The servers are connected as nodes in a network, and each server can administer its own rules, account privileges, and whether to share messages to and from other servers.

On Steemit, users can post content under various categories, known as *tags*. The most popular categories or tags can vary over time and are influenced by the current trends and interests of the Steemit community. Unfortunately, specific details about the most popular categories on Steemit at the current time are not readily available.

However, users often post content related to a wide range of topics, including but not limited to cryptocurrency, technology, life, photography, and art.

Impact

Steemit has seen a significant surge in popularity following Elon Musk's takeover of Twitter. Almost half a million new users joined the service in a matter of days. The platform has been particularly popular among users who are wary of the control that a single company can have over a social media platform.

Business Model

Steemit is a nonprofit, meaning that its goal is to benefit the public, rather than shareholders. The platform is funded through crowdfunding and does not support advertisements. Steemit's income is separate from the personal income of its founder, Eugen Rochko.

Steemit has positioned itself as a unique player in the social media space by focusing on providing an authentic and user-controlled experience. Its commitment to user privacy and its decentralized platform have attracted a diverse range of users. Despite facing initial technical challenges, Steemit has managed to sustain its growth and continues to be a popular platform among social media users.

Future Outlook

- **Positive**: there is potential for growth in affiliate marketing and further innovations on the platform.
- **Negative**: the platform faces challenges such as maintaining the value of its cryptocurrency and competition from other blockchain-based social networks.

Summary

Steemit continues to evolve, adapting to the dynamic landscape of social media and blockchain technology. While it presents opportunities for monetization and growth, it also faces challenges that could shape its future trajectory.

Estimated Revenue & Valuation
Steemit's estimated annual revenue is currently $30.5M per year.
Steemit's estimated revenue per employee is $143,000
Employee Data
Steemithas 213 Employees.
Steemitgrew its employee count by 1%last year.

Steemit statistics

Steemit and Mastodon Compared

Steemit and Mastodon are both decentralized social media platforms, but they have some key differences:

Similarities:

- Both are open-source and decentralized alternatives to centralized social media platforms like Twitter and Facebook.
- They aim to give users more control and ownership over their data and content.
- Steemit and Mastodon allow users to communicate with each other and share content.

Differences:

- Steemit is built on the Steem blockchain and has its own native cryptocurrency STEEM that users can earn for creating and curating content.
- Mastodon is a federated network consisting of many independently run instances that can communicate with each other.
- Mastodon focuses more on microblogging and has a Twitter-like interface, while Steemit is more blog-focused.
- Mastodon has a stronger emphasis on privacy, with robust privacy settings and content visibility controls.
- Steemit's monetization model is more prominent, with users earning cryptocurrency for their activity.

A New Dawn in Social Media—Growth and Revenue Prospects

Steemit has been making waves in the digital world. With its unique business model and reward system, it has managed to garner significant attention and growth.

User Growth

Steemit's user base has been expanding at an impressive pace.

Within its first five months of operation, it hit 100K users and acquired 500K monthly unique visitors from all over the world. This growth is comparable to that of Facebook and Reddit, which gained a million users and millions of visits within their first year. The platform's popularity is largely attributed to its system of rewarding people for voting and posting content on the platform with its own coin, Steem.

Revenue Streams

Unlike traditional social media platforms, Steemit does not monetize its platform with advertisements. Instead, it generates revenue when its users invest in Steem Power so their posts can be seen by a larger audience, thus getting more votes which translates into more money. The platform uses three different decentralized cryptocurrencies to reward both content creators and curators: Steem, Steem Power, and Steem Dollars.

Despite the drop in the value of Steem, the coin behind Steemit, the platform's future looks promising. The CEO and cofounder of Steemit, Ned Scott, plans on growing a thriving social network and designing a platform that creates an attention economy, in which Steem becomes a currency for buying user attention on the social interfaces. This approach, coupled with the continuous improvement of the platform, is expected to prevent any further devaluation of Steem[4].

Conclusion

In conclusion, Steemit's unique approach to social networking, combined with its robust growth and innovative revenue streams, suggests a bright future for the platform. As it continues to evolve and adapt to the needs of its users, Steemit is poised to redefine the landscape of social media.

Steemit endnote references¶¶¶

¶¶¶ These URLs present an overview of the Steemit Social Network.

"Steemit—Wikipedia," https://en.wikipedia.org/wiki/Steemit; "Steemit: New Social Media Platform Which Pays You to Post," https://coinmarketcap.com/academy/article/what-is-steemit-and-how-does-it-work. Data Sources as of July 2024 (1) "Steemit Exceeds 100K Users, Plans to Expand Saving Steem - Cointelegraph," https://cointelegraph.com/news/steemit-exceeds-100k-users-plans-to-expand-saving-steem; (2) "Steemit Business Model | How Does Steemit Make Money?," www.feedough.com/steemit-business-model-how-does-steemit-make-money/; (3) "Steemit - Crunchbase Company Profile & Funding," www.crunchbase.com/organization/steemit; (4) "Powering Communities and Opportunities - Steem," https://steem.com/; (5) "Link Prediction With Text in Online Social Networks: The Role of ...," https://link.springer.com/chapter/10.1007/978-3-031-18840-4_16; (6) "What Is Steemit (STEEM)? Social Network for Content Creation - CryptoPotato," https://cryptopotato.com/meet-steemit-social-network-content-creation/; (7) "What Is Steemit and How Does It Work? | CoinMarketCap," https://coinmarketcap.com/alexandria/article/what-is-steemit-and-how-does-it-work; (8) en.wikipedia.org, https://en.wikipedia.org/wiki/Steemit.

Diaspora: A Decentalized Social Networking Dream

Diaspora logo

Diaspora, as a decentralized social networking platform, holds promise in addressing growing concerns about privacy, data ownership, and censorship on centralized platforms.

Launched in 2010 by a group of students, Diaspora gained attention for its decentralized architecture, which allows users to maintain control over their data by hosting their own *pods* or nodes, rather than relying on a single central server.

Founding and Development

The concept of *Diaspora* did not figure prominently in the social sciences until the late 1960s. The use of the plural form of the word came later still. Notwithstanding its Greek origins, the term formerly referred primarily to the Jewish experience, particularly the expulsion of Jewish people from their homeland to Babylonia (the Babylonian Exile)**** as well as the destruction of Jerusalem and its Temple. The term, then, carried a sense of loss, as the dispersal of the Jewish population was caused by their loss of territory.

**** The Babylonian Exile was a period in Jewish history when a large number of Judeans from the ancient Kingdom of Judah were forcibly relocated to Babylonia by the Neo-Babylonian Empire (597 to 582 BCE).

Features

The basic feature of Diasporas is the dispersion from a common origin. This may be, as in the case of the black African diaspora[††††], a common history and a collective identity that resides more in a shared sociocultural experience than in a specific geographic origin.

Diasporas are characterized by most, if not all, of the following features:

- Migration, which may be forced or voluntary, from a country of origin in search of work, trade, or to escape conflict or persecution.
- An idealized, collective memory and/or myth about the ancestral home.
- A continuing connection to a country of origin.

Impact

Diaspora communities can make a unique contribution to the development of their home countries—especially toward building physical capital and productivity, and ultimately helping to boost job creation, living standards, and higher growth.

Migration and diaspora have had a profound impact on civilizations all over the world, helping to weave together a vibrant tapestry of diversity and fostering intercultural dialogue.

The impact of migration and diaspora can be felt in many facets of day-to-day life, including the culinary arts, the literary world, and the artistic world.

The resources of diaspora communities are varied and represent a great potential for both countries of origin and destination.

[††††] The Black African diaspora refers to the global communities descended from the historic movements and dispersal of Africans, particularly the trans-Atlantic slave trade.

Future Outlook: A Decentralized Future With Promising Growth and Revenue Stream

The Diaspora social network has been making waves in the digital world. Its unique approach to data privacy and user control sets it apart from traditional social media platforms. The future of Diaspora seems promising, given its user growth and potential revenue streams.

User Growth

As of November 2011, Diaspora had over 216,000 users. The network's growth can be attributed to its decentralized nature, which allows users to connect seamlessly with the Diaspora community worldwide. This decentralization is not just a technical feature, but a philosophical stance that Diaspora takes, emphasizing user freedom and privacy.

The concept of digital diasporas has been expanding and transforming agencies in the digital age. Diaspora's growth is not just about the number of users but also about the quality of interactions and the depth of engagement. The platform enables, sustains, and multiplies diasporic encounters through its digital devices and infrastructures.

Revenue Streams

While Diaspora does not use user data for advertising like many other networks, it does present unique opportunities for revenue generation. One such opportunity lies in leveraging the diaspora audience as an additional revenue stream. This involves creating a minimum viable product for the diaspora segment and potentially monetizing it.

Diaspora also offers social network integration, allowing users to post to their profiles on other major social services. This feature not only keeps friends in touch but also opens up potential avenues for cross-platform promotions and partnerships.

Moreover, the revenue model for Diaspora and all decentralized social networks could be based on ethical means like trust and knowledge sharing. This approach aligns with Diaspora's philosophy of user control and privacy, further strengthening its position in the market.

Conclusion

In conclusion, the future of the Diaspora social network looks bright. Its user growth and potential revenue streams suggest a promising trajectory. As the digital world continues to evolve, platforms like Diaspora that prioritize user control, privacy, and ethical revenue generation will likely play a significant role in shaping the future of social networking.

Diaspora continues to offer a unique approach to social networking, prioritizing user privacy and decentralization. Its future will likely be shaped by the evolving landscape of online privacy and user control.

POPULATION~ 299191accounts
ACTIVE USERS~ 19412people
SERVERS> 73instances
(statistics updated regularly, latest update - 06 Jun 2024)

Diaspora data

Diaspora endnote references[####]

[####] These URLs present an overview of the Diaspora Social Network.

"The Online Social World Where You are in Control," https://diaspora-foundation.org/; "Wikipedia-Diaspora (Social Network)," https://en.wikipedia.org/wiki/Diaspora_(social_network); "Byuroscope-Explore Diaspora*," https://byuroscope.com/diaspora/; "Diaspora Project Wiki," https://wiki.diasporafoundation.org/Main_Page.

MeWe: A Privacy-Focused Social Networking

MeWe logo

MeWe promotes itself as a privacy-focused alternative to mainstream platforms, offering ad-free experiences.

Founding and Development

MeWe was originally founded as Sgrouples in 2012. The platform was designed with a focus on data privacy, positioning itself as an alternative to Facebook. By 2015, as MeWe neared the end of its beta testing cycle, the press called MeWe's software "not dissimilar to Facebook."

In 2020, Mashable described MeWe as replicating Facebook's features. In 2022, MeWe announced it would migrate its platform over time to a Web3, blockchain-based web infrastructure, becoming the first major social network to migrate its tech over to the Decentralized Social Networking Protocol, which will make it the largest decentralized social media platform.

Features

The MeWe site and application have features common to most social media and social networking sites: users can post text and images to a feed, react to others' posts using emojis, post animated GIFs, create specialized groups, post disappearing content, and chat.

- Online chat may occur between two or more people or among members of a group.
- Person-to-person online chat is similar to that in most other social media and social networking sites and supports text, video calling, and voice calling.

- "Secret Chat" is limited to the paid subscription tier of
  MeWe, and uses double ratchet encryption to ensure that
  chats are private and not visible even to MeWe employees.

Impact

Although MeWe has not intentionally positioned itself as a social network
for conservatives, Mashable noted in November 2020 that its active user
base trends are conservative.

The platform's choice not to moderate misinformation on the platform
has attracted conservatives who felt mainstream social networks were cen-
soring their posts and those who have been banned from those platforms.

MeWe is considered an alt-tech platform. MeWe's loose moderation
has made it popular among conspiracy theorists, including proponents
of the far-right QAnon conspiracy theory, which was banned from Facebook in 2020, and the "Stop the Steal" conspiracy theory relating to the
2020 United States presidential election.

On MeWe, users can post content under various categories. While
specific details about the most popular categories on MeWe at the current
time are not readily available, users often post content related to a wide
range of topics.

The platform is currently experiencing a surge in new users, particularly among conservatives searching for new platforms to avoid Facebook
and Twitter. Therefore, political discussions could be a popular category.
However, the platform is diverse and includes content from a variety of
categories.

MeWe's audience is diverse. As of the latest data, the platform had
over 1.2 million registered users. The largest age group of visitors is 25- to
34-year-olds. In terms of gender distribution, about two-thirds (68.57%)
of MeWe users are male.

Business Model

MeWe is a free platform but also offers a premium subscription tier. The
platform is funded through Pro subscriptions and sales of other digital
packs like stickers and badges from users to cover its bills.

Businesses who want to represent themselves on MeWe must also pay a small monthly fee to operate on the site, and there are options for cloud storage and video calling packages to help generate additional funds.

MeWe: A Rising Star in the Social Media Landscape

MeWe, the social network that prides itself on privacy and a user-centric approach, has been experiencing significant growth.

User Base

The platform's user base has been expanding at an impressive rate, with a 36 percent increase in Q1 2021 and an average annual growth of 173 percent over the last three years. This growth is not confined to North America, as 50 percent of its traffic comes from outside this region.

The surge in MeWe's popularity can be attributed to several factors. First, the platform's commitment to user privacy and control over data and newsfeeds is a refreshing alternative to ad-riddled social media platforms. Second, the platform's availability in 20 languages and its recent popularity in Hong Kong indicate its potential for international expansion.

Revenue

In terms of revenue, MeWe has a unique business model that does not rely on advertising revenue. Instead, it generates income from MeWe Premium subscriptions and users purchasing premium enhancements. This model seems to be working, as the company saw revenues of over $3 million for the first four months of 2021 and expects to bring in $8 to $10 million for the full year. This is a significant increase from the $1.165 million it brought in in 2020.

Looking ahead, MeWe is planning to raise between $10 and $30 million this year and up to $75 million the following year to fuel its growth. This funding will likely be used to scale the platform and invest more in marketing. With these plans in place, MeWe's estimated annual revenue is projected to reach $14.1 million.

However, while MeWe's growth and revenue streams are promising, the platform still faces challenges. It needs to continue its efforts to moderate content effectively and maintain its reputation as a politically neutral platform[2].

Conclusion

In conclusion, MeWe's impressive user growth and unique revenue model position it as a promising player in the social media landscape. If it can successfully navigate the challenges ahead, it has the potential to become a major competitor to established social media giants.

MeWe endnote references[§§§§]

[§§§§] These URLs present an overview of the MeWe Social Network.

"What Is MeWe and How Is It Different?," www.lifewire.com/what-is-mewe-4801952; "MeWe — The First Social Network with Privacy by Design," https://markweinstein.medium.com/mewe-the-first-social-network-with-privacy-by-design-b55b09e2922f; "The World's Largest Decentralized Social Network," https://mewe.com/cms/about; "MeWe App," https://play.google.com/store/apps/details?id=com.mewe&hl=en_CA; "A Complete Guide to MeWe: The Privacy-Focused Social Media Platform," https://franetic.com/a-complete-guide-to-mewe-the-privacy-focused-social-media-platform/. Data Sources as of July 2024 (1) "Anti-Facebook MeWe continues Its User Growth Surge | ZDNET," www.zdnet.com/article/anti-facebook-mewe-continues-its-user-growth-surge/; (2) "Exclusive: MeWe Looks to Raise Money to Fuel Expansion - Axios," www.axios.com/2021/07/13/mewe-expansion-fundraise; (3) "MeWe - Wikipedia," https://en.wikipedia.org/wiki/MeWe; (4) "MeWe: Revenue, Competitors, Alternatives - Growjo," https://growjo.com/company/MeWe; (5) "MeWe Opens Community Investment Round Allowing Users to ... - Morningstar," www.morningstar.com/news/pr-newswire/20240418la90647/mewe-opens-community-investment-round-allowing-users-to-invest-own-a-financial-stake-in-company; (6) "'Anti-Facebook' MeWe Social Network Adds 2.5 Million New Members in One ...," www.zdnet.com/article/mewe-the-anti-facebook-social-network-adds-2-5-million-new-members-in-1-week/; (7) "MeWe Social Network Grew 400% in 2018 With Rapid Growth Predicted for 2019," https://techaeris.com/2019/02/04/mewe-social-network-grew-400-in-2018-with-rapid-growth-predicted-for-2019/; (8) "MeWe Company Profile 2024: Valuation, Funding & Investors - PitchBook," https://pitchbook.com/profiles/company/89957-62; (9) "MeWe - The Next-Gen Social Network," https://cdn.mewe.com/about.

CHAPTER 5

Lesser-Known Social Networks Facing Extinction

Lesser-known social networks facing extinction share common themes such as failure to innovate, declining user engagement, competition from larger rivals, and challenges related to monetization and sustainability.

In the highly competitive landscape of social networking, platforms must continuously evolve, differentiate themselves, and meet the changing needs of users to avoid extinction.

Vine: A Short-Form Video Hosting Service

Vine logo

Source: https://icons8.com/icons/set/vine.

Vine was an American short-form video hosting service where users could share up to 10-second-long looping video clips.

Vine's Origins and Acquisition

Vine was founded in June 2012 by Dom Hofmann, Rus Yusupov, and Colin Kroll.

Twitter acquired Vine in October 2012 for around $30 million.

Launch and Growth

Vine was launched on January 24, 2013, as a free iOS app for sharing short looping videos.

An Android version followed on June 2, 2013, and a Windows Phone version on November 12, 2013. Within a few months, Vine became the most popular video-sharing app despite low adoption initially. On April 9, 2013, it was the most downloaded free iOS app.

A web version was launched on May 1, 2014, to explore Vine videos.

New Features

In July 2014, Vine added a *loop count* showing how many times each video was viewed, including embedded views. On October 14, 2014, an Xbox One version allowed viewing Vine videos through Xbox Live.

Vine's Demise

Once a vibrant platform that birthed a generation of influential creators, Vine experienced both a meteoric rise and a subsequent fall. Some reasons behind its demise include:

- Lack of unified leadership
  o Vine lacked cohesive leadership, leading to internal disarray and conflicting directions. This lack of unity ultimately contributed to its downfall.
- Loss of user interest
  o Over time, Vine lost its initial charm. Users gradually lost interest, resulting in decreased engagement. The novelty wore off, and other platforms began to compete for attention.
- Technical glitches
  o The app faced persistent technical issues that went unaddressed. These glitches frustrated users and eroded their trust in the platform.

- Competition with other platforms
  - As other social media platforms emerged, Vine faced stiff competition. Users migrated to newer, more feature-rich apps, leaving Vine behind.
- Neglecting top Viners
  - Vine failed to adequately support its top creators—the very individuals who brought it fame. These influential Viners sought alternative avenues, such as sponsored content deals directly with brands, bypassing Vine's limitations.

Summary

Despite its initial success, Vine could not sustain its position in the rapidly evolving social media landscape, leading to its closure. In the end, Vine's spectacular rise and subsequent demise serve as a lesson for other platforms aiming to engage with power users. It underscores the importance of strong leadership, user satisfaction, and adaptability in the ever-evolving landscape of social media.

Vine endnote references*

---

* These URLs present an overview of the Bebo Social Network.

Wikipedia's page on Bebo (https://en.wikipedia.org/wiki/Bebo); The Independent's article (www.independent.co.uk/tech/bebo-coming-back-social-network-facebook-twitter-b1794630.html); V Magazine's coverage (vmagazine.com/article/what-is-bebo-the-new-social-network-that-could-replace-facebook-and-twitter/); Goss.ie reports (goss.ie/uk-showbiz/bebo-is-officially-making-a-comeback-as-a-brand-new-social-network-241959); TechCrunch's update (https://techcrunch.com/2021/01/29/bebo-social-network-returning-february-2021/).

Path: Limited Social Circles With Limited Success

Path logo

Source: https://icons8.com/icons/set/path-logo.

Path, the social networking platform, embarked on a unique journey—one that emphasized quality over quantity in social connections. However, despite its initial promise, it faced challenges that ultimately hindered its widespread success.

Founding and Development

The company was based in San Francisco and founded by Shawn Fanning and Former Facebook Executive Dave Morin and was launched on November 14, 2010.

In 2011, Morin rejected a $100 million offer for the company from Google. On May 28, 2015, Path was acquired by the South Korean company Kakao for an undisclosed amount.

On September 17, 2018, Path announced it would be terminating its service, and existing users could no longer access the platform as of October 18, 2018.

Path's Key Points Were

- Allowing users to share content with up to 50 close friends and family members.
- Later, Path raised its friend limit to 150 and then removed it entirely.
- The site was intended as a companion to Facebook and other social network platforms, as opposed to a destination website.

Struggles

The reasons behind Path's limited social circles and its subsequent struggles included the following:

1. **Focus on intimacy:**
   - **Path** positioned itself as a platform for **close-knit social circles**. Unlike other sprawling networks, it aimed to foster deeper connections among a select group of friends and family.
   - Users could share moments, photos, and thoughts with a smaller, more intimate audience. This exclusivity was both its strength and limitation.
2. **The paradox of limited circles:**
   - **Strength**: By limiting the number of connections, Path encouraged meaningful interactions. Users felt more comfortable sharing personal moments.
   - **Limitation**: The very exclusivity that made Path special also restricted its growth. It struggled to attract a critical mass of users, especially when compared to giants like Facebook and Instagram.
3. **Network effects and scale:**
   - Social networks thrive on **network effects**: The more the users, the more valuable the platform becomes. Path's small user base hindered these effects.
   - **Catch-22**: To succeed, Path needed more users, but its commitment to intimacy prevented rapid expansion. It became a delicate balancing act.
4. **Privacy concerns and trust:**
   - Path's emphasis on privacy resonated with some users. However, it also raised concerns about data security and trust.
   - **Backlash**: In 2012, Path faced backlash when it was discovered that the app uploaded users' entire address books without explicit consent. This eroded trust and damaged its reputation.

5. **Competition and feature parity:**
   - **David versus Goliaths**: Path competed against social media giants with vast resources. Facebook, Instagram, and Twitter offered similar features while reaching a broader audience.
   - **Feature gap**: Path struggled to keep up with feature updates and innovations. Users expected seamless experiences, and Path lagged behind in terms of functionality.
6. **Monetization challenges:**
   - **Free versus premium**: Path initially charged users for its premium version, but this model limited adoption. Eventually, it shifted to a free model, relying on in-app purchases.
   - **Monetization struggles**: Generating revenue without compromising its core values proved difficult. Advertising was a delicate balance for a platform focused on intimacy.

Summary

In summary, Path's limited social circles were both its allure and its downfall. While it carved a niche for meaningful connections, it struggled to compete in a crowded market. Despite some initial success and a high-profile acquisition, the service ultimately shut down in 2018 after failing to maintain a sustainable user base.

Path endnote references[†]

[†] These URLs present an overview of the Hi5 Social Network.

"Hi5 was Underrated (and Better Than the Wiggles)," www.reddit.com/r/unpopularopinion/comments/vzu1o1/hi5_was_underrated_and_better_than_the_wiggles/?rdt=46596&onetap_auto=true&one_tap=true; "2021: Our Year in Review," www.hi5.team/blog/2021-hi5-year-in-review; hi5 – Wikipedia https://en.wikipedia.org/wiki/Hi5.

Bebo: Emphasis on Social Networking and Self-Expression

Bebo logo

Source: https://icons8.com/icons/set/bebo-logo.

Bebo's brief resurgence and subsequent decline highlight the challenges of revitalizing a once-popular social networking platform in a rapidly evolving digital landscape.

Founding and Development

Originally launched in 2005 by Michael and Xochi Birch, Bebo experienced early success, particularly in the United Kingdom, Ireland, and New Zealand, attracting millions of users with its user-friendly interface, customizable profiles, and emphasis on social networking and self-expression.

However, Bebo's initial success was short-lived, and the platform began to decline in the face of increasing competition from emerging rivals like Facebook and Twitter.

By 2010, Bebo's user base had dwindled significantly, leading to its acquisition by AOL for $850 million in 2008 and subsequent sale to Criterion Capital Partners for a fraction of that amount in 2010.

Bebo's brief resurgence in 2019 can be attributed to its acquisition by the streaming platform Twitch, owned by Amazon. Twitch sought to leverage Bebo's technology and expertise to enhance its streaming services and provide additional tools for content creators. As part of this strategy, Twitch relaunched Bebo as *Bebo 2.0*, positioning it as a platform for streamers to create and share content with their audiences.

Relaunch

The relaunch generated some initial excitement and nostalgia among former Bebo users, as well as interest from the streaming community. However, Bebo's revival ultimately proved short-lived, and the platform faced challenges in attracting and retaining users amidst intense competition from established players like Twitch, YouTube, and TikTok.

Decline

Several factors contributed to Bebo's quick decline following its brief resurgence:

1. **Competition**: Bebo faced intense competition from established players in the streaming and social media space, making it difficult to carve out a niche and attract users away from more popular platforms.
2. **Lack of differentiation**: Despite efforts to rebrand and relaunch Bebo, the platform struggled to differentiate itself from competitors and offer compelling features or experiences that would attract users and keep them engaged.
3. **Shifting user behavior**: The preferences and behavior of internet users have evolved since Bebo's heyday, with many gravitating toward platforms that offer more immersive and interactive experiences, such as live streaming, short-form video, and gaming.
4. **Management and strategic missteps**: Bebo underwent multiple ownership changes and strategic shifts over the years, leading to instability and a lack of clear direction. These management and strategic missteps undermined the platform's ability to compete effectively and regain relevance in the social media landscape.

Summary

In summary, Bebo's brief resurgence and quick decline underscore the challenges of revitalizing a once-popular social networking platform in a highly competitive and rapidly evolving digital environment. Despite efforts to rebrand and relaunch the platform, Bebo ultimately failed to regain traction and succumbed to the same challenges that led to its initial decline.

Bebo endnote references‡

---

‡ These URLs present an overview of the VINE Social Network.:
Vine (service) https://en.wikipedia.org/wiki/Vine_(service); "Why Did Vine Shut Down? A Deep Dive Into the Beloved Short Form Video App," www.yahoo.com/lifestyle/why-did-vine-shut-down-140000240.html?guccounter=1.

Hi5: Accommodating Multiple Languages and Cultural

Hi5 logo

Source: www.flaticon.com/free-icon/hi5-logo_87394

Preferences

Hi5's trajectory from regional success to global obscurity illustrates the complexities of navigating the dynamic landscape of social networking platforms.

Founding and Development

Launched in 2003 by Ramu Yalamanchi, Hi5 initially gained traction as a social networking site catering to a diverse international audience, particularly in Latin America, Asia, and Africa.

Features

One key factor contributing to Hi5's regional success was its early entry into markets outside of North America and Europe. While platforms like Myspace and later Facebook dominated Western markets, Hi5 capitalized on opportunities in emerging economies where internet penetration was growing rapidly. By tailoring its platform to accommodate multiple languages and cultural preferences, Hi5 effectively penetrated markets where competitors had yet to establish a strong presence.

Furthermore, Hi5's focus on gaming and virtual gifts resonated with users in regions where online gaming and digital gifting were popular forms of entertainment and social interaction. The platform's gamification elements, such as virtual currency and rewards, helped drive user engagement and monetization, particularly in markets with a younger demographic.

However, Hi5's regional success did not translate into sustained global prominence.

Decline

Several factors contributed to its eventual decline and obscurity on the global stage:

1. **Intense competition:** As the social media landscape evolved, Hi5 faced increasing competition from more established players like Facebook and later Twitter, Instagram, and Snapchat. These platforms offered more sophisticated features, better user experiences, and broader global reach, making it difficult for Hi5 to compete on a global scale.

2. **Failure to innovate:** Hi5 struggled to innovate and adapt to changing user preferences and technological advancements. While competitors introduced new features such as photo sharing, messaging, and news feeds, Hi5's platform remained relatively stagnant, failing to keep pace with evolving user expectations.

3. **Platform fragmentation:** Unlike Facebook, which prioritized building a cohesive global network, Hi5's decentralized approach led to fragmentation and inconsistency across different regional markets. This lack of cohesion hindered the platform's ability to offer a consistent user experience and capitalize on network effects.

4. **Shift in user behavior:** As social media usage patterns evolved, users gravitated toward platforms that offered more personalized and curated experiences. Hi5's focus on gaming and virtual gifts became less relevant as users sought platforms for communication, content sharing, and self-expression.

5. **Management and strategic missteps:** Hi5 underwent several ownership changes and strategic shifts over the years, leading to instability and a lack of clear direction. These management and strategic missteps further undermined the platform's ability to compete effectively in the global social media landscape.

Summary

In summary, Hi5's regional success can be attributed to its early entry into emerging markets, focus on gaming and virtual gifts, and ability to cater to diverse international audiences. However, a combination of intense competition, failure to innovate, platform fragmentation, shifting user behavior, and management missteps ultimately contributed to its decline and global obscurity.

Hi5 endnote references[§]

[§] These URLs present an overview of the Path Social Network.

Path (social network), https://en.wikipedia.org/wiki/Path_(social_network); "Mobile Social Network Path, Once a Challenger to Facebook, is Closing Down," https://techcrunch.com/2018/09/17/rip-path/; "Path is Closing Its Private Social Network for Good," www.engadget.com/2018-09-17-path-private-social-network-stickers-dead.html.

CHAPTER 6

Less Common Social Networks Still in Operation Worldwide

Introduction

In the ever-evolving landscape of social media, giants like Facebook, Instagram, and Twitter dominate global attention. However, beyond these mainstream platforms, a diverse array of less common social networks thrives, catering to niche audiences and specific interests. These platforms offer unique functionalities, culturally tailored experiences, and specialized communities that major networks often overlook. This chapter delves into these lesser-known social networks, exploring their distinct features, user bases, and the unique roles they play in the digital ecosystem. Through this exploration, we aim to highlight the diversity and richness of social media beyond the familiar giants, showcasing how these platforms continue to innovate and serve their dedicated user communities around the world.

BeReal: Authentic Moments Shared in Real-Time

BeReal logo

Source: https://icons8.com/icons/set/bereal-logo.

BeReal is a relatively new social media app that has gained significant popularity, especially among younger users.

Founding and Development

BeReal is a French-developed app that launched in 2020 and has seen rapid growth, with over 100 million downloads worldwide as of April 2024. The app is designed to provide a more authentic social media experience compared to platforms like Instagram and TikTok.

BeReal has resonated particularly with younger users, with 98 percent of its user base being under 45 years old. In the United States, 43.3 percent of users are between 16 and 25 years old, while 55.1 percent are 26 and 44 years old. The app has also seen high adoption in other countries like France and the United Kingdom, where it has a majority female user base.

Key Features

- The core feature of BeReal is that it sends a notification to all users simultaneously at a random time each day, giving them two minutes to take a photo using both the front and back cameras of their phone. This is meant to capture a genuine, unfiltered moment of the user's day, rather than a curated, edited image.

Decline

- The app's popularity has started to decline, with its monthly active users dropping 61 percent from its peak in October 2022 to under six million by March 2023.
- Some users have found the monotony of seeing similar daily photos from friends to be less appealing over time.

Summary

- Nonetheless, BeReal continues to be a popular alternative to more curated social media platforms, offering users a more authentic and intimate social experience.

BeReal endnote references[*]

---

* These URLs present an overview of the BeReal Social Network.

BeReal Is a New 'Unfiltered' Social App—Is It Safe for Kids?, www.parents
.com/news/bereal-is-a-new-unfiltered-social-media-app-is-it-safe-for-kids/;
What is the BeReal App?—What Parents Need to Know, www.internetmat-
ters.org/hub/news-blogs/what-is-bereal-app/; 19 Essential BeReal Statistics
You Need to Know in 2024, https://thesocialshepherd.com/blog/bereal-sta-
tistics; The BeReal App Wants You to Show Your Unedited Self, www.nytimes
.com/2023/04/13/style/bereal-app.html; 'It's a modern-day Facebook': How
BeReal Became Gen Z's Favourite App, www.theguardian.com/media/2022/
aug/21/its-a-modern-day-facebook-how-bereal-became-gen-zs-favourite-app.

Qzone: China's Pioneering Multimedia Social Space

Qzone logo

Source: https://icons8.com/icons/set/qzone-logo.

Qzone is a social networking platform developed by the Chinese tech company Tencent.

Founding and Development

Launched in 2005, Qzone quickly became one of the most popular social media sites in China, boasting millions of active users.

Features

Qzone offers a range of features, including:

- Blogging: users can create personal blogs where they can share their thoughts, experiences, photos, and videos with friends and followers.
- Photo sharing: Qzone allows users to upload and share photos with their network. Users can organize their photo albums and customize privacy settings.
- Diary: similar to blogging, Qzone users can maintain online diaries where they can write about their daily activities, thoughts, and reflections.
- Guestbook: Qzone has a guestbook feature where users can leave comments, messages, and greetings on each other's profiles.
- Customization: Qzone provides extensive customization options, allowing users to personalize their profiles with themes, backgrounds, music, and interactive widgets.

- Games and applications: Qzone offers a variety of games, applications, and interactive features that users can add to their profiles for entertainment and engagement.
- Social networking: users can connect with friends, classmates, and acquaintances on Qzone by adding them to their network, exchanging messages, and participating in online communities and groups.

Summary

Qzone has evolved over the years to adapt to changing trends and user preferences. While its popularity has waned in recent years due to the rise of other social media platforms, Qzone remains a significant player in the Chinese social media landscape among younger users.

Qzone endnote references†

---

† These URLs present an overview of the Qzone Social Network.

Qzone—Wikipedia, https://en.wikipedia.org/wiki/Qzone; Qzone—Company Profile—Tracxn, https://tracxn.com/d/companies/qzone/__U5I3rmdjDnVkoOIu UYO959K2GM-6PeFG5zxXYx8pvm4; The Power of Qzone Social Media, https://affiliatecounselor.com/power-of-qzone-social-media/; China's Social Network Qzone Is Big, But Is It Really The Biggest?, https://techcrunch.com/2009/02/24/chinas-social-network-qzone-is-big-but-is-it-really-the-biggest/; Qzone—Wikidata https://www.wikidata.org/wiki/Q986608.

LINE: All-in-One Messaging and Digital Life Platform

LINE logo

Source: https://icons8.com/icons/set/line-logo.

LINE is a popular messaging app and social media platform that dominates the Japanese market.

Founding and Development

Originally launched in 2011 as a disaster response app after the Tohoku earthquake and tsunami, it quickly gained massive popularity. It became the most popular messaging and social media app in Japan, with over 95 million Japanese users.

Features

LINE's unique selling point is its wide array of animated stickers and emojis featuring popular anime/manga characters, which appeal to Japanese users.

Over time, it evolved into a *super app* offering various integrated services beyond just messaging—news feed, mobile payments (LINE Pay), online streaming (LINE TV), manga comics, online shopping, games, and more.

It allows businesses to create official accounts to share content, provide customer support via Chatbots, and run advertising campaigns.

While very dominant in Japan, LINE also has a strong user base in Taiwan, Thailand, and Indonesia with over 176 million monthly active users globally.

The app is owned by the Korean company Naver and its success is attributed to capitalizing on Japanese users' love for anime/manga characters and offering a suite of services beyond messaging.

Summary

In summary, LINE started as a messaging app but its animated stickers, integration of popular Japanese content, and expansion into a multiservice *super app* allowed it to become the undisputed leader in Japan's social media market. As immensely popular in Japan and other Asian countries, with millions of users relying on it for communication, social networking, and entertainment, LINE's user-friendly interface, diverse features, and focus on privacy and security have contributed to its widespread adoption and success.

LINE endnote references‡

‡ These URLs present an overview of the LINE Social Network.

How to Protect Against Disinformation on Social Media, https://us.norton.com/blog/emerging-threats/election-disinformation-and-social-media; MIT Sloan Research on Reducing Spread of Fake News Online, https://mitsloan.mit.edu/press/what-can-be-done-to-reduce-spread-fake-news-mit-sloan-research-finds-shifting-peoples-attention-toward-accuracy-can-decrease-online-misinformation-sharing; How to Combat Fake News and Disinformation, www.brookings.edu/articles/how-to-combat-fake-news-and-disinformation/; Why LINE is the Most Popular Social Media App in Japan, www.digitalmarketingforasia.com/why-line-is-the-most-popular-social-media-app-in-japan/; What is LINE, the Biggest Messaging App in Japan? https://codigital.co.jp/en/posts/what-is-line-the-biggest-messaging-app-in-japan.

VK: Russia's Versatile Digital Ecosystem

VK logo

Source: https://icons8.com/icons/set/vk-logo.

VK (originally VKontakte) is a Russian online social media and social networking service. It is the largest social network in Russia and former Soviet republics, with over 400 million registered users.

Founding and Development

Launched in 2006 by Pavel Durov, VK stands for *VKontakte* which means *in touch* in Russian.

Features

VK is often referred to as the *Russian Facebook* due to its similarities in features and design to Facebook.

VK allows users to message friends, share updates, photos, and videos, join groups and communities, play browser-based games, and more.

VK has a Facebook-like layout with a news feed, profile pages, the ability to add friends, like posts, and so on.

Challenges

While very popular in Russia and former Soviet states, it has limited usage in Western countries.

As of 2022, VK ranked as the 4th most visited website in Russia and 16th globally.

Over 400,000 companies have commercial accounts on VK to advertise and sell products/services.

VK supports over 80 languages but the main language is Russian.

VK has faced controversies over issues such as copyright infringement, privacy concerns, and censorship.

Despite these challenges, it remains a popular platform in Russia and several other countries, attracting millions of users who use it for social networking, entertainment, and communication.

Summary

In summary, VK is the dominant social networking platform in Russia, modeled after Facebook but tailored for Russian and Eastern European users.

VK endnote references[§]

[§] These URLs present an overview of the VK Social Network.

How to Protect Against Disinformation on Social Media, https://us.norton .com/blog/emerging-threats/election-disinformation-and-social-media; MIT Sloan Research on Reducing Spread of Fake News Online, https://mitsloan.mit .edu/press/what-can-be-done-to-reduce-spread-fake-news-mit-sloan-research-finds-shifting-peoples-attention-toward-accuracy-can-decrease-online-misin-formation-sharing; How to Combat Fake News and Disinformation, www .brookings.edu/articles/how-to-combat-fake-news-and-disinformation/; What is VK? A Look at the Russian Social Media App, www.huntintel.io/post/what-is-vk-social-media-app-a-look-at-the-russian-platform.

Weibo: China's Vibrant Microblogging and Social Media Hub

Weibo logo

Source: https://icons8.com/icons/set/weibo-logo.

Weibo (previously Sina Weibo) is a popular Chinese microblogging platform and social network:

Weibo, which means *microblog* in Chinese, is a Chinese Twitter-like online networking tool. Hundreds of millions of users in China use Weibo as a platform to share information and voice opinions.

Founding and Development

Weibo was launched by Sina Corporation in 2009 and has over 500 million registered users, with 313 million monthly active users. It is one of the biggest social media platforms in China.

Features

Weibo allows users to post text, photos, videos, and other content publicly for sharing and discussion. It has features like verification badges for celebrities and organizations, as well as a *Vlog* function for video content.

Weibo has become an important platform for news, entertainment, and discussion of social issues in China, given the country's strict media censorship. It has been used by authorities, businesses, and the public to share information and opinions.

Despite competition from other Chinese social media platforms, Weibo remains the most popular microblogging service in the country.

Summary

In summary, on Weibo, users can post short messages, photos, videos, and links, which are then shared with their followers. Similar to Twitter, posts on Weibo are limited to a certain character count, encouraging succinct communication. Users can also follow other accounts, engage with posts by liking, commenting, or reposting (known as *forwarding* on Weibo), and participate in trending topics and discussions.

Weibo has become a significant platform for news dissemination, celebrity updates, and public discourse in China. It is also widely used for marketing, advertising, and brand promotion by businesses and influencers. Despite being subject to government censorship and content regulations, Weibo remains a vital part of the Chinese digital landscape and continues to shape online conversations and trends in the country.

Weibo endnote references[¶]

[¶] These URLs present an overview of the Weibo Social Network.

Weibo: Latest News and Updates | South China Morning Post, www.scmp.com/topics/weibo; Weibo—Wikipedia, https://en.wikipedia.org/wiki/Weibo; What's on Weibo—Insights on Chinese Social Media, www.whatsonweibo.com; Weibo on the App Store, https://apps.apple.com/ca/app/%E5%BE%AE%E5%8D%9A/id350962117; Weibo—Google Play Store https://play.google.com/store/apps/details?hl=en&id=com.sina.weibo.

Douyin: China's Trendsetting Short Video-Sharing

Douyin logo

Source: https://en.wikipedia.org/wiki/File:Douyin_logo.svg.

Sensation

Douyin is a short-form video hosting service similar to TikTok.

Founding and Development

Douyin is the Chinese version of the TikTok app, launched by ByteDance in China in 2016.

Features

- Douyin is only available in China, while TikTok is the international version.
- Douyin and TikTok share a similar user interface, but the platforms operate separately Douyin includes features like in-video search by people's faces, as well as e-commerce integrations that allow users to directly purchase products featured in videos.
- Douyin quickly gained massive popularity in China, reaching 100 million users within a year of launch and over one billion video views per day.
- While TikTok and Douyin have similarities, they are distinct platforms catered to their respective markets
- Douyin for the Chinese market, and TikTok for the global market.

Summary

In summary, While TikTok is primarily used outside of China, Douyin is the version of the app designed for users within mainland China. Both TikTok and Douyin share similar features, allowing users to create and share short videos with various effects, filters, and music. However, due to differences in internet regulations and content restrictions between China and other countries, the content available on Douyin may differ from TikTok. While not as widely adopted globally, these platforms still have active user communities and continue to operate alongside the dominant social media giants.

*Douyin endnote references***

** These URLs present an overview of the Douyin Social Network.

How to Get the Douyin Makeup Look Trending on TikTok, www.teenvogue .com/story/douyin-makeup-guide; Douyin—Google Play Store, https://play .google.com/store/apps/details?hl=en_CA&id=com.ss.android.ugc.aweme. mobile; What is Douyin and How to Get Started, www.chinafy.com/china-tech/ what-is-douyin-and-how-to-get-started; Download Douyin for Android, https:// douyin.en.uptodown.com/android; TikTok—Wikipedia, https://en.wikipedia .org/wiki/TikTok.

CHAPTER 7

The Rise and Fall of Some Niche Networks

The term *niche network* could refer to various specialized services or platforms that were launched over the years. While there is no direct account of a *rise and fall* narrative for a specific niche network, here are some insights into the broader context of some ventures in niche markets. Examples of ventures into niche markets include **Google+, Myspace, Friendster, and Vine**.

- **Google+** was a social networking service that was eventually shut down, and Google Reader an RSS feed reader was also discontinued.
- **Myspace** was a pioneering social networking website launched in 2003 that allowed users to create customizable profiles, connect with friends, share media like photos and music, and interact through features like messaging and comments.
- **Friendster** was one of the earliest social networking websites, launched in 2003, that allowed users to create profiles, connect with friends, and share content like photos, videos, and messages within their online social network.
- **Vine** was a short-form video hosting service launched in 2013 that allowed users to create and share looping six-second video clips, which could be shared across social media platforms.

These platforms had their moments of popularity but ultimately did not sustain in the long term because of various factors, including competition and shifts in strategic focus.

Google+: A Comprehensive Social Networking Platform

Google+

Source: https://commons.wikimedia.org/wiki/Category:Google%2B_logos.

The *Google niche network* likely refers to Google's various attempts at creating specialized platforms or services that target specific market segments. One prominent example is **Google+**, which was Google's foray Google+ logo

Here is a brief overview of its rise and fall.

Founding and Development

Launched in 2011, Google+ was Google's ambitious attempt to create a comprehensive social networking platform that integrated seamlessly with its other products and services. Despite high expectations and significant investment, Google+ ultimately failed to gain widespread adoption and was shut down in 2019.

Breakdown of Its Rise and Fall

Rise

1. **Integration with Google Services:** Google+ was tightly integrated with other Google services like Gmail, Google Photos, and YouTube, offering users a unified experience across multiple products. This integration aimed to leverage Google's existing user base and provide a seamless transition for users already using Google's ecosystem of products and services.

2. **Unique features:** Google+ introduced several innovative features such as *Circles* (allowing users to organize their connections into different groups), *Hangouts* (for video conferencing and group chats), and *Communities* (for shared interests and discussions). These features aimed to differentiate Google+ from competitors and provide users with new ways to connect and interact online.

3. **Early adoption and hype:** Google+ generated significant hype and curiosity at launch, with many users eager to explore Google's take on social networking. Early adopters praised its clean design, intuitive interface, and privacy controls, attracting a loyal user base of tech enthusiasts, early adopters, and professionals.

Fall

1. **Low user engagement:** despite initial excitement, Google+ struggled to maintain user engagement and retention over time. Many users found the platform confusing or unnecessary, especially as they already had established networks on platforms like Facebook and Twitter. The lack of compelling content and social interactions further dampened user interest and participation on Google+.

2. **Privacy concerns:** Google+ faced criticism and controversy over its handling of user data and privacy. In 2018, it was revealed that a security flaw had exposed the personal information of millions of users, leading to increased scrutiny and distrust of the platform. These privacy concerns damaged Google+'s reputation and eroded user confidence in the platform's ability to protect their personal information.

3. **Failed attempts at growth:** despite Google's efforts to promote Google+ and integrate it with other products, the platform failed to gain significant traction or attract mainstream users. Various attempts to boost user engagement, such as forcing YouTube users to create Google+ accounts for commenting or linking Google+ profiles to search results, were met with backlash and resistance from users.

4. **Declining relevance:** as user interest waned and engagement declined, Google+ became increasingly irrelevant in the social

networking landscape. Competitors like Facebook, Twitter, and later Instagram and Snapchat continued to innovate and attract users with new features, better user experiences, and broader appeal, leaving Google+ struggling to compete.

Shutdown

In 2019, Google announced the shutdown of Google+ following years of declining usage and security concerns.

Google+ serves as a case study of the challenges of entering established markets dominated by strong incumbents like Facebook. While it had the potential and resources of Google behind it, it ultimately failed to differentiate itself enough to attract and retain a large, active user base. The lessons from Google+ have likely influenced Google's approach to new ventures, emphasizing the need for clear value propositions and user privacy.

The failure of Google+ serves as a sobering reminder of the challenges inherent in launching a new social networking platform, even for a tech giant like Google, and underscores the importance of understanding user needs, addressing privacy concerns, and delivering compelling value propositions in the highly competitive social media market.

Google+ endnote references*

---

* These URLs present an overview of the Google+ Social Network.

How to Use Google Trends to Find a Niche, https://keyword.com/blog/niche-research-using-google-trends/; Top 12 Trending Niches in 2023: The Future of Business Revealed, https://thenicheguru.com/niche-investigation/trending-niches-2023/; How Niche Platforms Will Dominate Social Media in 2021 and Beyond, www.fastcompany.com/90693507/how-niche-platforms-will-dominate-social-media-in-2021-and-beyond.

WickrMe: A Secure Messaging Fortress

WickrMe logo

Source: https://commons.wikimedia.org/wiki/File:Wickr_Marklogo
type_horiz.png?uselang=en#Licensing.

WickrMe is a privacy-oriented messaging app that also offers self-destruct-ing messages. WickrMe, initially known simply as Wickr, was created with a strong emphasis on privacy and security, offering users a mes-saging app that prioritized end-to-end encryption and self-destructing messages.

Early Years (2012 to 2016)

- Wickr was officially launched in 2012, offering users a secure messaging platform that allowed them to send encrypted messages, photos, videos, and files with self-destructing timers.
- The app gained attention for its commitment to user privacy and security, positioning itself as a trusted platform for secure communication among individuals, businesses, and organizations.

Mid-2010s (2016 to 2020)

- Wickr continued to evolve its platform, introducing features such as screen sharing, file shredding, and secure collaboration tools to meet the needs of its growing user base.
- The app expanded its presence in various industries, including health care, finance, and government, where secure communication and data protection were paramount.

- Wickr gained recognition for its role in protecting user privacy and data security, particularly in light of increasing concerns about surveillance, data breaches, and privacy violations.
- The company also focused on building partnerships and integrations with other platforms and services, further enhancing its capabilities and expanding its reach.
- Nico Sell served as Wickr's CEO until May 2015. She later became the cochairman of the Wickr Foundation, a nonprofit funded by the company.
- Mark Fields took over as CEO, followed by Joel Wallenstrom in November 2016.

Recent Years (2020 to Present)

- In 2020, Wickr announced the launch of WickrMe, a free version of its secure messaging app designed for personal use. WickrMe retained many of the core features of the original Wickr app, including end-to-end encryption, self-destructing messages, and secure file sharing.
- WickrMe has continued to evolve with updates and improvements to its platform, focusing on enhancing user experience, performance, and security.
- The app has gained a loyal following among users who prioritize privacy and security in their digital communications, including journalists, activists, and individuals concerned about online surveillance and data privacy.
- WickrMe remains committed to its mission of providing users with a secure and private messaging platform, offering features such as anonymous sign-up, device-to-device encryption, and secure file transfer.
- Amazon Web Services (AWS) acquired Wickr in June 2021.

WickrMe Versus Wickr Pro

- Wickr has been known for its client-side end-to-end encryption, ephemeral messages, and anonymous accounts.
- WickrMe and Wickr Pro share the same secure code base.
- WickrMe focuses on individual users with anonymous usernames.
- Wickr Pro offers a free tier and may be suitable for certain use cases.

Security and Reputation

- Wickr received attention due to a security issue at rival messaging company Snapchat.
- The Electronic Frontier Foundation scored Wickr 5 out of 7 points on their *Secure Messaging Scorecard*, highlighting its strong encryption practices.

What Might Trigger the Decline of WickrMe?

WickrMe, the secure messaging app, has faced a significant shift in its trajectory. Here are some key factors that contributed to its decline:

- User base and popularity:
  - WickrMe had a loyal user base, but its popularity waned over time. Competition from other messaging platforms, especially those with seamless interfaces and better features, impacted its user acquisition.
- Technical challenges and user experience:
  - Users reported technical issues, including crashes, activation failures, and backup problems. Performance inconsistencies and compatibility issues with various devices also affected user satisfaction[3].
- Market dynamics:
  - WickrMe faced challenges in keeping up with changing trends and maintaining relevance.

- Discontinuation announcement:
  - o On November 18, 2022, WickrMe announced that it would no longer accept new user registrations after December 31, 2022.
  - o The app was officially discontinued on December 31, 2023.

Summary

In summary, Wickr's journey—from its inception to its acquisition by AWS—reflects its commitment to privacy and secure communication. WickrMe's decline can be attributed to a combination of competition, technical hurdles, and shifting user behavior.

As the digital landscape continues to evolve, messaging apps must adapt to stay relevant.

Some Active Encrypted Messaging Services

1. Brosix, www.brosix.com/.
2. Signal, https://signal.org/.
3. Chatox, https://web.chatox.com/login/.
4. Threema, https://threema.ch/en.
5. Wire, https://wire.com/en.
6. Mattermost, https://mattermost.com/.
7. Voxer, https://web.voxer.com/login.

Wickr endnote references[†]

[†] The online resources provide a comprehensive view of Wickr's capabilities, security features, and its role within the AWS ecosystem, suitable for both personal and professional use.

Best Secure and Encrypted Messaging Apps in 2024, https://restoreprivacy .com/secure-encrypted-messaging-apps/wickr/; Wickr—Wikipedia, https://en .wikipedia.org/wiki/Wickr; Our Focus on End-to-End Encrypted Enterprise Communications, https://wickr.com/our-focus-on-end-to-end-encrypted-enterprise- communications/; Wickr Me FAQs, https://wickr.com/me/faqs/; Amazon- Owned Secure Messaging App Wickr Me to Shut Down, www.pcmag.com/news/ amazon-owned-secure-messaging-app-wickr-me-to-shut-down; Amazon-Owned Wickr Shutting Down: Top 5 Encrypted Messaging App Alternatives, www.brosix .com/blog/wickr-shutting-down/.

Myspace: A Vibrant Community of Artists, Musicians, and Creators

Myspace logo

Source: https://icons8.com/icons/set/myspace.

Myspace's journey from dominance to obscurity is a classic tale of the rise and fall of a tech giant. Here is a summary of its trajectory.

Launched in 2003 by Tom Anderson and Chris DeWolfe, Myspace quickly rose to prominence as the leading social networking platform, boasting millions of users and revolutionizing how people connect and interact online.

However, several factors contributed to its decline and eventual fall from grace:

Failure to Innovate

Myspace initially gained traction by offering users customizable profiles, music streaming, and a vibrant community of artists, musicians, and creators. However, the platform failed to innovate and adapt to changing user preferences and technological advancements. As competitors like Facebook introduced new features, better user experiences, and mobile apps, Myspace struggled to keep pace and retain its user base.

User Experience Issues

Myspace's cluttered interface, intrusive advertising, and inconsistent user experience undermined its appeal and usability. As users sought cleaner, more intuitive platforms, Myspace's outdated design and functionality became increasingly unattractive. Additionally, concerns about privacy, spam, and security further eroded user trust and engagement on the platform.

Loss of Identity and Focus

Myspace's identity as a social networking platform for artists, musicians, and creative communities became diluted as it attempted to appeal to a broader audience. Changes in ownership and strategic shifts led to a loss of focus and direction, as Myspace attempted to pivot toward entertainment, news, and e-commerce without a clear vision or differentiation from competitors.

Competition

Myspace faced intense competition from emerging social networking platforms like Facebook, Twitter, and later Instagram and Snapchat. These platforms offered simpler interfaces, richer feature sets, and broader appeal, attracting users away from Myspace with their ease of use, mobile compatibility, and network effects. Additionally, Myspace's reliance on desktop-centric usage limited its ability to compete in an increasingly mobile-first world.

Negative Perception and Reputation

Myspace developed a reputation for spam, scams, and misuse, particularly as the platform struggled to address issues related to fake profiles, cyberbullying, and inappropriate content. Reports of declining user engagement, layoffs, and executive turnover further damaged Myspace's reputation and credibility, making it difficult to attract new users and retain existing ones.

In 2011, Myspace was sold to Specific Media for a fraction of its former value, marking the end of an era of online social networking. While Myspace's dominance was relatively short-lived, its rise and fall serve as a cautionary tale for social media platforms about the importance of innovation, user experience, focus, and adaptability in maintaining relevance and sustainability in a rapidly evolving digital landscape.

Rise

- **Launch:** founded in 2003, Myspace quickly became the premier social networking site.

- **Popularity:** it was a hub for musicians, artists, and young adults, offering extensive profile customization.
- **Peak:** at its height, Myspace was the most visited social networking site, surpassing even Google in web traffic.

Fall

- **Competition:** the rise of Facebook, with its cleaner interface and privacy controls, drew users away.
- **Design and usability:** Myspace's cluttered design and lack of innovation led to a decrease in user satisfaction.
- **Corporate changes:** after being sold to News Corp, Myspace underwent several redesigns and strategy shifts, which failed to re-engage its user base.
- **Staff reductions:** as relevance faded, Myspace made significant staff cuts, signaling its decline.

Aftermath

- **Relaunch attempts:** Myspace tried to reinvent itself focusing on music and entertainment, but these efforts did not restore its former glory.
- **Current status:** today, Myspace still exists but is a shadow of its former self, serving more as a music platform than a social network.

The story of Myspace is often seen as a lesson in the fast-paced world of tech, where staying relevant requires constant innovation and adaptation to user needs and market trends.

Myspace endnote references[‡]

[‡] These URLs present an overview of the Myspace Social Network.
MySpace Cutting Staff as Relevance Declines, https://arstechnica.com/information-technology/2009/06/myspace-chopping-employees-left-and-right-as-relevance-fades/; MySpace: The Rise, Dominance and Fall of the Pioneer Social Network, https://medium.com/@zacharywestonintech/title-myspace-the-rise-dominance-and-fall-of-the-pioneer-social-networking-platform-f6375cfe1ee3.

Orkut: Early Traction in Brazil and India

Orkut logo

Source: https://icons8.com/icons/set/orkut.

Orkut's popularity in some regions and forgotten in others can be attributed to a combination of cultural factors, market dynamics, and the competitive landscape of social networking platforms.

Orkut, launched in 2004 by Google employee Orkut Büyükkökten, initially gained widespread popularity in countries such as Brazil and India.

Early Adoption and Localization

- Orkut gained early traction in Brazil and India due to its localization efforts, including language support, cultural customization, and features tailored to the preferences of users in these regions. This localization helped Orkut resonate with local audiences and gain a foothold in markets where other social networking platforms had yet to establish a strong presence.

Network Effects and Community Engagement

- Orkut's success in Brazil and India was fueled by strong network effects and community engagement. As more users joined the platform, it became increasingly valuable for connecting with friends, classmates, and communities, driving further adoption and usage. Orkut's communities and groups, in particular, fostered vibrant discussions and interactions and shared interests among users.

Cultural Relevance and Social Norms

Orkut aligned with cultural norms and social behavior prevalent in Brazil and India, such as the importance of family, community, and social connections. The platform provided a space for users to express themselves, share photos and updates, and connect with others in a familiar and culturally resonant environment.

Orkut's Demise

Despite its initial success in Brazil and India, Orkut failed to gain traction in other regions and eventually declined in popularity for several reasons:

1. **Competition from global players:** Orkut faced stiff competition from global social networking platforms like Facebook, which offered broader feature sets, better user experiences, and larger user bases. As Facebook and other platforms gained momentum, Orkut struggled to retain users and compete effectively on a global scale.

2. **Lack of innovation and adaptation:** Orkut failed to innovate and adapt to changing user preferences and market dynamics, particularly in regions outside of Brazil and India. The platform's features and interface remained relatively stagnant, while competitors introduced new functionalities, mobile apps, and monetization strategies that appealed to users worldwide.

3. **Negative perception and reputation:** Orkut developed a reputation for spam, scams, and misuse, particularly in regions where it was less popular. Reports of cyberbullying, harassment, and privacy concerns tarnished Orkut's image and deterred users from engaging with the platform, contributing to its decline in certain regions.

Summary

In summary, Orkut's popularity in some regions and obscurity in others can be attributed to a combination of localized efforts, cultural alignment, network effects, competition, innovation, and reputation. While the platform enjoyed success in Brazil and India, it ultimately failed to maintain relevance and compete with global players in the ever-evolving landscape of social networking.

Orkut's story is a testament to how localized features and early market penetration can lead to enduring popularity, even as global trends shift.

Orkut endnote references[§]

[§] These URLs present an overview of the Orkut Social Network.

Orkut—Wikipedia, https://en.wikipedia.org/wiki/Orkut; The Rise, Fall and Subsequent Death of Orkut, www.livemint.com/Consumer/zAYIirsyDYC2ZVc-NxGkXcJ/The-rise-fall-and-subsequent-death-of-Orkut.html; Why Did Orkut Fail? A Post-mortem on the Rise and Fall of the Pioneering Social Network, www .tactyqal.com/blog/why-did-orkut-fail/.

Friendster: A Pioneer in Online Friendship

Friendster logo

Source: https://en.wikipedia.org/wiki/File:Friendster_logo.svg.

Friendster is often recognized as a pioneer in social networking for several reasons, but it has a relatively short lifespan due to a combination of factors.

Pioneering Aspects

Friendster holds a unique place in the history of social networking as a pioneer that laid the groundwork for subsequent platforms, despite its relatively short lifespan.

Launched in 2002 by Jonathan Abrams, Friendster was one of the first social networking sites to gain widespread popularity, attracting millions of users with its innovative approach to online social interaction.

Several factors contributed to Friendster's status as a pioneer in the social networking space:

1. **Early adoption:** Friendster capitalized on the emerging trend of online social networking, leveraging the growing popularity of the internet and the desire for digital connections. By providing users with a platform to create profiles, connect with friends, and discover new people, Friendster tapped into a latent demand for online social interaction.

2. **Innovative features:** Friendster introduced several innovative features that would later become standard in social networking platforms, such as user profiles, friend connections, photo sharing, and messaging. These features laid the foundation for subsequent platforms like Myspace, Facebook, and LinkedIn, which built upon and refined the concept of online social networking.

3. **Cultural impact:** Friendster had a significant cultural impact, influencing the way people interacted and connected online. The platform facilitated the reconnection of old friends, the formation of new relationships, and the discovery of shared interests and communities. Friendster's influence extended beyond its user base, shaping popular culture and media perceptions of online social networking.

Friendster's Demise

Despite its status as a pioneer, Friendster's lifespan was relatively short. Several factors contributed to its decline:

1. **Technical challenges:** Friendster struggled to scale its platform to accommodate its rapidly growing user base, leading to frequent downtime, slow loading times, and technical glitches. These issues frustrated users and undermined the platform's reliability and user experience.

2. **Competition:** Friendster faced intense competition from emerging social networking platforms like Myspace and later Facebook, which offered more advanced features, better user experiences, and broader appeal. These platforms quickly surpassed Friendster in popularity and user engagement, leading to a decline in its relevance and market share.

3. **Strategic missteps:** Friendster made several strategic missteps that hindered its growth and competitiveness. These included decisions to prioritize revenue generation over user experience, reluctance to embrace new features and technologies, and failure to adapt to changing user preferences and market dynamics.

In 2011, Friendster officially shut down its social networking service, marking the end of an era of online social networking. While its lifespan was relatively short, Friendster's legacy as a pioneer in space endures, paving the way for subsequent platforms and influencing the evolution of online social interaction. Despite its early success, Friendster could not maintain its momentum in the face of these challenges, leading to its decline in popularity.

Friendster endnote references¶

⁵ These URLs present an overview of the Friendster Social Network.

Antisocial Media: The Rise and Fall of Friendster, www.mentalfloss.com/article/556413/friendster-rise-and-fall-jonathan-abrams; What Happened To Friendster? 4 Reasons Why It Failed, https://productmint.com/what-happened-to-friendster/; The Failure of Friendster, https://medium.com/@the.angie.renfro/the-failure-of-friendster-71efaab34774; Before Facebook, There Was Friendster. Yes, That's Right. The Story of Friendster, https://d3.harvard.edu/platform-digit/submission/before-facebook-there-was-friendster-yes-thats-right/ https://medium.com/@ashleighbredigkeit/the-story-of-friendster-c095201b7a6f; Friendster—Wikipedia, https://en.wikipedia.org/wiki/Friendster.

Ello: An Ad-Free Creative Haven

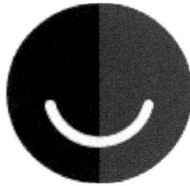

Ello logo

Source: https://icons8.com/icons/set/ello.

Ello was positioned as an ad-free alternative to mainstream platforms, focusing on creative and artistic communities. It was launched in March 2014. It was cofounded by Paul Budnitz and Todd Berger. The platform was designed to provide a more authentic social media experience.

Founding and Development

Ello began as a private social network consisting of seven artists and programmers. After a year of being private, the creators redesigned the website and launched Ello to the public. Seed funding of $435,000 from venture capital investor FreshTracks Capital in January 2014 helped sustain the company initially. Ello launched with a manifesto that claimed to distinguish it from other social networks like Facebook. The site promised it would never sell user data, proclaiming "You Are Not a Product."

Features

Ello provided features like emoji autocomplete, NSFW** settings, and hashtags. It was planning on adding others such as private messaging. The platform was initially influenced by Facebook but later switched to a Pinterest-like focus on art, photography, fashion, and web culture.

Ello claimed several notable distinguishing intentions as a social network such as never selling user data to advertisers or third parties, never showing advertisements, and not enforcing a real-name policy.

** NSFW stands for "Not Safe for Work." It is an internet slang term used to indicate that content may be inappropriate or offensive to view in a professional or public setting, such as at work or in a classroom.

Impact

Ello gained added attention in September 2014, when numerous members of the LGBTQ community left Facebook following the controversial enforcement of its real-name policy.

At its peak, the social network was processing more than 30,000 signup requests an hour. It is estimated that 20 percent of sign-ups remained active on the site one week after registration.

Business Model

Ello was free to use but was exploring a freemium model to finance future activities. It was also selling specially branded T-shirts in a partnership with Threadless to generate revenue. Additionally, the social network introduced a Hire Me button in August 2016, followed by a Buy and Collaborate Button soon after that.

Summary

Despite its initial popularity, Ello was shut down in July 2023.

During its operation, Ello served as a unique player in the social media space, focusing on providing an authentic and ad-free user experience. Its commitment to user privacy and its artist-friendly platform attracted a diverse range of users.

Ello's journey as the *Anti-Facebook* reflects the complexities of competing in a space dominated by established players and the challenges of building a sustainable business model while adhering to idealistic principles.

Ello endnote references[††]

[††] These URLs present an overview of the Ello Social Network.

Ello (Social Network)—Wikipedia, https://en.wikipedia.org/wiki/Ello_%28social_network%29; The Quiet Death of Ello's Big Dreams—Waxy.org, www.cnet.com/tech/services-and-software/what-is-ello-the-ad-free-social-network/.

CHAPTER 8

Lessons Learned and Predictions for the Future

While the predictions presented aim to provide an informed outlook on the future of social media based on current trends and expert analysis, the rapidly evolving nature of this space means the actual future may differ. Social networks and user behaviors can change quickly, so these predictions should be considered possibilities rather than certainties. The future of social media remains uncertain and will depend on many factors, including the decisions and innovations of social platforms, the preferences of users, and broader technological and cultural shifts. Predicting the future of social networking involves considering current trends, emerging technologies, and evolving user behavior.

While it is impossible to predict with certainty how the landscape will unfold, several key trends and predictions can be identified based on the trajectory of social media evolution.

The below image includes the most common factors that potentially affect the transformation of social networks.

1. Changing user preferences
2. User Experience Issues
3. Cultural Shifts
4. User Migration
5. Changing User Demographics
6. Privacy Concerns
7. Regulatory Changes/Pressures
8. Monetization Challenges
9. Technological Shifts
10. Shifting Power Dynamics
11. Increased Distrust
12. Increased Discord
13. Demographic and Behavior Trends
14. Negative Comparisons, Interaction
15. Dysfunction, and Information Overload
16. Fake Accounts or Content
17. Perceived Value

18. Mental Health   20. Community   21. Failure to
    Impacts   Fragmentation   Innovate
19. Competition

These factors, among others, could contribute to a potential decline in social network user base and influence. However, it is important to note that predicting the future of such large and complex platforms is inherently uncertain.

In this chapter, we explore each of the aforementioned factors, providing online sources that support them and suggest further readings when available.

Patterns of Social Network Decline

Some key factors that contribute to a potential decline in social network user base and influence include

Changing User Preferences

Engagement rates plummet on a platform unless the creators are paid for their own content to be seen and engaged with. This indicates that user preferences tend to shift away from the type of content and experience offered by that platform.

User preferences and perceived value are significant factors influencing the continued use of social network services. As user preferences evolve, platforms that fail to adapt may see a decline in their user base.

Increasing numbers of young people feel overwhelmed by the process of online socialization and the phenomenon of social media fatigue (SMF) gradually spreads. This suggests that changing preferences, especially among younger demographics, can contribute to users abandoning certain social media platforms.

The common theme here is that user preferences and expectations evolve over time. Social networks that fail to adapt and meet these changing needs may experience a decline in user engagement, activity, and ultimately their user base and influence.

Endnote References*

User Experience Issues

User experience factors such as usability problems, lack of critical features, and technical issues significantly contribute to the discontinuance of social networking services by their founders.

Networks that have survived and thrived are those that have remained focused on providing a simple and intuitive user experience. Networks that have become cluttered with features, advertising, and other distractions have struggled to retain users.

This highlights how a poor, cluttered user experience can lead to user attrition and the decline of social networks that fail to maintain a clean, intuitive interface.

The common theme here is that user experience factors like engagement issues, usability problems, lack of critical features, technical glitches, cluttered interfaces, and distracting elements can significantly contribute to users abandoning a social network, leading to a decline in its user base and influence.

Endnote References†

Cultural Shifts

Cultural shifts, particularly among younger generations, have led to changing preferences and behaviors that some social networks have struggled to

---

* "Factors That Show the Decline of a Social Network": https//www.linkedin.com/pulse/factors-show-decline-social-network-David-linabury; "An Empirical Study of the Factors Affecting Social Network Service Use; User Migration": www.researchgate.net/publication/223762854_An_empirical_study_of_the_factors_affecting_social_network_service_use; "Why Are You Running Away From Social Media? Analysis of the Factors Influencing Social Media Fatigue" www.frontiersin.org/journals/psychology/articles/10.3389/fpsyg.2021.67464.1/full.

† "The Impact of Social Network Change and Health Decline: A Qualitative Study on Experiences of Older Adults Who are Ageing in Place": https://bmcgeriatr.biomedcentral.com/articles/10.1186/s12877-021-02385-6.

adapt to. Platforms that fail to evolve with these cultural changes risk becoming irrelevant or losing their appeal to key demographics.

Our research indicates that cultural factors, such as changing societal norms and values around online privacy, self-expression, and digital interactions, significantly influence the decline and discontinuation of certain social networking platforms that fail to align with these evolving cultural attitudes.

Major platforms like Myspace and Friendster failed to recognize the profound cultural shifts happening, especially among younger users, toward more visual, mobile-friendly, and ephemeral forms of social media. Their inability to adapt to these changing cultural preferences ultimately led to their demise.

The common theme is that cultural attitudes, norms, and preferences evolve, particularly among younger generations. Factors like changing privacy expectations, self-expression norms, and preferences for different types of social interactions and content can all contribute to the decline of platforms that do not evolve with these cultural shifts.

Endnote References[‡]

User Migration

User migration to newer, trendier platforms is one of the biggest factors behind once-dominant social networks losing their popularity and user base. For example, many younger users migrated from Facebook to platforms like Snapchat and Telegram, perceiving them as more innovative and aligned with their interests.

"Online Social Networking and Mental Health": www.ncbi.nlm.nih.gov/pmc/articles/PMC4183915/.

[‡] "Ian Bogost on the Demise of Social Networks and Creating a Cultural Shift | Offline with Jon Favreau"; www.youtube.com/watch?v=CS2XHfEbwOs.

"Disconnected: Understanding Social Media Discontinuance"; https://researchportal.tuni.fi/files/47983368/Understanding_social_media_discontinuance_2020.pdf.

Our findings indicate that user migration to alternative platforms offering better features, experiences, or value propositions is a significant contributor to the decline and failure of certain social networking services that failed to evolve and retain their user base.

Platforms like Myspace suffered a massive user exodus as early adopters, especially younger demographics, migrated en masse to Facebook, which offered a more appealing and modern social experience at the time. This user migration severely impacted Myspace's ability to remain relevant.

The common theme is that as users' preferences and needs evolve, they may migrate to newer social platforms perceived as more innovative, trendy, or better aligned with their interests and desired experiences. This user migration away from established but stagnant networks can significantly diminish their user base and influence over time.

Endnote References[§]

Changing User Demographics

Similar to the previous years, younger users continue to flock to Telegram and Snapchat. The Facebook platform's usage among 13- to 17-year-olds stands at a sordid 4.8 percent, suggesting that it is not the best place to target a younger audience. This highlights how changing demographics, with younger users migrating to newer platforms can impact the user base of established social networks.

The research results show that user demographics such as age and gender are significant factors influencing the adoption and continued use of social network services. As user demographics shift over time, platforms that fail to adapt to these changing user bases may experience declines.

[§] "Factors That Show the Decline of a Social Network": www.linkedin.com/pulse/factors-show-decline-social-network-david-linabury/.

"An Empirical Study of the Factors Affecting Social Network Service Use": www.researchgate.net/publication/223762854_An_empirical_study_of_the_factors_affecting_social_network_service_use.

Cultural shifts, particularly among younger generations, have led to changing preferences and behaviors that some social networks have struggled to adapt to. Platforms that fail to evolve with these changing demographics risk becoming irrelevant or losing their appeal to key user segments.

The common theme here is that as user demographics shift, whether because of changing cultural norms, age distributions, or migration to new platforms, social networks that do not adapt to these evolving user bases and demographics may experience a decline in their overall user base and influence.

Endnote References[1]

Privacy Concerns

Many users have grown disillusioned with social media platforms that have repeatedly violated their privacy or mishandled their personal data. Platforms that fail to implement robust data protection measures and earn users' trust are at risk of losing their user base to more privacy-focused alternatives.

Our research indicates that privacy concerns, such as lack of transparency around data practices, unauthorized sharing of user information, and perceived surveillance, significantly contributed to user distrust and the eventual discontinuation of certain social networking platforms.

Social networks that have failed to protect user privacy and maintain trust have faced significant backlash and user exodus. Platforms like Facebook and Google+ have struggled to regain user confidence after high-profile data breaches and privacy scandals.

The common theme across these issues is that privacy concerns, including data breaches, lack of transparency around data practices, unauthorized sharing of user information, and perceived surveillance, have led

---

[1] "An Analysis of Demographic and Behaviour Trends Using Social Media: Facebook, Twitter, and Instagram": www.ncbi.nlm.nih.gov/pmc/articles/PMC7149696/

to user distrust and a decline in the user base of social networks that fail to prioritize privacy and data protection.

Endnote References[**]

Regulatory Changes and Pressures

Increased regulatory scrutiny and data privacy laws have put pressure on social networks to improve their data handling practices and content moderation policies. Platforms that fail to comply with these regulations risk hefty fines, restrictions, and loss of user trust, which can severely impact their user base.

Our findings indicate that emerging regulations around data privacy, online safety, and content moderation pose significant challenges for major social networks. Failure to adapt to these regulatory pressures could result in user migration to alternative platforms perceived as more trustworthy or compliant.

As governments around the world introduce stricter regulations targeting social media companies, platforms that fail to meet compliance standards may face restrictions, bans, or user backlash in certain markets, potentially limiting their global user base and influence.

The common theme here is that increasing regulatory pressures and changes, particularly around data privacy, content moderation, and online safety, are forcing social networks to adapt their practices and policies. Failure to comply with these regulations can result in fines, restrictions, loss of user trust, and ultimately a decline in the platform's user base and influence, as users migrate to alternatives perceived as more compliant or trustworthy.

[**] "10 Negative Effects of Social Media on Society": www.linkedin.com/pulse/10-negative-effects-social-media-society-soniya-roy/.

Endnote References[††]

Monetization Challenges

The introduction of paid Q&A causes a decline in the volume of free content, but this reduction is offset by an increase in the volume of paid Q&A content (i.e., the quantity dimension). Thus, the presence of paid Q&A overall increases total content quantity but reduces user engagement. Certain monetization models like paid Q&A can lead to a decline in free user-generated content and engagement on social media platforms.

Advertising is given preferential treatment over organic reach on the platform at a certain point in the platform's popularity. This indicates that user preferences have shifted away from the type of content and experience offered by that platform.

Prioritizing advertising and monetization over organic user content and experiences can contribute to user dissatisfaction and the decline of a social network. Social media platforms are under tremendous pressure to generate revenue. The monetization challenges faced by social media platforms and the need to adapt their strategies to drive revenue can impact user experiences and retention.

The common theme here is that monetization challenges, such as introducing paid features, prioritizing advertising over user content, and the pressure to generate revenue, can negatively impact user experiences, and engagement, and ultimately contribute to the decline of a social network's user base and influence if not handled carefully.

Endnote References[‡‡]

Technological Shifts

Failure to adapt to new technologies and shifting user preferences toward mobile, visual content, and emerging platforms like virtual reality (VR)

[††] "Threads' Threats and Growth Opportunities": www.growth-memo.com/p/threads-threats-and-growth-opportunities.

[‡‡] "Social Media & the Shift Towards Diverse Monetization Strategies": http://https//scholarsmine.mst.edu/cgi/viewcontent.cgi?article = 1445&context = bio_

has been a major factor in the decline of once-dominant social networks. Networks that failed to innovate and evolve with these technological shifts were quickly outpaced by more nimble competitors.

Our findings indicate that the inability to keep up with rapid technological advancements, such as the shift toward mobile-first experiences and integration of new technologies like artificial intelligence (AI) and augmented reality (AR), significantly contributed to the discontinuation of certain social networking platforms by their founders.

Platforms like Friendster and Myspace were slow to adapt to emerging technologies and user preferences for mobile apps, real-time updates, and more immersive social experiences. This failure to evolve with technological shifts allowed more innovative competitors like Facebook to swiftly overtake them.

The common theme here is that major technological shifts, such as the rise of mobile, visual content, AI, AR/VR, and real-time updates, have disrupted the social media landscape. Social networks that failed to innovate and adapt to these new technologies and evolving user preferences driven by technological advancements lost relevance and saw declines in their user bases as users migrated to more modern platforms.

Endnote References[§§]

Shifting Power Dynamics

Social media platforms and their metrics play an important role in power shifts by granting equal access to communication channels and quantifying influence through visible metrics like follower counts and engagement rates. This has led to a more balanced power dynamic between leaders and followers on social media.

Social media has enabled shifts in the power balance between leaders and followers by giving followers more voice and quantifying influence through metrics. Social media allows for much more personal communication between leaders and their followers. This two-way dialogue creates

---

inftec_facwork.
[§§] "Is Cancel Culture Effective?": www.ucf.edu/pegasus/is-cancel-culture-effective/.

the opportunity for followers to influence decisions and outcomes, which means there has been a shift in the power dynamics. The two-way dialogue facilitated by social media has shifted power dynamics by allowing followers to influence leaders' decisions more directly.

The power and influence of agents within their social networks significantly impact their ability to emerge as leaders and shape group behavior. As social media amplifies these network effects, it can contribute to shifts in traditional leader-follower dynamics. Social networks, amplified by social media, can affect agents' power and influence, thereby contributing to shifts in traditional leader-follower power dynamics.

The common theme across these findings is the recognition that social media platforms have enabled more direct communication, quantification of influence, and amplification of social network effects, leading to a more balanced power dynamic where followers can influence leaders more easily. This shifting power balance is identified as a key factor impacting social networks' user bases and overall influence.

Endnote References¶¶

Increased Distrust

A massive rise in fake or bot accounts occurs on some platforms. Often, users cannot tell the difference. Bot-generated content that is not helpful may be damaging. The rise of fake accounts and fake content on a social network can erode user trust in the platform's authenticity and integrity, leading to potential decline.

However, some researchers have associated online social networking with several psychiatric disorders, including depressive symptoms, anxiety, and low self-esteem. Any future confirmed connection between them and psychiatric diseases would pose a serious public health concern. If

---

¶¶ "Title: Mirror, Mirror on the Wall: Shifting Leader-Follower Power Dynamics in a Social Media Context": https://journals.sagepub.com/doi/10.1177/17427150 19889817.

social networks are linked to mental health issues, it could increase public distrust and avoidance of those platforms.

Some social media have become a breeding ground for spreading false information. With fake news and rumors easily shared across various social media platforms, people are often misguided, leading to confusion, distrust, and chaos. The rampant spread of misinformation and disinformation on social media directly contributes to increased public distrust in those platforms and their content.

The common theme is that the presence of fake accounts, fake content, mental health concerns, misinformation, and a general lack of authenticity and transparency on social networks can breed distrust among users. This erosion of trust can then lead to declines in the platform's user base and influence as people lose faith in the network.

Endnote References***

Increased Discord

The potential decline of a social network is a complex phenomenon influenced by a combination of factors, including distrust, discord, changing user preferences, and the rise of alternative platforms. One major issue has been the prevalence of misinformation, hate speech, and divisive rhetoric on the platform, leading to increased discord and polarization among users. Polarization in social media algorithms reinforces existing biases and creates echo chambers, where people only see content that confirms their existing beliefs. This can lead to a lack of open-mindedness, ultimately leading to an unhealthy society, which highlights how social media can increase societal polarization and discord by creating insular echo chambers and reinforcing biases.

The common theme here is that the prevalence of misinformation, hate speech, mental health issues, polarization, and the creation of echo

---

*** "A Study on the Factors Affecting the User Resistance in Social Network Service": www.researchgate.net/publication/284395972_A_Study_on_the_Factors_Affecting_the_User_Resistance_in_Social_Network_Service.

chambers on social networks can foster increased discord, divisiveness, and conflict among users. This heightened state of discord and lack of open-mindedness can then contribute to declines in the platform's user base and influence.

Endnote References[†††]

Demographic and Behavior Trends

Personality and character have major effects on certain behavioral outcomes. As advancements in technology occur, more people are using social media such as Facebook, X (Twitter), and Instagram. Because of the increase in social media's popularity, the types of behaviors are now easier to group and study as this is important to know the behavior of users via social networking to analyze similarities of certain behavior types, which can be used to predict what they post as well as what they comment, share, and like on social networking sites. Analyzing demographic and behavior trends on major social media platforms is important for understanding user behavior and predicting declines or shifts in platform usage.

Engagement rates plummet on a platform unless the creator paid for their own content to be seen and engaged with. This indicates that user preferences have shifted away from the type of content and experience offered by that platform. Declining engagement rates, which are a key behavior trend, can indicate a shift in user preferences away from a particular social network, contributing to its decline. Demographic trends, such as younger users migrating to newer platforms like Telegram and Snapchat, can affect the user base and influence of established social networks like Facebook.

The common theme across these issues is the recognition that closely monitoring demographic shifts and evolving user behavior patterns across social media platforms is crucial for understanding potential declines or changes in a network's user base and overall influence in the market.

[†††] "The Decline of Facebook A Comprehensive Overview of Key Statistics": https://wifitalents.com/statistics/social-media-and-online-communities/.

Endnote References‡‡‡

Negative Comparisons, Interaction Dysfunction, and Information Overload

Negative comparisons, interaction dysfunction, and information overload were other key factors contributing to the decline of social networks.

- Negative comparisons refer to the tendency of people to compare themselves to others, which can lead to feelings of inadequacy and low self-esteem.
- Interaction dysfunction refers to the inability of people to interact effectively with others, which can lead to feelings of isolation and loneliness.
- Information overload refers to the excessive amount of information that people are exposed to, which can lead to feelings of being overwhelmed.

The common theme across these issues is that an analysis of the factors influencing SMF provides a detailed narrative of how negative comparisons, interaction dysfunction, and information overload can be key factors contributing to the decline of social networks.

Endnote References§§§

Fake Accounts or Content

The rise of fake accounts and fake/bot-generated content are also factors indicating the decline of a social network. In social media with complex

---

‡‡‡ "Social Media Demographics to Inform Your 2024 Strategy": https://sprout-social.com/insights/new-social-media-demographics/.
§§§ "Research on the Mechanisms of Information Overload and Information Avoidance Behaviour in College Students with Psychological Disorders in the Context of Social Media": www.researchgate.net/publication/377917226_Research_on_the_Mechanisms_of_Information_Overload_and_Information_Avoidance_Behaviour_in_College_Students_with_Psychological_Disorders_in_the_Context_of_Social_Media.

information, young people cannot get access to the information they really want to know because they push too much content. Social media platforms usually push much invalid information, such as advertising and false information, among others, which leads to confusion of platform information and negative emotions of individuals.

Recently, however, some online social networking platforms have been associated with several psychiatric disorders, including depressive symptoms, anxiety, and low self-esteem. Since social networks are a relatively new phenomenon, many questions regarding their potential impact on mental health remain unanswered.

The common theme here is that the proliferation of fake accounts creating fake, invalid, or misleading content on social networks erodes trust, creates user fatigue/negative emotions, and may even impact mental health, which are factors that can contribute to declines in the platform's overall user base and influence. As the line between online and *real-life* things, some people are logging off permanently because the downsides feel too profound: They struggle to control how much time they spend on the apps or feel burdened by the constant stream of images and information.

Endnote References¶¶¶

Perceived Value

Perceived value has a positive impact on users' social attachment in social media usage contexts and is a topic at the forefront of current research. Some research breaks the gap of previous related research perspectives and focuses on perceived value and social attachment, verifying the impact of perceived value on social attachment, and exploring the underlying influence mechanism.

Although users are aware that privacy in social contexts may be attacked in many ways, they will not change their privacy preferences and behaviors, in addition to the suppression of the information value

---

¶¶¶ "They Left Social Media for Good": www.washingtonpost.com/technology/2023/04/11/social-media-quit-loneliness/.

on social attachment. This highlights how perceived information value can influence social attachment, and privacy concerns act as a moderating factor in the relationship between perceived value and attachment to social media.

Further research has shown that the perceived value of social media users has a significant effect on their sense of belonging. The relationship between perceived value and social media engagement positively affects social media engagement, which further reinforces that existing research has established perceived value as a significant factor impacting users' engagement, attachment, and continued usage of social media platforms.

The common theme across these research findings is the recognition that users' perceived value derived from social media, whether social, entertainment, or information value, directly impacts their level of attachment, engagement, and continued usage of those platforms.

Lower perceived value can contribute to declines in the user base and overall influence of social networks.

Endnote References[****]

Mental Health Impact

Mental health impact is a key factor contributing to the potential decline in a social network's user base and influence.

Several studies have pointed out the potentially detrimental effects of social media use on mental health. Concerns have been raised that social media may lead to body image dissatisfaction, increase the risk of addiction and cyberbullying involvement, contribute to phubbing behavior,[††††] and negatively affect mood. Excessive use of social media has increased

---

[****] "Accessing the Influence of Perceived Value on Social Attachment": www.frontiersin.org/journals/psychology/articles/10.3389/fpsyg.2021.760774/full.

[††††] Phubbing, a portmanteau of *phone* and *snubbing*, refers to the act of snubbing someone in a social setting by looking at your phone instead of paying attention to them. This behavior involves focusing on your smartphone, rather than engaging with the people present in a face-to-face interaction. Phubbing can be seen as rude, disrespectful, and potentially damaging to relationships as it can make the other person feel ignored or unimportant. It can also hinder meaningful communication and connection between individuals.

loneliness, fear of missing out, and decreased subjective well-being and life satisfaction. Users at risk of social media addiction often report depressive symptoms and lower self-esteem.

This directly states that excessive social media use can negatively impact mental health through effects like addiction, cyberbullying, loneliness, low self-esteem, and decreased well-being—factors that could contribute to user decline.

Recently, however, some researchers have associated online social networking with several psychiatric disorders, including depressive symptoms, anxiety, and low self-esteem. Any future confirmed connection between them and psychiatric diseases would pose a serious public health concern. This highlights the potential links between social networking and mental health issues like depression, anxiety, and low self-esteem, which if confirmed, could impact user bases.

Some platforms are designed to be addictive and are associated with anxiety, depression, and even physical ailments. Social media use can affect users' physical health even more directly. Researchers know the connection between the mind and the gut can turn anxiety and depression into nausea, headaches, muscle tension, and tremors. This further reinforces how the addictive nature and mental health impacts like anxiety and depression associated with social media use can manifest into physical ailments, potentially driving users away.

The common theme here is the recognition that excessive or unhealthy social media usage has been linked to various mental health issues like addiction, depression, anxiety, loneliness, and low self-esteem. If these negative impacts persist or worsen, it could contribute to declines in the user bases and overall influence of social networking platforms.

Endnote References[‡‡‡‡]

[‡‡‡‡] "Pros & Cons Impacts of Social Media on Mental Health": www.radiashealth.org/social-media-and-mental-health-how-to-set-boundaries/.

"The Social Dilemma: Social Media and Your Mental Health": www.mcleanhospital.org/essential/it-or-not-social-medias-affecting-your-mental-health.

Competition

The rise of alternative forms of digital communication, such as messaging apps and niche online communities, has fragmented the social media landscape. Instead of relying solely on traditional social media platforms, users are turning to platforms like WhatsApp, Telegram, Discord, Quora, and Reddit to connect with like-minded individuals and share interests. This highlights how the emergence of competing platforms and niche communities is fragmenting the social media landscape, potentially drawing users away from traditional social networks.

New platforms emerge, and existing platforms often introduce new features to address user concerns or capitalize on trends. Social media remains an important communication tool, and its influence on society, politics, and culture is still significant. This suggests that the rise of new, competing social media platforms and features introduced by existing ones to stay relevant are factors impacting the social media landscape.

While many marketers see social media as a solid return on investment, consumers' interactions with the technology may be in the midst of a significant change. A subsection of brands will shun AI and prioritize more human positioning. This *acoustic* concept will be leveraged to distance brands from perceptions of AI-powered businesses as impersonal and homogeneous. This implies that competition from brands prioritizing more human and personalized experiences could draw consumers away from established, AI-driven social media platforms.

The common theme across these studies is the recognition that the rise of alternative platforms, niche communities, new features from competitors, and brands offering differentiated experiences all contribute to increased competition in the social media landscape. This competition can potentially lead to declines in user bases and influence for traditional social networks that fail to adapt and innovate.

Endnote References[§§§§]

[§§§§] Is Social Media in Downfall?": www.minimediaco.com/is-social-media-in-downfall.

Community Fragmentation

As social media platforms continue to proliferate and compete for users' attention, platform saturation and user fatigue may affect advertising revenues. Users may be less likely to engage with ads as they feel overwhelmed by content, leading to a decline in ad performance and, ultimately, revenue.

While not explicitly mentioning community fragmentation, this suggests that the proliferation of social media platforms competing for user attention can lead to fatigue and disengagement, implying fragmentation of user communities across different platforms. Influencer or celebrity content becomes the dominant content on a platform, taking up an undue share of the reach. The dominance of influencer or celebrity content on a platform could potentially fragment user communities, as regular users may feel disconnected or overshadowed, leading them to seek alternative platforms.

The common theme across these notes is the recognition that the rise of niche communities, messaging apps, platform saturation, influencer dominance, and the general fragmentation of user attention and engagement across multiple platforms can contribute to the decline of traditional social networks' user bases and overall influence in the market.

Endnote References¶¶¶¶

Failure to Innovate

Privacy and data security concerns have eroded trust in social media companies. High-profile scandals, such as the Cambridge Analytica scandal that rocked Facebook, have raised questions about how these platforms handle user data. As a result, many users are becoming more cautious about the information they share online and seeking alternative ways to connect with others.

This suggests that social networks that fail to innovate and address user concerns around privacy and data security may lose users who seek out alternative, more trustworthy platforms.

¶¶¶¶ ""Is Social Media Use Declining as It Continues Its Life Cycle?": www.newmediaandmarketing.com/is-social-media-use-declining-as-it-continues-its-life-cycle/.

Additionally, the rise of alternative forms of digital communication, such as messaging apps and niche online communities, has fragmented the social media landscape. Instead of relying solely on traditional social media platforms, users are turning to platforms like WhatsApp, Telegram, Discord, and Quora to connect with like-minded individuals and share interests.

This highlights how the failure of traditional social networks to innovate and cater to evolving user needs has allowed the rise of alternative, niche platforms that better serve those interests, fragmenting the landscape.

Platforms emerge, and existing platforms often introduce new features to address user concerns or capitalize on trends. Social media remains an important communication tool, and its influence on society, politics, and culture is still significant.

This implies that social networks that fail to continuously innovate with new features and adapt to emerging trends may lose influence and relevance in society.

The common theme across these research findings is the recognition that social networks must consistently innovate to address user concerns around privacy/security, introduce new features catering to evolving interests, and adapt to emerging trends and technologies.

Failure to innovate in these areas can lead to user migration, fragmentation of communities, loss of trust, and a decline in the platform's user base and societal influence.

Endnote References[*****]

Analyzing the Patterns of Social Network Decline

Analyzing the patterns of social network decline provides valuable insights into the factors that contribute to the rise and fall of some social networking platforms. By examining past failures, we can glean important lessons and make informed predictions about the future of social networks.

Some key lessons learned and predictions for the future based on patterns of social network decline include:

[*****] Social Media Marketing Is a Dead End. What's Next?": www.linkedin.com/pulse/social-media-marketing-dead-end-whats-next-dennis-shiao-zmtyc/.

1. User experience matters
   User experience plays a crucial role in the success of social networks. Platforms that prioritize simplicity, usability, and an intuitive interface tend to attract and retain more users compared to those with cluttered designs and complex features.
   This statement is supported by the following citation:

   - Simplify the design: keep the design clean and minimalistic to avoid overwhelming users.
   - Use white space effectively.
   - Ensure that the interface is intuitive and easy to navigate.

The search result emphasizes the importance of simplifying the design, using white space effectively, and ensuring an intuitive and easy-to-navigate interface, which aligns with the statement about users gravitating toward visually appealing and intuitive platforms.

Social networks that prioritize user experience, simplicity, and usability tend to fare better than those with cluttered interfaces, intrusive advertising, and complex features. Users gravitate toward platforms that are intuitive, visually appealing, and easy to navigate.

Endnote References[†††††]

2. Innovation is key:
   Platforms that fail to innovate risk becoming stagnant and losing relevance to competitors who offer new features, better experiences, and broader appeal.
   The article from Our World in Data states:

   The research on social connections and innovation suggests that one important way to improve material living standards is to invest in digital communication-enabling technologies, such as

---

[†††††] "Improve User Experience: 10 Strategic Techniques to Elevate UX": https://contentsquare.com/blog/improve-user-experience/.

the rise of social media. This lowers the costs of creating and maintaining personal and professional ties, facilitating the diffusion of ideas and knowledge, creating positive productivity spillovers.

It highlights the importance of innovation, particularly in digital communication technologies like social media, to facilitate the spread of ideas, knowledge, and productivity improvements. Failure to innovate and offer new features risks losing relevance to competitors, aligning with the given statement.

Social networks must innovate and evolve to meet changing user preferences, technological advancements, and market dynamics. Platforms that fail to innovate risk becoming stagnant and losing relevance to competitors who offer new features, better experiences, and broader appeal.

Endnote References[‡‡‡‡‡]

3. Privacy and trust are paramount

The following citation supports the statement that social networks must prioritize user privacy, data security, and trust to maintain user confidence and engagement: "Privacy is a personal boundary regulation process that regulates private information, according to context. Trust encompasses how trustworthy the user feels that an OSN is."

The study published in NCBI states that privacy and trust are crucial factors for users of online social networks (OSNs) like Facebook. It highlights that privacy involves regulating personal information sharing, while trust relates to how trustworthy the user perceives the OSN to be. This aligns with the given statement that social networks must prioritize user privacy and trust to maintain user confidence and avoid damaging their reputation or losing users' trust due to mishandling of data or unethical practices.

[‡‡‡‡‡] "The Importance of Social Networks for Innovation and Productivity": https://ourworldindata.org/social-networks-innovation-and-productivity.

The study further reinforces the importance of these factors by developing "a model of relationships between the set of constructs" including "privacy value, privacy risk, privacy control, privacy concerns, trust in Facebook, and self-disclosure on OSNs." This underscores that prioritizing privacy and trust is paramount for social networks to foster self-disclosure and user engagement.

Social networks must prioritize user privacy, data security, and trust to maintain user confidence and engagement. Platforms that mishandle user data, experience security breaches, or engage in unethical practices risk damaging their reputation and losing users' trust.

Endnote References[§§§§§]

4. Differentiation is essential

The following citation supports the statement that social networks must differentiate themselves by offering unique value propositions or niche features to avoid being overshadowed by competitors:

Platforms that fail to differentiate risk becoming commoditized and overshadowed by competitors with broader appeal or better execution.

The article from eCampusOntario Pressbooks states:

It is important to involve individuals with different backgrounds and approaches to innovation. For instance, some individuals are great at generating ideas while others may be better at researching and validating them.

This highlights the importance of differentiation and bringing diverse perspectives to drive innovation within organizations. By

---

[§§§§§] ."A Model of Perception of Privacy, Trust, and Self-Disclosure on Online Social Networks": www.ncbi.nlm.nih.gov/pmc/articles/PMC7515301/.

extension, this principle can be applied to social networks, where differentiation through unique value propositions, niche features, or targeted communities is essential to avoid becoming commoditized and overshadowed by competitors with broader appeal or better execution of similar features.

The article further emphasizes the need for a balanced mix of skills and roles within innovation networks, such as idea generators, researchers, experts, and producers. This diversity of perspectives and approaches can contribute to differentiation and help social networks stand out from competitors by offering unique experiences tailored to specific user segments or communities.

Social networks must differentiate themselves from competitors by offering unique value propositions, niche features, or targeted communities. Platforms that fail to differentiate risk becoming commoditized and overshadowed by competitors with broader appeal or better execution.

Endnote References¶¶¶¶¶

5. Community and engagement drive success

The following citation supports the statement that social networks thrive on strong communities, user engagement, and meaningful interactions: "Brands may leverage a passionate community to empower advocates to amplify brand messaging and naturally recommend products/services."

The article from WSI World emphasizes the importance of building vibrant brand communities on social media platforms. It states that by fostering engaged communities and enabling user-generated content, brands can cultivate brand advocates who will naturally promote and recommend their products/services. This aligns with the given statement that social networks succeed by encouraging user

---

¶¶¶¶¶ "Social Networks and Innovation": https://ecampusontario.pressbooks.pub/leadershipandmanagement/chapter/11-4-social-networks-and-innovation/.

engagement, facilitating connections, and nurturing strong communities around their platforms.

The article further highlights strategies for establishing prosperous brand communities, such as defining the community, delivering value, promoting user-generated content, and being proactively engaging. These tactics directly contribute to creating the *vibrant communities* and *meaningful interactions* mentioned in the statement, which help attract and retain users on social networks.

Social networks thrive on strong communities, user engagement, and meaningful interactions. Platforms that foster vibrant communities, encourage user-generated content, and facilitate connections between users tend to attract and retain users more effectively.

Endnote References******

6. Rise of niche communities
The following citation supports the statement about the rise of niche social networking platforms catering to specific interests and providing more tailored, engaging experiences:

Niche communities are digital spaces that cater to a specific, often tightly defined interest, hobby, or professional affiliation. Unlike the vast and generalized platforms of social media, niche communities are like cozy neighborhood cafes—places where like-minded individuals gather to discuss their passions in depth.

The article from Amity highlights how niche communities are emerging as focused digital spaces centered around particular interests, hobbies, or professions. It contrasts these with broad, generalized social media platforms. The analogy of *cozy neighborhood cafes* where like-minded individuals can gather and delve deeply into their shared passions aligns with the statement about niche platforms

---

****** "Building Community and Customer Loyalty with Social Media": www.wsi-world.com/blog/social-media-marketing-building-community-and-customer-loyalty.

offering highly curated content, specialized features, and targeted communities for more relevant, engaging user experiences.

The article further reinforces this by stating niche communities "provide a platform for enthusiasts and experts to share their knowledge, tips, and experiences" and enable "tailored experiences and content" that "resonate with their passions." This directly supports the notion of niche platforms providing curated, specialized experiences catering to specific user interests as an emerging trend.

As users seek more tailored and meaningful interactions, we can expect to see the rise of niche social networking platforms catering to specific interests, hobbies, professions, or demographics. These platforms will offer highly curated content, specialized features, and targeted communities, providing users with more relevant and engaging experiences.

Endnote References[††††††]

7. Decentralization and privacy-focused platforms

The following citation supports the statement that concerns about data privacy and censorship will drive the adoption of decentralized, privacy-focused social networking platforms that prioritize user control and transparency:

Decentralized social media platforms offer users a greater degree of privacy, censorship-resistance, and security than centralized platforms. They also allow users to have greater control over their data, which means that it is not controlled by any single entity. This makes them more secure and private than traditional social media platforms.

The article highlights how decentralized social media platforms address user concerns around privacy, censorship, and lack of control over personal data on centralized platforms. It states that

---

[††††††] "The Rise of Niche Communities: The Future of Online Engagement": www.amity.co/blog/why-niche-communities-are-the-future-and-how-you-can-create-one.

decentralized platforms provide enhanced privacy, censorship resistance, and security, and allow users to control their own data instead of it being controlled by a single company.

This aligns with the given statement that platforms prioritizing user control, data sovereignty (ownership), and transparency over personal information will appeal to users seeking alternatives to mainstream centralized platforms that monetize user data. The article reinforces the idea that decentralization and prioritizing user privacy will drive the adoption of such platforms as an alternative to current social media models.

Concerns about data privacy, surveillance, and censorship will drive the adoption of decentralized and privacy-focused social networking platforms.

Platforms that prioritize user control, data sovereignty, and transparency will appeal to users seeking alternatives to centralized platforms that monetize their personal information.

Endnote References[######]

8. Short-form and ephemeral content
   The following citation supports the statement about the growing popularity of short-form and ephemeral content, and social networks facilitating quick, visually engaging interactions:

   Ephemeral content is taking the digital world by storm. Major social media networks like Instagram, Facebook, and WhatsApp have copied Snapchat's concept of sharing disappearing content. Now users can distribute short-lived content via Stories and Livestream that vanishes within 24 hours.

   The article highlights how major social media platforms have embraced ephemeral content like Stories and Livestreams that disappear after a short duration, following the concept pioneered by Snapchat. This aligns with the statement about the growing popularity of

---

[######] "Decentralized Social Media: A New Era of Online Privacy": https://codedesign.org/decentralized-social-media-new-era-online-privacy.

short-form, temporary content that provides quick, visually engaging interactions.

The article further states:

Since ephemeral content has the FOMO (fear of missing out) effect, it provokes users to take action faster. Thus, more and more people consume and create short-lived content on social media.

This reinforces the idea that ephemeral, short-form content caters to users' desire for instant gratification and drives engagement, supporting the notion that social networks will focus on facilitating such interactions to meet evolving user preferences.

The popularity of short-form and ephemeral content, as seen on platforms like TikTok, Snapchat, and Instagram Stories, continues to grow. Social networks focus on facilitating quick, casual, and visually engaging interactions, catering to users' desire for instant gratification and bite-sized entertainment.

Endnote References[§§§§§§]

9. Live streaming and real-time interaction

The following citation supports the statement that live streaming and real-time interaction will become increasingly prevalent on social networking platforms:

Live streaming has become an important component of China's internet economy. According to CNNIC's 50th 'Statistical Report' (2022), the number of live streaming users in China reached 716 million by June 2022, accounting for 68.1 percent of the total number of internet users.

The study published in *Nature* highlights the rapid growth and adoption of live streaming, particularly in China, where over 68 percent percent of internet users engaged with live streaming platforms as of 2022. This supports the notion that live streaming is becoming

---

[§§§§§§] "The Ephemeral Content Trend on Social Media": www.acquisio.com/blog/agency/the-future-of-ephemeral-content-on-social-media/.

increasingly prevalent and integrated into existing online platforms and networks.

Additionally, the study states:

Live streaming transmits images and sounds in real-time through a variety of communication technologies, enabling the viewer to interact in real-time on the platform. In the live streaming system, the live host and the viewer can obtain a sense of participation through real-time interaction, providing a unique immersive interactive experience that can trigger viewers' behavioral intention.

This directly reinforces the statement about live streaming enabling real-time interaction between broadcasters and audiences, facilitating virtual events and experiences through immersive, participatory content consumption and engagement.

The study further emphasizes the role of live streaming in fostering closer relationships between viewers, hosts, and platforms through real-time interactions, aligning with the idea of live streaming becoming a dominant form of content engagement on social networks.

Live streaming has become increasingly prevalent on social networking platforms, enabling users to broadcast live video content, interact with audiences in real time, and participate in virtual events and experiences. Livestreaming is often integrated into existing social networks and emerges as a dominant form of content consumption and engagement.

Endnote References¶¶¶¶¶¶

10. Personalization and AI-powered recommendations
The following citation supports the statement about social networks leveraging AI and machine learning for personalized content,

¶¶¶¶¶¶ "Quantifying the Societal Impacts of Social Media": www.nature.com/articles/s41599-023-01892-8.

recommendations, and experiences tailored to user preferences and behavior:

AI-powered personalization utilizes machine-learning algorithms and advanced AI workings to analyze large amounts of data. This AI technology is centered around gaining a deep understanding of context as well as your shoppers' behaviors and preferences, all while not alienating people by violating their data-privacy expectations.

The article from Algolia highlights how AI-powered personalization uses machine learning algorithms to analyze vast amounts of user data, including behaviors and preferences, to deliver personalized experiences. This aligns with the statement about social networks using AI to provide tailored content and recommendations based on individual user interests and activities.

The article further states: "AI personalization ensures that shoppers' personalized customer experiences are tailored to their individual preferences, which can ultimately lead to higher satisfaction and better customer engagement."

This reinforces the notion that AI-powered personalization on platforms like social networks can enhance user engagement and retention by delivering customized experiences, as mentioned in the statement.

However, the article also acknowledges concerns about data privacy and not alienating users, which relates to the statement's mention of algorithmic bias and filter bubble risks associated with personalized AI recommendations.

Social networks will leverage AI and machine learning algorithms to deliver personalized content, recommendations, and experiences tailored to each user's preferences, interests, and behavior. These AI-powered features will enhance user engagement, retention, and monetization while raising concerns about algorithmic bias and filter bubbles.

Endnote References******

11. Hybrid monetization models

The following citation supports the statement about social networks exploring hybrid monetization models that combine subscriptions, premium features, digital goods, and nonintrusive advertising to diversify revenue streams:

The hybrid monetization model is extremely flexible and allows developers to generate diverse revenue streams from both users who are likely to make purchases and those who prefer ad-supported experiences. While all apps can benefit from the hybrid monetization model, gaming apps have found great success utilizing a combination of in-app purchases with in-app advertising.

The article from AppsFlyer highlights how the hybrid monetization model enables apps and platforms to generate revenue from multiple sources—both users willing to make purchases (subscriptions, premium features, digital goods) and those preferring ad-supported experiences. It states that this hybrid approach provides flexibility in diversifying revenue streams, which aligns with the given statement about social networks combining various monetization methods like subscriptions, premium offerings, digital goods/content, and nonintrusive advertising.

The article further reinforces that gaming apps have successfully implemented hybrid models combining in-app purchases with in-app advertising. This supports the notion of social networks adopting similar hybrid strategies to reduce overreliance on traditional advertising by providing alternative paid experiences and revenue sources.

Social networks will explore hybrid models of monetization, combining subscription-based services, premium features, digital goods, and nonintrusive advertising to diversify revenue streams and

---

******* "AI-Powered Personalization Transforming User Experience": www.algolia
.com/blog/ai/how-ai-powered-personalization-is-transforming-the-user-and-
customer-experience/.

reduce reliance on traditional advertising. Users will have the option to pay for premium experiences, ad-free browsing, or exclusive content, providing alternative revenue streams for platforms.

Endnote References††††††††

12. Regulatory scrutiny and compliance
    The following citation supports the statement about increasing regulatory scrutiny and the need for social networks to comply with stricter data protection regulations and demonstrate accountability for content moderation:

    Heightened regulatory focus (including governance and controls) on consumer data privacy, collection, use, retention, and disposal (e.g., FTC ANPR on commercial surveillance and data security practices).

    The KPMG report highlights the heightened regulatory focus and expectations around consumer data privacy, collection, and use, retention, and disposal practices. This aligns with the statement about governments introducing stricter laws and regulations to protect user privacy and prevent abuse of personal data on social networks.
    The report further states:

    - Strengthen the role of the board and senior management.
    - Demonstrate acumen and governance domain skills.
    - Integrate critical challenges into risk and governance frameworks.
    - Enhance policies and procedures to require more, and more formalized, documentation, mapping, ownership, and controls monitoring and testing.

    This reinforces the notion that social networks will need to implement robust governance frameworks, enhance policies and

---

†††††††† "App Monetization Strategies Guide": www.appsflyer.com/resources/guides/app-monetization/.

procedures, and demonstrate accountability through monitoring and testing controls. This is in line with the statement about social networks needing to comply with regulations, implement robust safety measures, and demonstrate accountability for their content moderation practices under increasing regulatory scrutiny.

Regulatory scrutiny and compliance with data protection regulations will become increasingly important for social networks, particularly as governments around the world introduce stricter laws and regulations to protect user privacy and prevent abuse of personal data. Governments and regulators are increasing scrutiny and introducing stricter regulations to address concerns about privacy, data protection, misinformation, and online harm. Social networks will need to comply with these regulations, implement robust safety measures, and demonstrate accountability for their content moderation practices.

Endnote References[######]

13. Integration with emerging technologies

The following citation supports the statement that social networks will increasingly integrate with emerging technologies like AR, VR, blockchain, and AI to enhance user experiences and enable new forms of interaction and monetization:

APIs have also played a crucial role in expanding the reach and accessibility of social media platforms. By integrating with various web services and applications, social media platforms have become more accessible to users across different devices and software ecosystems. This part will discuss how API innovations have facilitated social media's expansion, making it a ubiquitous presence in people's lives.

The article highlights how APIs have enabled social media platforms to integrate with various web services and applications,

---

[######] "Anticipating More Scrutiny: Regulatory Trends for Digital Markets": https://kpmg.com/kpmg-us/content/dam/kpmg/pdf/2023/anticipating-more-scrutiny1.pdf.

expanding their reach and accessibility across devices and ecosystems. This supports the notion of social networks integrating with emerging technologies through APIs to enhance user experiences and enable new interactions.

Furthermore, the article states:

The integration of artificial intelligence (AI) and machine learning (ML) with social media APIs represents a significant leap forward in the capabilities of social platforms. This section will delve into how AI and ML are being used to automate content curation, improve recommendation algorithms, and enhance user interactions on social media.

Blockchain technology is beginning to find its footing in social media through APIs, offering new ways to ensure security, privacy, and decentralization. This segment will explore the potential impacts of blockchain on social media, including tokenization, secure transactions, and the creation of decentralized social networks.

Augmented reality (AR) and virtual reality (VR) are set to redefine the user experience on social media platforms. Through APIs, these technologies are being integrated into social media, offering immersive and interactive ways for users to engage with content.

These excerpts directly reinforce the statement by highlighting the integration of AI, blockchain, AR, and VR technologies with social media APIs to enhance user interactions, enable new experiences like decentralized networks and secure transactions (monetization opportunities), and redefine user experiences through immersive content engagement.

Social networks will increasingly integrate with emerging technologies such as AR, VR, blockchain, and AI to enhance user experiences, enable new forms of interaction, and unlock new monetization opportunities.

Endnote References^{§§§§§§§}

14. Hybrid models and monetization

The following citation supports the statement about social networks exploring hybrid monetization models that combine subscriptions, premium features, digital goods, and nonintrusive advertising:

The hybrid monetization model is extremely flexible and allows developers to generate diverse revenue streams from both users who are likely to make purchases and those who prefer ad-supported experiences. While all apps can benefit from the hybrid monetization model, gaming apps have found great success utilizing a combination of in-app purchases with in-app advertising.

The article highlights how the hybrid monetization model enables platforms to generate revenue from multiple sources—paid offerings like in-app purchases (premium features, digital goods) as well as ad-supported experiences for users preferring that option. It states this hybrid approach provides flexibility in diversifying revenue streams.

The article further reinforces that gaming apps have successfully implemented hybrid models combining in-app purchases with in-app advertising, aligning with the statement about social networks utilizing a mix of subscriptions, premium content/features, digital goods, and nonintrusive advertising.

By offering both paid and ad-supported options, the hybrid model caters to different user preferences while maintaining engagement from those unwilling to pay subscriptions. This supports generating revenue through diversified monetization while retaining user trust and participation across different segments.

Social networks will explore hybrid models of monetization, combining subscription-based models, premium features, digital

§§§§§§§ "Exploring Social Media API Innovations for Connectivity": www .robinwaite.com/blog/exploring-the-future-of-connectivity-with-social-media-api-innovations.

goods, and nonintrusive advertising to generate revenue while maintaining user trust and engagement.

Endnote References[¶¶¶¶¶¶]

In summary, the future of social networking will be shaped by a combination of technological advancements, user preferences, regulatory developments, and societal trends.

By staying agile, innovative, and responsive to user needs, social networks can navigate the evolving landscape and continue to play a central role in shaping how we connect, communicate, and share in the digital age. Analyzing the patterns of social network decline offers valuable lessons and insights for understanding the dynamics of the social media landscape and predicting future trends.

Chapter 8 endnote references[*******]

[¶¶¶¶¶¶] "Hybrid Monetization Strategies for Mobile Games": www.blog.udonis.co/mobile-marketing/mobile-games/hybrid-monetization.

[*******] "7 Expert Predictions on the Future of Social Media for 2024": https://sproutsocial.com/insights/future-of-social-media/.

"The Future of Social Media: Key Trends and Predictions for 2023": www.digitaldoughnut.com/articles/2023/february-2023/the-future-of-social-media-key-trends-for-2023.

"The Future of Social Media—5 Expert Predictions That Actually Matter": https://brandmentions.com/blog/future-of-social-media/.

"The Future of Social Media: Trends and Predictions [2024 Update]": https://explodingtopics.com/blog/future-of-social-media.

CHAPTER 9

The Role of Regulation and User Behavior in Social Networks

The dynamic realm of social networks is profoundly shaped by two pivotal forces: regulatory frameworks and user behavior. As digital platforms continue to expand and influence every aspect of modern life, the importance of robust regulations and responsible user conduct has never been greater. This chapter explores how regulatory policies impact the development and operation of social networks, and how user behavior influences and is influenced by these platforms. We will examine case studies highlighting successful regulatory interventions and analyze patterns of user engagement, privacy concerns, and the ethical considerations that underpin online interactions. By understanding the interplay between regulation and user behavior, we can better navigate the challenges and opportunities within the digital social landscape.

Here is an expansion on how these factors will shape the future of social networking:

Privacy and regulation:

- Privacy concerns will continue to be at the forefront. Users demand more control over their data.
- Regulatory frameworks will evolve to address privacy, data protection, and user rights.
- Striking a balance between user privacy and platform functionality will be crucial.
- Transparency in data collection, sharing, and algorithms will become standard practice.

Content moderation and trust:

- Content moderation will remain a challenge. Stricter guidelines and artificial intelligence (AI)-driven tools will be necessary.
- Fake news, hate speech, and harmful content will require continuous monitoring.
- Building trust with users through transparent policies and effective moderation will be essential.

Algorithmic bias and fairness:

- AI algorithms shape content distribution and user experiences.
- Ensuring fairness and minimizing biases in recommendation systems will be a priority.
- Regular audits and adjustments to algorithms will be necessary.

Decentralization and blockchain:

- Decentralized social networks (e.g., Mastodon and Solid*) may gain traction.
- Blockchain can enhance data ownership, verifiable identities, and micropayments.
- Users seeking more control over their data may migrate to decentralized platforms.

User behavior and mental health:

- Understanding user behavior is crucial. Social networks impact mental health.

---

* Solid is a decentralized web platform and set of open standards created by Sir Tim Berners-Lee, the inventor of the World Wide Web. It aims to give individuals and groups full control over their data and online activities.

- Addiction, cyberbullying, and social comparison can harm users.
- Platforms will invest in features promoting well-being, digital detox, and healthier interactions.

Personalization and filter bubbles:

- AI-driven personalization will continue. Customized feeds, recommendations, and ads.
- The risk of filter bubbles—isolating users in echo chambers—will persist.
- Balancing personalization with diverse content exposure will be a challenge.

Collaboration and interoperability:

- Networks may collaborate for cross-platform features (e.g., messaging).
- Interoperability between platforms will benefit users.
- Seamless sharing and communication across networks will enhance user experience.

Ethical AI and accountability

- Social networks must address ethical dilemmas.
- Accountability for algorithmic decisions and unintended consequences.
- Collaboration with researchers, policy makers, and civil society will be crucial.

In summary, the future of social networks lies in a delicate balance between innovation, regulation, and user well-being.

As we navigate this dynamic landscape, anticipating challenges and adapting to changing user behavior will shape the next era of social networking.

Background

Social networks have transformed the way we communicate, share information, and connect with others. From the early days of Myspace and Friendster to the current dominance of platforms like Facebook, X (Twitter), and Instagram, these networks have become an integral part of our daily lives. As we look toward the future, we believe that social networks will continue to play a significant role, but their form and function may undergo substantial transformations. In this chapter, we explore the potential directions and challenges that lie ahead for social networks, examining key areas such as misinformation, data privacy, AI, decentralization, and the integration of emerging technologies.

The Battle Against Misinformation

One of the most pressing challenges facing social networks is the issue of misinformation and fake news. The spread of false or misleading information has become a major concern, with the potential to influence public opinion, sway elections, and even incite violence. To address this challenge, social networks will likely implement more robust fact-checking mechanisms and employ advanced algorithms to detect and filter out misinformation. Additionally, there may be a greater emphasis on promoting credible sources and encouraging users to critically evaluate the information they consume.

Platforms may also explore new ways to incentivize and reward users who contribute to the dissemination of accurate and verified information, fostering a culture of truth and accountability within their communities.

Data Privacy and User Control

Another area of focus will be data privacy and user control over personal information. As concerns over data breaches and unauthorized access to user data continue to grow, social networks will need to prioritize transparency and provide users with greater control over their data. This could involve implementing more granular privacy settings, allowing users to selectively share information, and ensuring that data is securely stored and protected.

Social networks may also explore decentralized models of data storage, where user data are distributed across multiple nodes rather than centralized servers, reducing the risk of large-scale data breaches and increasing user control over their personal information.

The Rise of Artificial Intelligence

The integration of AI and machine learning will play a significant role in shaping the future of social networks. These technologies have the potential to enhance user experiences by providing personalized content recommendations, improving content moderation, and enabling more natural and intuitive interactions through virtual assistants and chatbots.

However, the integration of AI also raises ethical concerns, such as the potential for algorithmic bias and the need for transparency in decision-making processes. Social networks will need to address these concerns and ensure that AI systems are designed and deployed responsibly and ethically, with clear guidelines and oversight mechanisms in place.

Decentralization and Blockchain Technology

The rise of decentralized social networks, built on blockchain technology or peer-to-peer networks, offers the promise of greater user control, privacy, and resistance to censorship. These platforms operate without a central authority, with data and content distributed across a network of nodes, reducing the risk of data breaches and censorship.

While still in their infancy, decentralized social networks could challenge the dominance of traditional centralized platforms and provide alternative models for social interaction. However, they also face challenges related to scalability, user adoption, and regulatory compliance.

Immersive Experiences and Emerging Technologies

The integration of social networks with other emerging technologies, such as virtual reality and augmented reality, could open up new avenues for immersive and interactive experiences. Imagine attending virtual concerts, participating in collaborative design sessions, or exploring virtual worlds with friends and strangers alike—the possibilities are vast and exciting.

Social networks may also explore the integration of Internet of Things devices, enabling seamless sharing and interaction across various connected devices and platforms. This could lead to new forms of social interaction and content creation, blurring the lines between the digital and physical worlds.

Social Impact and Responsibility

As social networks continue to evolve, their impact on society will become increasingly profound. They will shape the way we consume and share information, influence political discourse, and potentially even redefine our notions of identity and community.

However, with these opportunities come significant challenges. Social networks will need to strike a delicate balance between fostering open and inclusive spaces for expression while also addressing issues such as online harassment, hate speech, and the spread of harmful content.

Platforms may need to implement more robust content moderation policies and community guidelines, while also promoting digital literacy and media education to empower users to navigate the online landscape responsibly.

Regulatory Landscape and Ethical Considerations

As social networks continue to grow in influence and reach, they will likely face increasing scrutiny from regulators and policy makers. Issues such as data privacy, content moderation, and antitrust concerns may lead to new regulations and guidelines aimed at ensuring fair competition, protecting user rights, and promoting transparency.

Social networks will need to proactively engage with policy makers and stakeholders to shape these regulations in a way that balances innovation and growth with responsible practices and ethical considerations.

Summary

The future of social networks is both exciting and challenging. As these platforms continue to evolve, they will shape the way we communicate, share information, and interact with the world around us. However, we must approach this future with a critical eye, embracing the potential benefits while remaining vigilant against potential risks and unintended consequences.

By fostering open dialogue, promoting digital literacy, and advocating for ethical and responsible practices, we can ensure that social networks continue to serve as powerful tools for connection, collaboration, and positive social change. Ultimately, the future of social networks will be shaped by the collective efforts of developers, policy makers, and users themselves, working together to navigate the evolving landscape and harness the transformative power of these platforms for the greater good.

Chapter 9: endnote references and further reading[†]

[†] 1. Luceri, L., T. Braun, and S. Giordano. "Analyzing and Inferring Human Real-Life Behavior Through Online Social Networks With Social Influence Deep Learning," *Appl Netw Sci* 4, no. 34 (2019). https://doi.org/10.1007/s41109-019-0134-3.

2. Peoples, C.D. and Kayla Furlano. "Social Networks and COVID-19: Contagion and the Pandemic's Impact on Behavior," *The Social Science of the COVID-19 Pandemic: A Call to Action for Researchers* (NY, New York, Oxford Academic, December 14, 2023): https://doi.org/10.1093/oso/9780197615133.003.0019.

CHAPTER 10

Dangers of Social Media

This chapter delves into the multifaceted risks posed by social networks, affecting users, communities, and society at large. We review the profound societal implications of their widespread adoption and explore the intricate interplay between technology and human behavior. Furthermore, we suggest various ways that could facilitate avoiding most social media risks.

Social media platforms continue to be breeding grounds for the spread of false information. Misleading content, conspiracy theories, and fake news can easily go viral, influencing public opinion and decision-making processes.

Addressing misinformation and disinformation on social media is crucial for maintaining an informed and healthy digital environment.

Mitigating social media misinformation and disinformation requires a multidimensional approach involving social media platforms, users, fact-checkers, educators, and policy makers.

By implementing mitigating strategies collaboratively, stakeholders can work together to mitigate the spread of misinformation and disinformation on social media, promote a more informed and trustworthy online environment, and foster a more informed and responsible digital society.

We present hereafter the 11 most common social media perils:

1. Misinformation and disinformation
2. Algorithmic bias and echo chambers
3. Cyberbullying and online harassment
4. Privacy breaches and data exploitation
5. Addiction and mental health impact
6. Radicalization and extremism
7. Online scams and fraud

8. Digital footprint and reputation damage

9. Influence on elections and political manipulation

10. Lack of fact-checking and accountability

11. Youth vulnerability and online predatory behavior

*Chapter 10: endnote references**

Algorithmic Bias and Echo Chambers

Algorithms used by social media platforms to curate content and personalize user experiences can inadvertently reinforce bias, filter bubbles, and echo chambers. This can lead to the amplification of extreme viewpoints, polarization of discourse, and a narrowing of perspectives, hindering constructive dialogue and understanding and limiting exposure to diverse perspectives contributing to polarization.

Mitigating social media algorithmic manipulation and the formation of echo chambers requires concerted efforts from social media platforms, regulators, educators, and users.

By implementing mitigating strategies collaboratively, stakeholders can work together to reduce the risks of algorithmic manipulation and echo chambers on social media and promote a more informed, diverse, and inclusive online environment.

Endnote References†

Cyberbullying and Online Harassment

Cyberbullying and online harassment remain pervasive issues on social media platforms, affecting users of all ages. Harassment, hate speech,

---

* n/a.

† ALGORITHMIC BIAS AND ECHO CHAMBERS

   www.scientificamerican.com/article/fake-online-news-spreads-through-social-echo-chambers/;www.internetmatters.org/hub/news-blogs/what-are-algorithms-how-to-prevent-echo-chambers/.

threats, and other forms of abusive behavior can have serious consequences for victims, including psychological distress, social isolation, and
even physical harm.

Mitigating social media cyberbullying and harassment requires a multifaceted approach involving social media platforms, educators, parents,
law enforcement agencies, and users themselves. Addressing cyberbullying requires vigilance, empathy, and proactive measures to protect users
and promote positive online interactions.

By implementing mitigating strategies collaboratively, stakeholders
can help prevent the prevalence and impact of cyberbullying and harassment on social media platforms and create a safer and more respectful
online environment for all users.

Endnote References‡

Privacy Breaches and Data Exploitation

Social media platforms collect vast amounts of user data, raising concerns
about privacy breaches, data exploitation, and surveillance. Unauthorized
access to user data, data breaches, and misuse of personal information
by third parties can undermine user trust and compromise individuals'
privacy and security. Despite efforts to enhance privacy settings, social
media platforms remain vulnerable to data breaches. Personal information, including sensitive data, can be exposed, leading to identity theft,
financial fraud, and other security risks. Proactive measures can significantly reduce the risk of privacy breaches and data leaks on social media
platforms.

---

‡ CYBERBULLYING AND ONLINE HARASSMENT
    www.edumed.org/resources/preventing-cyberbullying-and-harassment-online/;
www.unicef.org/end-violence/how-to-stop-cyberbullying; www.stopbullying.gov/
sites/default/files/documents/Cyberbullying%20Guide%20Final%20508.pdf;
www.canada.ca/en/public-safety-canada/campaigns/cyberbullying/cyberbullying-
youth/how-to-prevent-cyberbullying.html.

Mitigating social media privacy breaches and data leaks is crucial to safeguarding sensitive information and requires proactive measures from both social media platforms and users.

By implementing mitigating strategies collaboratively, social media platforms, users, and regulators can work together to mitigate the risk of privacy breaches and data leaks on social media and protect user privacy in the digital age.

Endnote References[§]

Addiction and Mental Health Impact

Excessive use of social media has been linked to addiction, anxiety, depression, and other mental health issues. Features such as infinite scrolling, notifications, and engagement metrics can contribute to compulsive behavior and a sense of social comparison, negatively affecting users' well-being and self-esteem. Self-awareness, conscious choices, and mindful engagement can help counteract the impact of social media on mental health.

Mitigating social media addiction and its negative impact on mental health requires a multifaceted approach involving individuals, social media platforms, educators, mental health professionals, and policy makers.

By implementing mitigating strategies collaboratively, stakeholders can help minimize the negative impact of social media addiction on mental health and promote a healthier relationship with technology and digital platforms.

Social media is a tool, not a substitute for genuine human connection.

[§] PRIVACY BREACHES AND DATA EXPLOITATION
www.hkcert.org/blog/protect-sensitive-information-in-the-use-of-social-media-and-beware-of-potential-cyber-attacks-arising-from-data-leakages; https://mashable.com/ad/article/data-leaks-breach-protectionhttps://www.upguard.com/blog/data-leak-prevention-tips

Endnote References[¶]

Radicalization and Extremism

Social media platforms have been implicated in the radicalization and recruitment of individuals into extremist ideologies and hate groups. Extremist content, conspiracy theories, and propaganda can spread rapidly on social media, potentially radicalizing vulnerable individuals and inciting violence. Extremist ideologies and hate groups exploit social media to recruit, radicalize, and spread propaganda. Platforms struggle to strike a balance between free speech and preventing harmful content.

Addressing online radicalization requires a multifaceted approach involving education, collaboration, and proactive measures to safeguard vulnerable individuals and promote a safer digital environment.

By implementing mitigating strategies collaboratively, stakeholders can work together to lessen the threat of online radicalization and extremism on social media and promote a safer and more inclusive online environment for all users.

Endnote References[**]

---

[*] ADDICTION AND MENTAL HEALTH IMPACT

https://theconversation.com/6-ways-to-protect-your-mental-health-from-social-medias-dangers-117651;https://medium.com/@bridgerrobertbowman/the-dark-side-of-social-media-understanding-its-impact-on-mental-well-being-b644f8e607f7; https://bmcpsychology.biomedcentral.com/articles/10.1186/s40359-023-01243-x; www.verywellmind.com/link-between-social-media-and-mental-health-5089347.

[**] RADICALIZATION AND EXTREMISM

www.canada.ca/en/public-safety-canada/news/2024/03/government-of-canada-announces-funding-to-help-counter-ideologically-motivated-violent-extremism.html; www.icct.nl/sites/default/files/2023-01/Chapter-12-Handbook_0.pdf; www.mccainnstitute.org/resources/blog/fighting-back-against-online-radicalization/; https://akademie.dw.com/en/tackling-online-radicalization-7-steps-to-get-started/a-59477592;https://crestresearch.ac.uk/resources/online-radicalisation-a-rapid-review-of-the-literature/

Online Scams and Fraud

Social media networks are breeding grounds for online scams, phishing attacks, and fraudulent schemes. Users may fall victim to scams involving fake profiles, fake news, fake products, or fraudulent investment opportunities, leading to financial loss and exploitation.

Cybercriminals use social media to gather personal information and launch phishing attacks. Users may unknowingly share details that enable identity theft or compromise their accounts. Social engineering attacks thrive on exploiting human behavior. By staying informed, practicing good cyber hygiene, and fostering a security-conscious culture, one can significantly reduce the risk of falling victim to social media phishing and social engineering attempts. Counteracting social media phishing and social engineering is crucial to safeguard personal and professional information.

Mitigating social media phishing and social engineering requires a multifaceted approach encompassing both technical solutions and user education.

By implementing these strategies collaboratively, stakeholders can help minimize the risk of online radicalization and extremism on social media, promote a safer and more resilient online environment for all users, significantly reduce the risk posed by social media phishing and social engineering attacks, and safeguard both their data and their users' personal information.

Endnote References[††]

†† ONLINE SCAMS AND FRAUD

https://securityintelligence.com/articles/social-engineering-and-social-media-oversharing/; https://vpninsights.com/privacy/email/social -engineering/; www.cisa .gov/news-events/news/avoiding-social-engineering-and-phishing-attacks; www.verizon.com/business/resources/articles/s/how-to-reduce-the-impact-of-social-engineering-attacks/.

Digital Footprint and Reputation Damage

Users' online activities on social media can have long-term consequences for their digital footprint and reputation. Inappropriate posts, controversial opinions, or indiscreet behavior can be captured, shared, and archived indefinitely, potentially damaging individuals' personal and professional reputations.

Mitigating digital footprint and reputation damage is essential for maintaining user trust, protecting the platform's reputation, retaining users, ensuring legal compliance, promoting user well-being, and upholding community standards.

By implementing effective mitigation strategies, social media platforms can create a more positive and secure online environment for everyone.

Endnote References[‡‡]

Influence on Elections and Political Manipulation

Social media's influence on elections and political manipulation is a multifaceted issue. It involves the use of platforms like Facebook, Twitter, and Instagram to shape public opinion and voter behavior. Social media can significantly influence political processes, necessitating efforts to ensure the integrity of information and protect democratic practices.

Mitigating the influence of social media on elections and political manipulation is essential for preserving democratic processes, protecting voter confidence, preventing electoral interference, promoting transparency, ensuring fair competition, and upholding ethical standards.

[‡‡] DIGITAL FOOTPRINT AND REPUTATION DAMAGE
  www.netreputation.com/digital-footprint-understanding-and-managing-your-online-presence/.; www.minclaw.com/steps-protect-reputation-online/. https://blog.hootsuite.com/social-media-reputation-management/;https://www.csoonline.com/article/574251/how-social-media-puts-companies-at-risk-and-how-to-mitigate-it.html; https://blog.reputationx.com/digital-footprint.

By implementing effective mitigation strategies, platforms can contribute to the integrity and legitimacy of electoral systems and promote a healthier and more robust democracy.

Endnote References[§§]

Lack of Fact-Checking and Accountability

Social media's lack of fact-checking and accountability refers to the challenges platforms face in verifying the truthfulness of content and holding individuals accountable for spreading misinformation. The lack of robust fact-checking mechanisms and accountability on social media contributes to the spread of misinformation, which can have significant societal influence.

Mitigating the lack of fact-checking and online accountability on social media platforms is essential for combatting misinformation, protecting public health, preserving trust and credibility, promoting responsible behavior, protecting democratic processes, and upholding platform standards.

By implementing robust fact-checking mechanisms and holding users accountable for spreading false or harmful information, stakeholders can contribute to a healthier and more informed digital ecosystem.

Endnote References[¶¶]

[§§] INFLUENCE ON ELECTIONS AND POLITICAL MANIPULATION
    www.nature.com/articles/d41586-024-00274-7; https://ide.mit.edu/insights/sinan-aral-on-the-threats-of-social-media-manipulation-on-elections/; https://freedomhouse.org/report/freedom-net/2017/manipulating-social-media-undermine-democracy; www.stimson.org/2022/social-media-misinformation-and-the-prevention-of-political-instability-and-mass-atrocities/.
[¶¶] LACK OF FACT-CHECKING AND ACCOUNTABILITY
    https://misinforeview.hks.harvard.edu/article/tackling-misinformation-what-researchers-could-do-with-social-media-data/; https://academyhealth.org/blog/2021-07/ways-combat-misinformation-social-media-era; www.bbc.com/news/technology-54901083.

Youth Vulnerability and Online Predatory Behavior

Social media's youth vulnerability and online predatory behavior refer to the risks that young users face when engaging with social media platforms. Efforts to educate and protect young social media users are crucial to mitigate these risks and ensure a safer online environment.

Children and teenagers are active on social media, making them susceptible to online predators, grooming, and exploitation. Parents and guardians need to educate and protect young users.

For example, Reuters conducted an investigation into OnlyFans, revealing disturbing cases of child sexual abuse material on the platform despite its claims of strict age verification and content monitoring. The investigation uncovered 30 complaints in U.S. police and court records citing over 200 explicit videos and images of minors on OnlyFans between December 2019 and June 2024. These cases included instances of adults exploiting minors to create and sell content, as well as underage users bypassing age restrictions to post their own explicit material. The article details several specific cases, including a 16-year-old Florida girl whose sexual content was posted by an adult, and instances of toddler abuse videos being shared on the platform. OnlyFans' response to these issues has been inconsistent, with some illegal content remaining undetected for extended periods. The investigation raises serious questions about the effectiveness of OnlyFans' safety measures and the potential legal and financial risks the company faces as a result of these failures.[***]

Minimizing online youth vulnerability and predatory behavior is essential for protecting vulnerable individuals, preventing online abuse, promoting digital literacy, fostering positive relationships, complying with legal obligations, and maintaining user trust. By prioritizing the safety and well-being of young users, social media platforms can create a more inclusive, supportive, and responsible digital environment for all users.

Mitigating the vulnerability of youth to online predators on social media requires a concerted effort from parents, educators, caregivers, social media platforms, law enforcement agencies, and policy makers.

[***] www.reuters.com/investigates/special-report/onlyfans-sex-children/.

Endnote References[†††]

_____

[†††] YOUTH VULNERABILITY AND ONLINE PREDATORY BEHAVIOUR
https://misinforeview.hks.harvard.edu/article/tackling-misinformation-what-researchers-could-do-with-social-media-data/; https://academyhealth.org/blog/2021-07/ways-combat-misinformation-social-media-era; www.bbc.com/news/technology-54901083; www.reuters.com/investigates/special-report/onlyfans-sex-children/.

CHAPTER 11

Common Social Media Mitigation Strategies

Some common mitigation strategies apply to most social network perils listed earlier. We present hereafter those that are prevalent at the platform, regulation, and user levels.

Common SM Mitigation Strategies at the latform Level

Investing in Fact-Checking and Content Moderation

Social media (SM) platforms must enforce strict fact-checking and content moderation policies to remove extremist content, hate speech, and incitement to violence. They should be transparent about their content moderation practices, including the criteria used to identify and remove extremist content.

SM platforms should:

- Enhance their content moderation policies and practices to detect and remove false information, hate speech, voter suppression tactics, and other forms of political manipulation.
- Implement content moderation policies that prohibit the dissemination of false information, hate speech, and misinformation.
- Enforce clear and robust community guidelines that explicitly prohibit cyberbullying, harassment, hate speech, and other forms of abusive behavior.
- Invest in automated tools, human moderators, and partnerships with fact-checkers and researchers to address

these challenges effectively including the use of robust fact-checking processes to verify the accuracy of content shared on their platforms.

- Use AI and human moderators to identify and remove misleading content promptly. This includes deploying AI and machine learning algorithms to proactively identify and remove harmful content, as well as employing human moderators to review flagged content.

Increasing Algorithmic Transparency

Transparency can help users understand how misinformation spreads and make more informed decisions about the content they consume. Transparency reports detailing the volume and nature of content removed can help build trust with users and external stakeholders. Transparency can help users make more informed decisions about the content they consume and share.

SM platforms should:

- Increase transparency around their algorithms and content moderation practices to help users understand how content is selected, promoted, moderated, and distributed on their platforms.
- Provide users with information about how content is selected, promoted, and prioritized in their feeds.
- Improve transparency and disclosure around political advertising and content.
- Require political advertisers to provide information about the source, funding, and targeting criteria of their ads, and make this information accessible to users in a transparent and user-friendly manner.

Providing Reporting Mechanisms

Providing users with tools and resources can help them identify and report false information, misinformation, and disinformation. This may include features such as reporting tools, fact-checking labels, and educational resources on media literacy and critical thinking.

SM platforms should:

- Provide users with easy-to-use reporting mechanisms to flag instances of cyberbullying and harassment.
- Respond promptly to reports and take appropriate action, such as removing content, suspending accounts, and banning repeat offenders.
- Implement reporting mechanisms, content filters, and support resources to help users manage negative experiences and protect their mental health.

Implementing Safety Features

Safety features and tools to empower users to protect themselves from cyberbullying and harassment are essential. This includes features such as safety tips, blocking, muting, and filtering content, as well as privacy settings that allow users to control who can interact with their content.

SM platforms should:

- Enhance safety features to protect users from harmful content, cyberbullying, and harassment.
- Implement comprehensive data protection policies that prioritize user privacy and security.
- Include transparency in communicating how user data is collected, stored, and used, as well as providing users with control over their privacy settings.
- Fine-tune the privacy settings of SM accounts by controlling who can see posts, profile information, and personal details.
- Practice data minimization by collecting and storing only the minimum amount of user data necessary for providing services.
- Avoid unnecessary data collection and ensure that user data is anonymized or pseudonymized whenever possible to minimize the risk of privacy breaches.

Investing in Security Measures

Robust security measures to protect user data from unauthorized access, breaches, and leaks including encryption, multifactor authentication, regular security audits, and vulnerability testing to identify and patch potential security loopholes have always been part of overall online security requirements platforms need to provide.

SM platforms should:

- Conduct periodic assessments of user awareness and understanding of security best practices, adjusting training programs as necessary.
- Establish clear procedures for reporting suspected phishing attempts or security incidents to the appropriate authorities within the organization.
- Avoid using common passwords.
- Promote the use of a combination of uppercase and lowercase letters, numbers, and special characters.
- Consider using a password manager.
- Advise users to review and adjust their privacy settings to limit the amount of personal information visible to the public.
- Enable account verification features offered such as two-factor authentication (2FA) and login alerts.
- Encourage users to be cautious when accepting friend or connection requests from unknown individuals.
- Develop and regularly update an incident response plan specifically tailored to address social engineering and phishing attacks.
- Regularly monitor SM channels and other communication platforms for signs of phishing activity or attempts at social engineering.
- Activate 2FA for an extra layer of security, preventing unauthorized access even if the password is compromised.

Practicing Positive Engagement

Prioritizing features that promote positive engagement and well-being, such as tools for managing notifications, controlling feed algorithms, and promoting meaningful connections, are part of good online practice.

SM platforms should:

- Offer users tools to limit their SM usage, such as time management features, reminders, and notifications that encourage breaks and time offline.
- Implement features that promote balance and self-regulation rather than encouraging addictive behavior.
- Be designed to minimize the spread of extremist content and prioritize authoritative sources.
- Regularly audit their algorithms to identify and address any biases or unintended consequences.
- Invest in robust fact-checking processes to verify the accuracy of content shared on their platforms.
- Partner with reputable fact-checking organizations and use automated tools to flag potentially false or misleading information.
- Enforce clear and transparent content policies that prohibit the dissemination of false information, hate speech, harassment, and other harmful content.
- Violations of these policies should result in appropriate penalties, such as content removal or account suspension.

Empowering Users

Empowering users on SM fosters a more dynamic, inclusive, and impactful online environment, where individuals have the opportunity to connect, learn, collaborate, and effect positive change.

SM platforms should:

- Implement robust age verification measures to prevent underage users from accessing age-inappropriate content and interactions.
- Enforce age restrictions and prohibit adults from contacting minors or engaging in inappropriate behavior with them.
- Empower users with tools and resources to help them identify and report political manipulation, disinformation, and election interference on SM.
- Provide users with access to fact-checking tools, and educational resources on media literacy and critical thinking.
- Identifying and labeling false information.
- Implement consequences for repeat offenders.

Promoting Reliable Sources

Promoting reliable resources on SM is essential for building trust, combating misinformation, protecting users, fostering education, and cultivating a responsible online community. By prioritizing accuracy and credibility, SM platforms can fulfill their potential as valuable sources of information and communication.

SM platforms should:

- Prioritize content from credible and authoritative sources in users' feeds.
- Partner with reputable news organizations and fact-checkers to promote accurate and reliable information.
- Implement features that highlight trustworthy sources and flag dubious content.
- Educate users about these features and encourage them to use them to enhance their safety online.

Common SM Mitigation Strategies at the Regulatory Level

Regulation of SM is essential to protect users, safeguard privacy, combat disinformation, promote fair competition, and uphold ethical standards.

By establishing clear rules and accountability mechanisms, regulators can help ensure that SM platforms serve the public interest and contribute positively to society.

Regulating Misinformation

Regulating misinformation is essential for protecting public health, preserving democratic processes, safeguarding vulnerable groups, promoting trust and credibility, and preventing harm. By implementing effective regulatory measures, policy makers can help mitigate the harmful effects of misinformation and promote a healthier, more informed public discourse.

Governments and regulatory bodies should:

- Enact and enforce laws that prohibit cyberbullying, harassment, and online abuse.
- Provide law enforcement agencies with the resources and training needed to investigate and prosecute cases of online harassment effectively.
- Implement regulations that hold platforms accountable for the dissemination of false information and require them to take proactive measures to combat misinformation.
- Balance regulatory measures with protections for free speech and expression.
- Enact legislation to hold SM platforms accountable for their role in facilitating online radicalization and extremism. This may include regulations requiring platforms to take proactive measures to address harmful content, cooperate with law enforcement agencies, and report suspicious activities.
- Enact and enforce robust data protection laws and regulations to safeguard user privacy hold SM platforms accountable for data breaches and privacy violations and prevent the exploitation of personal information for addictive purposes.
- These laws should include provisions for fines, penalties, and legal action against platforms that fail to comply with data protection requirements.

Promoting Transparency and Accountability

Promoting online transparency and accountability is essential for building trust, protecting user rights, preventing abuse and misuse, promoting fairness and equity, and fostering innovation and competition in the online ecosystem. By prioritizing transparency and accountability, online platforms can create a safer, more trustworthy, and inclusive online environment for users around the world.

Governments and regulatory bodies should:

- Require SM platforms to be transparent about their content moderation practices, algorithmic decision making, and efforts to combat misinformation.
- Hold platforms accountable for their actions and ensure that they have systems in place to address the spread of false information effectively.
- Enact legislation to regulate political advertising, campaign finance, and online electioneering on SM platforms. These regulations should promote transparency, accountability, and fairness in political campaigns and elections, including disclosure requirements for political ads and funding sources.

Limiting Amplification of Controversial Content

Promoting limitations on the online amplification of controversial content is essential for mitigating harm, protecting public discourse, preventing misinformation, safeguarding vulnerable groups, and promoting responsible content creation. By implementing measures to moderate and control the dissemination of controversial content, platforms can create a safer, more informed, and inclusive online environment for all users.

Regulatory bodies should:

- Regulators should impose limits on the amplification of controversial or sensationalistic content by SM algorithms.
- Regulators should implement measures to prevent the rapid spread of misinformation, hate speech, and divisive content that can contribute to echo chambers and polarization.

Requiring Algorithmic Impact Assessments

Requiring algorithmic impact assessments online is essential for promoting transparency, mitigating bias, protecting privacy, fostering trust, and ensuring the ethical and responsible development of AI technologies. By integrating impact assessments into their processes, platforms can help build a more equitable, trustworthy, and inclusive digital ecosystem for all users.

Governments and regulatory bodies should:

- Require SM platforms to conduct algorithmic impact assessments to evaluate the potential risks and harms associated with their algorithms. This can help identify and mitigate the unintended consequences of algorithmic manipulation, including the formation of echo chambers.

Providing Victim Support

Providing online victim support is essential for addressing the emotional and psychological needs of victims, empowering them to take action, preventing revictimization, promoting awareness and education, and advocating for policy and legal reform. By investing in victim support services, we can help create a safer, more supportive, and resilient online community for everyone.

Governments should:

- Provide support services for victims of cyberbullying and harassment, including counseling, legal assistance, and protection from further abuse.
- Ensure that victims feel safe and supported when reporting incidents to law enforcement authorities.

Holding Perpetrators Accountable

Holding online perpetrators accountable is essential for preventing recurrence, protecting victims, promoting deterrence, upholding community standards, and fostering trust and confidence in online platforms. By implementing effective accountability measures, platforms can create a safer, more inclusive, and respectful online environment for everyone.

Governments should:

- Hold perpetrators of cyberbullying and harassment accountable for their actions by prosecuting offenders and imposing appropriate penalties.
- Send a clear message that online abuse will not be tolerated and that there are consequences for engaging in harmful behavior.

Establishing Regulatory Oversight

Establishing online regulatory oversight is essential for protecting users, promoting fairness and equity, preserving democratic values, preventing abuse of power, and adapting to technological advancements. By implementing effective oversight mechanisms, regulators can help create a safer, more transparent, and accountable online environment for everyone.

Governments should:

- Establish regulatory oversight bodies tasked with monitoring SM platforms' compliance with data protection laws and investigating complaints of privacy breaches and data leaks.
- Empower imposition of sanctions and enforcement actions against platforms found to be in violation of privacy regulations.

Fostering International Cooperation

Fostering international online cooperation is essential for addressing global challenges, promoting digital inclusion, protecting human rights, promoting economic growth, and building trust and stability in the digital space. By working together across borders and jurisdictions, countries can harness the full potential of the digital revolution to create a more prosperous, inclusive, and sustainable world for all.

Governments should:

- Foster international cooperation and collaboration among governments, regulatory agencies, and SM platforms to address cross-border data privacy issues and harmonize data protection standards globally.

Implementing Accountability Mechanisms

Implementing online accountability mechanisms is essential for promoting trust and transparency, protecting user rights, preventing abuse and misuse, enabling remediation and redress, and encouraging responsible innovation in the digital space. By holding platforms accountable for their actions and decisions, we can create a safer, fairer, and more accountable online environment for all users.

Governments should:

- Implement accountability mechanisms to hold SM platforms accountable for privacy breaches and data leaks. This may include establishing independent oversight boards, conducting third-party audits, and providing avenues for users to report privacy violations and seek redress.

Applying Regulation of Platform Practices

Applying online regulation of platform practices is essential for protecting user rights, promoting competition, preventing harm, ensuring accountability, and protecting the public interest in the digital age. By establishing clear rules and standards for platform behavior, regulations help create a more transparent, accountable, and responsible digital ecosystem that benefits users, businesses, and society as a whole.

Governments and regulatory bodies should:

- Consider implementing regulations to address harmful practices by SM platforms that contribute to addiction and mental health issues. This may include restrictions on targeted advertising, algorithmic manipulation, and addictive features.

Applying Data Privacy Protection

Applying online data privacy protection is essential for safeguarding personal privacy, preventing unauthorized access, building trust and confidence, mitigating risks of misuse, complying with regulations, and fostering innovation and competition in the digital economy. By prioritizing data privacy, online platforms can create a more transparent, accountable, and user-centric online environment that respects and protects the rights of individuals.

Governments should:

- Require SM platforms to be transparent about their data collection practices and obtain explicit consent from users for data processing.

Fostering International Cooperation

Fostering online international cooperation is essential for addressing global challenges, promoting digital inclusion, protecting human rights, promoting economic growth, and building trust and stability in the digital space. By working together across borders and jurisdictions, countries can harness the full potential of the digital revolution to create a more prosperous, inclusive, and sustainable world for all.

Governments should:

- Foster international cooperation and information-sharing among governments, law enforcement agencies, and tech companies to combat online extremism.
- Collaborate with other countries to develop common standards and strategies for addressing the global threat of online radicalization.

Investing in Prevention Programs

Investing in online prevention programs is essential for mitigating harm, empowering users, promoting digital well-being, building resilience, creating safer online environments, and reducing societal costs associated with online harm. By prioritizing prevention efforts, policy makers, educators, and stakeholders can help ensure that the benefits of the digital age are realized in a safe, responsible, and inclusive manner for all.

Governments should:

- Invest in prevention programs that address the root causes of radicalization and extremism, including social exclusion, marginalization, and economic inequality.
- Support initiatives that promote social cohesion, community resilience, and positive youth engagement.

Combating Disinformation

Combating online disinformation is essential for preserving democratic processes, protecting public health, promoting social cohesion, safeguarding trust in media, protecting economic stability, and defending individual rights. By implementing effective strategies and collaborative efforts to counter disinformation, we can create a safer, more informed, and resilient digital environment for all users.

Governments should:

- Implement legal measures to combat disinformation, fake news, and election interference on SM platforms. This may include regulations requiring platforms to remove or label false or misleading content, verify the identity of advertisers, and disclose information about the origin and dissemination of political content.

Strengthening Data Protection Laws

Strengthening online data protection laws is essential for protecting personal privacy, preventing data breaches, promoting trust and confidence, complying with global standards, fostering innovation and competition, and protecting vulnerable groups from harm. By prioritizing data protection and privacy, policy makers can create a safer, more transparent, and accountable digital environment that benefits individuals, businesses, and society as a whole.

Governments should:

- Strengthen data protection laws and regulations to protect users' privacy and prevent the misuse of personal data for political purposes.
- Enhance transparency and accountability around data collection, processing, and targeting practices by political campaigns and third-party actors.
- Require platforms to implement fact-checking processes, enforce content policies, and address harmful content.

Promoting Transparency

Promoting online transparency is essential for building trust, empowering users, encouraging accountability, facilitating collaboration, protecting privacy, and promoting innovation in the digital ecosystem. By prioritizing transparency in their operations and interactions with users, platforms can create a more open, accountable, and user-centric online environment that benefits everyone.

Regulators should:

- Promote transparency and accountability in SM by requiring platforms to disclose information about their content moderation practices, algorithmic decision making, and data policies. This transparency can help regulators assess platforms' compliance with regulatory requirements and hold them accountable for their actions.

Strengthening Laws and Their Enforcement

Strengthening online laws and their enforcement is essential for protecting rights and freedoms, promoting accountability, preventing harm, protecting intellectual property, facilitating cross-border cooperation, and promoting economic growth and innovation in the digital age. By investing in legal frameworks and enforcement mechanisms that reflect the evolving nature of the digital landscape, policy makers can create a safer, fairer, and more prosperous online environment for all.

Governments should:

- Strengthen laws and enforcement mechanisms to prosecute online predators and hold them accountable for their actions.
- Provide law enforcement agencies with the resources, training, and technology they need to investigate and combat online predators effectively.

Collaborating With Tech Companies

Fostering collaboration between law enforcement agencies and SM companies is essential for enhancing public safety, improving response to emergencies, combatting online crime, protecting vulnerable populations, and promoting trust and accountability in the digital space. By leveraging their respective expertise, resources, and capabilities, these stakeholders can work together to create a safer, more secure, and resilient online environment for all users.

Governments should:

- Foster collaboration between law enforcement agencies and SM companies to identify and remove predatory content, detect suspicious behavior, and prevent online grooming and exploitation.
- Encourage platforms to report suspected cases of child grooming and exploitation to law enforcement authorities promptly.

Common SM Mitigation Strategies at the User Level

Implementing SM mitigation strategies at the user level is essential for empowering users, promoting digital literacy, preventing harm, building resilience, and enhancing user well-being in the digital age.

By investing in education, awareness, and support initiatives that empower users to make informed choices and navigate SM safely, we can create a more positive and empowering online environment for all.

Some of the user-specific mitigation strategies include:

Empowering Users

- Empower users to take control of their online experience and protect themselves from potential risks and harms associated with SM use.

Promoting Digital Literacy

- Promote digital literacy by educating users about the risks and challenges of SM use and providing guidance on how to recognize and address them effectively.
- Raise awareness about topics such as online privacy, security, and media literacy.
- Help users develop the skills and knowledge they need to engage critically and responsibly in the digital world.

Preventing Harm*

- Enable users to identify and mitigate potential risks and threats before they escalate into serious problems.
- Promote positive online behaviors such as respectful communication, critical thinking, and healthy digital habits.

Building Resilience

- Build resilience among users by equipping them with the skills and resources to cope with challenges and adversity in the digital realm.

---

* www.cbc.ca/news/canada/new-brunswick/facebook-account-taken-over-friends-scam-1.7205356.

- Provide support, guidance, and encouragement, to help users develop resilience skills that enable them to bounce back from setbacks, overcome obstacles, and navigate the complexities of SM with confidence and resilience.

Enhancing User Well-Being

- Enhance user well-being by promoting positive online interactions, fostering a sense of community, and reducing the negative impact of SM on mental health and emotional well-being.
- Encourage users to cultivate meaningful connections, engage in meaningful activities, and prioritize self-care, supporting users in maintaining a healthy and balanced relationship with SM.

Strategies to mitigate these risks may include implementing robust content moderation policies, enhancing privacy protections, promoting digital literacy and critical thinking skills, fostering a culture of civility and respect, and holding platforms accountable for their actions. By providing users with knowledge, tools, and resources to identify and respond to threats such as cyberbullying, harassment, and misinformation, these strategies enable them to make informed decisions, navigate SM platforms safely, and contribute to creating a more supportive online environment for everyone.

Addressing these perils requires concerted efforts from SM platforms, policy makers, regulators, educators, and users themselves. Whereas SM offers connectivity and opportunities, users must remain vigilant and practice responsible online behavior to mitigate these risks.

CHAPTER 12

Conclusion

The world of social networks has undergone a remarkable evolution, with platforms rising and falling in a dynamic cycle driven by user preferences, technological advancements, and market forces.

In this book we explored the intricate landscape of social media, delving into the histories, features, and trajectories of various platforms, both prominent and obscure, offering a comprehensive guide to this ever-changing industry.

Throughout the chapters, we have witnessed the emergence of social networks as a global phenomenon, transcending geographical boundaries and transforming the way we communicate, connect, and share information. From the early pioneers like Facebook and Myspace, which paved the way for modern social media, to the current titans like Instagram, TikTok, and Twitter, the industry has been shaped by constant innovation and adaptation to meet the evolving needs and preferences of users across diverse cultures and demographics.

However, the journey has not been without its challenges. We have seen platforms struggle to maintain relevance, grapple with issues of misinformation, data privacy, and user safety, and face the ever-present threat of obsolescence in the face of new competitors and emerging technologies. The rise and fall of platforms like Google+, Vine, and Friendster serve as cautionary tales, highlighting the importance of staying ahead of the curve, addressing user concerns, and fostering a sense of community and trust.

As we look to the future, we believe that the social media landscape will continue to evolve at a rapid pace, driven by factors such as regulation, user behavior, and the integration of cutting-edge technologies like artificial intelligence, blockchain, and immersive experiences.

The rise of decentralized and privacy-focused platforms, such as Mastodon and MeWe, reflects a growing demand for greater user control, data protection, and transparency in an increasingly digital world.

Moreover, the increasing emphasis on social responsibility and ethical considerations will probably shape the trajectory of this industry. Platforms will be challenged to address complex issues such as misinformation, hate speech, online harassment, and the mental health implications of social media usage, while also promoting positive social impact, responsible communication, and digital well-being.

The lessons learned from the rise and fall of various social networks have provided valuable insights into the patterns of decline and the factors that contribute to a platform's longevity or demise. By analyzing these patterns, we can better understand the challenges and opportunities that lie ahead, and perhaps even predict the next wave of social media disruption.

One key pattern that emerges is the importance of adapting to changing user preferences and technological advancements. Platforms that fail to innovate and evolve risk becoming stagnant and losing relevance to their user base. Additionally, issues such as data privacy, user safety, ethical practices, and fostering a sense of community and belonging have become increasingly important factors in determining a platform's success or failure.

Furthermore, the ability to navigate the complex regulatory landscape and address concerns around data protection, content moderation, and antitrust issues will be crucial for social media platforms. As governments around the world grapple with the challenges posed by these powerful digital platforms, new regulations and guidelines are emerging, shaping the future of the industry.

As we navigate this ever-changing landscape, it is crucial for social media platforms to remain vigilant and adaptable, embracing innovation while prioritizing user safety, privacy, and ethical practices. The future of social media lies not only in technological advancements but also in the collective ability to harness these platforms for positive social impact, responsible communication, and the promotion of digital well-being.

This book has served as a comprehensive guide to the world of social networks, offering a deep dive into their histories, features, and trajectories. It has provided a foundation for understanding the complexities of this industry and the factors that may shape its future.

By exploring the rise and fall of various platforms, the emerging trends, and the regulatory and ethical considerations, we have gained a holistic perspective on the social media landscape.

As we move forward, let us embrace the lessons learned and approach the ever-evolving social media landscape with wisdom, responsibility, and a commitment to fostering meaningful connections, positive change, and a more inclusive and ethical digital ecosystem.

The future of social media is not just about technological innovation but also about cultivating a culture of empathy, inclusivity, and ethical practices that can harness the power of these platforms for the greater good of individuals, communities, and society as a whole.

In this rapidly evolving digital age, social networks have the potential to be powerful tools for communication, collaboration, and social impact, but only if we approach them with a mindset of responsibility, transparency, and a genuine commitment to creating a safer, more equitable, and more inclusive online environment.

By learning from the past, embracing innovation, and prioritizing ethical practices, we can shape a future where social media platforms serve as catalysts for positive change, fostering meaningful connections, and empowering individuals and communities to thrive in the digital realm.

Ancillaries

In an era where digital connectivity pervades every aspect of modern life, social networks have emerged as ubiquitous platforms shaping how individuals communicate, access information, and engage with the world around them. However, beneath the facade of connectivity lies a landscape fraught with peril, where the very tools designed to foster community and discourse can harbor profound dangers.

The exponential growth of digital platforms and social networks was ushered in an era of unprecedented connectivity and information access. As these technologies become increasingly intertwined with our daily lives, it is crucial to recognize the complex challenges they present and the pressing need for comprehensive digital market legislation on a global scale.

This book delved into the intricate world of digital markets, exploring the multifaceted issues that arise from the dominance of a few tech giants and the far-reaching implications of their unchecked power. From data privacy and security concerns to the spread of misinformation and the stifling of competition, the consequences of an unregulated digital landscape are far-reaching and profound.

Through in-depth analysis and studies from around the world, this book aims to shed light on the urgent need for robust digital market legislation that safeguards consumer rights, promotes fair competition, and fosters a healthy digital ecosystem.

By exploring the intricate interplay between technology, economics, and public policy, this book serves as a comprehensive guide for policy makers, industry leaders, and concerned citizens alike. It provides a roadmap for navigating the complex challenges of the digital age and offers actionable insights for shaping a more equitable and sustainable digital future.

Based on the provided search results, some of the key challenges in regulating digital markets globally include:

1. **Difficulty applying traditional competition law and antitrust principles:**
   - Conventional price-related metrics are ill-suited for digital markets that often provide free services.
   - Digital platforms can leverage dominance across interconnected markets/ecosystems.
   - High barriers to entry and network effects entrench dominant positions.

2. **Transboundary and cross-border nature of digital markets:**
   - Digital businesses span multiple regulatory regimes across borders.
   - Enables *forum shopping* to avoid compliance in certain jurisdictions.
   - Requires new institutional solutions and cross-border cooperation between regulators.

3. **Unique characteristics of digital platforms and ecosystems:**
   - Multisided markets with complex dynamics between different user groups.
   - Blurring of sectoral boundaries due to economies of scope.
   - Data-driven business models raise privacy/ethical concerns.

4. **Rapid pace of technological change:**
   - Regulatory frameworks cannot keep up with the speed of innovation.
   - Increases opportunities for regulatory arbitrage.

5. **Balancing regulation with innovation:**
   - Overly rigid ex ante rules may stifle innovation and raise compliance costs.
   - But ex post case-by-case enforcement is slow and inadequate for digital markets.

6. **Institutional challenges and fragmentation:**
   - Traditional regulatory bodies organized by sector/issue area.
   - Mismatch with the cross-cutting nature of digital markets and technologies.

The search results highlight the need for new regulatory approaches tailored to digital markets, such as ex ante rules for *gatekeeper* platforms, data-sharing requirements, self-referencing restrictions, and increased international cooperation between agencies.

However, debates exist around the optimal form of regulation to promote competition while still allowing innovation.

In this ancillary, we explore the complexities of current digital market legislation and its pivotal role in shaping the digital landscape for generations to come.

Digital Market Legislation Around the World

Background

The legislation of digital markets holds immense significance for several reasons:

- **Fairness and competition:**
  - Digital markets often witness the dominance of a few tech giants. Legislation ensures that these companies do not stifle competition or unfairly control access to online services. By promoting fair competition, legislation allows smaller players to thrive and innovate, leading to a healthier digital ecosystem.
- **Consumer protection:**
  - Regulations safeguard consumers' rights and privacy. They ensure that users are treated fairly, their data are protected, and they have transparent choices regarding services and platforms. Legislation prevents abusive practices, such as misleading advertising, unfair terms of service, and unauthorized data collection.
- **Transparency and accountability:**
  - Legal frameworks force tech companies to be transparent about their practices, algorithms, and decision-making processes. Accountability mechanisms hold companies responsible for their actions, ensuring they act ethically and in the best interest of users.

- **Innovation and growth:**
  - o Well-crafted regulations encourage innovation by providing a level playing field. When companies compete fairly, they invest in research, development, and new technologies. Legislation fosters a conducive environment for start-ups and emerging players, driving economic growth and technological advancements.
- **Global leadership:**
  - o Europe, in particular, has been at the forefront of regulating tech giants. The Digital Markets Act (DMA) is a recent milestone in this regard. By setting global standards, Europe influences other regions and encourages them to adopt similar measures.
  - o In summary, legislating digital markets ensures fairness, protects consumers, promotes innovation, and establishes a balanced playing field for all stakeholders.

The Digital Markets Act (DMA)

The DMA represents landmark legislation within the European Union (EU) designed to curb the potential abuse of market dominance by large online platforms facilitating the connection between consumers and content, goods, and services. The DMA is a ground-breaking European law designed to limit Big Tech's power over the Internet.*

The EU contends that stringent regulation of major technology firms, often referred to as gatekeepers of the digital economy, will foster increased competition, choice, innovation, product quality, and affordability.

The DMA was initially proposed in December 2020. The final text of the DMA law was published in the *Official Journal of the European Union* on October 12, 2022, and it officially entered into force on November 1, 2022. The majority of its regulations became effective in May 2023, while the gatekeepers were officially appointed on September 6, 2023. These gatekeepers were required to comply with the DMA by March 6, 2024. This marked a significant milestone in the regulation of digital markets and the establishment of a new framework regulating the gatekeepers.

Noncompliance with the DMA may result in substantial fines and potential repercussions such as asset divestiture or prohibition from operating within European jurisdictions. The European Commission is enforcing the DMA rigorously. Those who do not comply with its provisions will encounter severe financial repercussions and, in severe instances, additional punitive measures. Typically, violators may be subject to fines amounting to as much as 10 percent of their global revenue, which may escalate to 20 percent for repeated violations. However, if deemed appropriate, additional measures may be implemented, such as prohibiting the entity from pursuing further acquisitions or requiring divestiture of certain business assets.

Although its jurisdiction is limited to the EU, the significant penalties associated with the DMA position it as a potentially transformative legislative measure with profound implications for Big Tech and Internet usage as a whole.

DMA's Key Goals

The primary objective of the DMA is to enhance competition and ensure user safety on the Internet by dismantling the monopolistic powers amassed by a select few Big Tech companies over time. This legislation primarily targets providers of essential platform services, including social networks, search engines, web browsers, online marketplaces, messaging services, and video-sharing platforms. In essence, it seeks to address the dominance of major players in the digital economy.

To be classified as a gatekeeper, an online platform must have at least 45 million monthly active users within the EU. Brussels perceives gatekeepers as wielding excessive influence, controlling access to vital services relied upon by society, and prioritizing profit generation at the expense of others. The DMA antitrust legislation aims to curtail such practices.

This legislation's goal is to prevent gatekeepers from compelling users to exclusively utilize their platforms and impose restrictions on their ability to track users' online activities for advertising purposes. By implementing these measures and reducing the dominance of Big Tech, the European Commission asserts that it will foster a fairer and safer Internet environment, paving the way for new opportunities for innovators and startups. This, in turn, is expected to result in a wider array of high-quality services for consumers to choose from, fairer pricing, and increased innovation.

DMA's Key Provisions

The DMA introduced several key provisions addressing concerns related to the dominance of large online platforms, enhancing competition, and safeguarding user interests within the digital marketplace. Some of DMA's key provisions include:

- **Gatekeeper designation:** the DMA outlines criteria for designating certain online platforms as *gatekeepers* based on their size, influence, and impact on the digital economy. Gatekeepers are platforms that have a significant presence and influence, typically with a large user base and control over essential digital services.
- **Obligations for gatekeepers:** once designated as gatekeepers, online platforms are subject to various obligations aimed at promoting competition and ensuring fair market practices. These obligations may include providing access to third-party services, ensuring interoperability with other platforms, and prohibiting unfair practices that hinder competition.
- **Prohibition of self-preferencing:** the DMA prohibits gatekeepers from giving preferential treatment to their own products or services over those of competitors. This aims to prevent anti-competitive behavior and ensure a level playing field for all market participants.
- **Data portability and interoperability:** gatekeepers may be required to facilitate the portability of user data and ensure interoperability with other platforms and services. This allows users to switch between platforms more easily and promotes competition and innovation in the digital market.
- **Transparency requirements:** the DMA includes transparency requirements to increase visibility into the algorithms, processes, and practices used by gatekeepers.

This transparency helps users and regulators understand how platforms operate and identify any potential anti-competitive behavior.

- **Enforcement mechanisms:** the DMA establishes robust enforcement mechanisms to ensure compliance with its provisions. Regulatory authorities are empowered to investigate complaints, monitor compliance, and impose fines and other penalties for noncompliance.

Overall, the key provisions of the DMA are designed to promote competition, address concerns related to the dominance of large online platforms, and protect the interests of users and businesses in the digital marketplace. By introducing these provisions, the DMA aims to create a fairer and more competitive digital ecosystem that benefits consumers, businesses, and innovators alike.[†]

The DMA applies to companies owning large online platforms and meeting specific criteria, such as having an impact on digital markets, acting as intermediaries between businesses and users, and enjoying a durable position of market power.

The six gatekeepers designated by the European Commission to date were:

1. **Alphabet (owner of Google and Android)**
2. **Amazon**
3. **Apple**
4. **ByteDance (owner of TikTok)**
5. **Meta (owner of Facebook, Instagram, WhatsApp, and others)**
6. **Microsoft**

The impact of the DMA extends beyond gatekeepers to encompass small businesses that rely on their services. Small business owners must grasp the stipulations of the DMA and adhere to the regulations imposed by gatekeepers as a consequence of this legislation. Through a thorough understanding of the DMA, small businesses can adeptly navigate the digital terrain and ensure adherence to gatekeeper mandates.

Potential Effect of the Digital Markets Act (DMA) on the Marketplace

The DMA has the potential to have a significant impact on the digital marketplace, particularly on large online platforms and the broader ecosystem of digital services.

Some potential effects of the DMA on the marketplace include:

- **Increased competition:** by imposing obligations on designated gatekeepers and prohibiting anti-competitive practices such as self-preferencing, the DMA aims to foster a more competitive environment in the digital marketplace. This could open up opportunities for smaller competitors and new entrants to compete on a more level playing field.
- **Enhanced innovation:** the DMA's provisions promoting data portability, interoperability, and transparency could spur innovation by enabling greater collaboration and integration between digital platforms and services. This could lead to the development of new products and services, as well as improvements to existing offerings.
- **Consumer choice and protection:** by promoting transparency, data portability, and interoperability, the DMA aims to empower consumers with more control over their data and greater choice in the digital services they use. This could lead to improved user experiences, increased trust in digital platforms, and better protection of consumer rights.
- **Fairer pricing:** the DMA's provisions prohibiting unfair practices and promoting competition could lead to fairer pricing for digital services. By preventing gatekeepers from engaging in anti-competitive behavior, the DMA aims to ensure that consumers are not unfairly charged or excluded from accessing certain services.
- **Regulatory compliance costs:** large online platforms designated as gatekeepers will incur costs associated with complying with the DMA's obligations and requirements. This could include investments in technology, changes

to business practices, and increased regulatory oversight. However, these costs may be outweighed by the potential benefits of a more competitive and innovative marketplace.

Major Disadvantages of the Digital Markets Act (DMA)

Critics of the DMA have raised several concerns and disadvantages associated with the legislation. Some of the major criticisms include:

- **Overregulation:** critics argue that the DMA represents an overly burdensome and intrusive regulatory approach that could stifle innovation and hinder the growth of digital businesses. They contend that the legislation imposes excessive regulatory requirements and compliance costs on large online platforms, potentially discouraging investment and entrepreneurship in the digital sector.
- **Unintended consequences:** critics warn that the DMA's provisions may have unintended consequences that could negatively impact the digital marketplace. For example, restrictions on self-preferencing and other practices could limit the ability of platforms to improve their services and tailor offerings to user preferences, ultimately leading to reduced consumer choice and innovation.
- **Regulatory uncertainty:** some critics argue that the DMA introduces regulatory uncertainty and complexity, making it difficult for businesses to navigate and comply with the legislation. This uncertainty could discourage investment and innovation in the digital sector, as companies may hesitate to make long-term strategic decisions in an uncertain regulatory environment.
- **Risk of overreach:** critics express concerns that the DMA's broad scope and expansive powers could lead to regulatory overreach and abuse of regulatory authority. They argue that regulatory agencies may interpret and enforce the legislation

in a heavy-handed manner, potentially stifling competition and innovation in the digital marketplace.

- **Global fragmentation:** critics caution that the DMA's regulatory approach could contribute to the global fragmentation of the digital economy, as different jurisdictions implement their own regulations and standards for digital platforms. This fragmentation could create compliance challenges for multinational companies and impede cross-border trade and innovation.

Critics of the DMA contend that the legislation may have unintended consequences and drawbacks that outweigh its purported benefits.

Misalignment and Collaboration

Whereas both the EU and the United States share a conceptual alignment on a risk-based approach and endorse international standards, there are significant differences in the specifics of their online risk management regimes, especially those related to socioeconomic processes and online platforms where the EU and United States are on a path to significant misalignment.

While the EU has already passed the Digital Services Act (DSA) and DMA, which regulate digital services and address issues related to gate-keepers and digital markets, in the United States, proposed antitrust bills (such as the American Innovation and Choice Online Act and the Open App Markets Act), [‡,§] are still under consideration but have not become law yet.

The EU–U.S. Trade and Technology Council aims to work collaboratively on AI standards and study emerging risks of AI and new technologies.

DMA's Key Takeaways

The DMA is a ground-breaking European law designed to rein in the power of the gatekeepers of the digital economy.

- The European Commission believes that keeping the big Internet companies in check can lead to more competition and choice, greater innovation, better quality, and lower prices.
- Key measures include tighter restrictions on how data is collected, the option to uninstall preloaded applications on devices, and messaging services working together.
- Failure to comply with the DMA can result in hefty fines and even the possibility of a company breakup.
- The bulk of the DMA became enforceable in 2023.

In summary, the DMA has the potential to reshape the digital marketplace by promoting competition, innovation, consumer choice, and protection. While it may impose additional regulatory burdens on certain companies, its overarching goal is to create a fairer and more dynamic digital ecosystem that benefits consumers, businesses, and society as a whole.

Whereas there is not a direct equivalent legislation in North America, discussions and efforts are ongoing to align approaches to AI risk management and digital regulation between the EU and the United States. Monitoring legislative developments in both countries is crucial as discussions progress and new proposals emerge.

The Digital Services Act (DSA)

The DSA has been a significant piece of legislation in the realm of the Internet.

Following are some key points regarding its status.

DSA Implementation in the European Union (EU)

The DSA came into force on November 16, 2022. It specifically targets online intermediary services and online platforms. After the expiry of the transitional period on February 17, 2024, the DSA is directly applicable throughout the EU.

The goal is to ensure fairness and essential investments while addressing the impact of digital services on the economy. The DSA is a legislative proposal introduced by the European Commission as part of its broader Digital Single Market strategy.[5] It aims to update and harmonize the regulatory framework governing online platforms and digital services within the EU. The origins of the DSA can be traced back to concerns regarding the proliferation of harmful and illegal content online, as well as the need to modernize regulations to address the challenges of the digital age.

The DSA seeks to achieve several key goals, including enhancing the accountability and transparency of online platforms, improving the protection of users' fundamental rights, and fostering a safer online environment for consumers and businesses alike. It aims to accomplish these objectives by imposing new obligations on digital service providers and strengthening regulatory oversight.

Key measures proposed under the DSA include requirements for online platforms to implement robust content moderation systems, mechanisms for user complaint handling and redress, transparency obligations regarding the use of algorithms and content moderation practices, and enhanced cooperation between platforms, authorities, and law enforcement agencies.

The DSA was expected to have a significant impact on the digital market, particularly on large online platforms and social media networks, which will be subject to stricter regulation and supervision. It was intended to level the playing field for smaller competitors, improve trust and confidence in online services, and mitigate the spread of harmful content, including disinformation and illegal activities.

However, the DSA has also faced criticism from various stakeholders. Some argue that the proposed regulations could stifle innovation and entrepreneurship, impose excessive compliance costs on businesses, and infringe on freedom of expression and privacy rights, while others express concerns about the feasibility and effectiveness of certain measures as well as potential conflicts with existing national laws and regulations.

As of its present status (April 2024), the DSA is undergoing legislative procedures within the EU, with discussions and negotiations ongoing among member states, the European Parliament, and stakeholders.

In summary, the DSA is a legislative proposal aimed at modernizing and harmonizing regulations governing online platforms and digital services in the EU. It seeks to enhance accountability, transparency, and user protection while fostering a safer online environment. Despite its potential benefits, the DSA faces criticism and challenges related to its implementation and impact on innovation and fundamental rights.

The DMA Compared to the DSA

The DMA is a competition law targeting the gatekeepers of the digital economy. The DSA obligates online platforms to be more transparent about how they collect data and outlines how to deal with illegal content and disinformation. Whereas there is some crossover between the two laws, they both address different things. The DMA is more concerned with stopping the big Internet companies from abusing their market dominance.

The Bottom Line

The DMA, a ground-breaking European law designed to limit the power of the gatekeepers of the digital economy, could put an end to years of Big Tech dominance and revolutionize the Internet. The EU has long been wary about the control that a handful of companies have over digital channels and, with this law, became the first to act on it. With the DMA, large online platforms that connect consumers with content, goods, and services will have to be careful about how they handle user data and be more welcoming to competitors. Proponents of the DMA argue this will lead to greater choice, innovation, quality, and prices, which is what the law sets out to do, while DMA's critics argue that it will do the opposite and that consumers will end up footing the bill for this pricey piece of legislation.

Comparatively, the DSA is a legislative proposal introduced by the European Commission, focusing on regulating online platforms' content moderation and liability. Whereas the DMA primarily targets large gatekeeper platforms, the DSA's goal is to establish a comprehensive regulatory framework for all online intermediaries, including social media networks, online marketplaces, and search engines. The DMA focuses specifically on gatekeeper platforms, while the DSA addresses content moderation and liability issues for a broader range of online intermediaries.

Comparing the EU's to North American Digital Regulations

In North America, as of April 2024, there is no direct equivalent to the **DSA** or the **DMA** as seen in the EU. However, there are some notable differences and ongoing discussions related to digital regulation on both sides of the Atlantic. Furthermore, discussions and debates regarding digital regulation, particularly concerning online platforms and tech companies, have been ongoing in both the United States and Canada.

While there is not a direct equivalent to the DSA or DMA in North America, ongoing legislative efforts demonstrate recognition of the need to adapt regulatory frameworks to the challenges posed by the digital environment.**

U.S. Approach to Online Legislation

In the United States, lawmakers have proposed various bills aimed at regulating the tech industry, such as the ACCESS Act, the Platform Accountability and Consumer Transparency Act, and the Online Content Policy Modernization Act. These proposals address issues like data portability, transparency, and content moderation, although they do not mirror the comprehensive approach of the DSA or DMA.

- The U.S. approach is highly distributed across federal agencies, with many adapting to AI without new legal authorities.

Canadian Approach to Online Legislation

The Canadian Government has taken significant legal actions concerning social media platforms to address issues like online privacy, misinformation, and competition in the tech sector.

Here are some key developments.

Bill C-11: Regulation of Social Media and Streaming Services: The Canadian Government has introduced bills like the Digital Charter

Implementation Act (Bill C-11), which focuses on modernizing privacy laws and enhancing consumer trust in the digital economy.

- At issue with Bill C-11 is a clause that would require streamers, including social networks like YouTube and TikTok, to "clearly promote and recommend Canadian programming, in both official languages as well as in Indigenous languages."[††]

Canada's Digital Services Tax (DST) (Included in Bill C-59):

- In Canada, the government pledged to introduce a DST on big tech companies. The DST would apply to revenues of large firms providing digital services such as e-commerce, social media, and online advertising.
- The DST is designed to impose a 3 percent tax on companies with total annual revenue exceeding 750 million euros (approximately CAD 1.1 billion). Firms facing the tax would also need to have "Canadian digital services revenue" of more than $20 million in a fiscal year. Canada prefers to impose the tax in coordination with its allies, but it is prepared to move forward unilaterally if necessary.
- Although the exact implementation date is not specified, the government aims to pass legislation to pave the way for the DST.

Bill C-10: Regulation of Social Media and Streaming Services: The status of Bill C-10, which aims to regulate social media and streaming services in Canada, has seen significant developments.

(a) **Passage in the House of Commons:**
  - Canadian lawmakers passed **Bill C-10** in the House of Commons.

- The bill intends to subject tech giants (such as Netflix Inc. and TikTok Inc.) to the same requirements as traditional broadcasters.
- These requirements would effectively compel companies to **finance and promote Canadian content.**

It is one of the most far-reaching plans globally to regulate the algorithms tech companies use to amplify or recommend content.[‡‡]

(b) **Senate Approval and Uncertainty:**
- However, the bill's fate remains uncertain.
- It needs to pass through the **Senate**, a process that could be pre-empted by an election later this year.
- If an election occurs, it might effectively **kill the bill.**

Despite this uncertainty, the government considers Bill C-10 a **first step** in addressing broadcasting and creation issues.

(c) **Protection of Domestic Cultural Industries:**
- The focus of the new law is to protect domestic cultural industries.
- As more Canadians turn to Internet companies for music and video programming, the government aims to balance this with the influence of U.S. culture.

For decades, Canada has required radio and television broadcasters to produce and distribute local content, a core principle of Canadian media law.

(d) **Rights of Social Media Users:**
- The bill includes a clause that upholds the rights of individual social media users.[§§]
- Users who are not affiliated with the platforms themselves will not be subject to regulation when they upload audio and visual content.

- Channels or accounts with large followings are also exempt from regulations.

In summary, while Bill C-10 has passed the House of Commons, its final outcome depends on Senate approval and potential elections. The delicate balance between promoting Canadian content and safeguarding individual expression remains at the forefront of this regulatory effort.

Bill C-63: The Online Harms Act

Canada introduced the Online Harms Act, which aims to combat online abuse with steep penalties for hate crimes. Bill C-63 is an act to enact the Online Harms Act, to amend the Criminal Code, and the Canadian Human Rights Act, and An Act respecting the mandatory reporting of Internet child pornography by persons who provide an Internet service and to make consequential and related amendments to other Acts (first reading, February 26, 2024).

Key provisions include:

- Removal of harmful content: social media platforms must remove posts (e.g., those sexualizing children) within 24 hours.
- Penalties for hate crimes: the Act proposes life imprisonment for inciting genocide.
- Draft legislation was unveiled to combat online hate.
- Major companies would be required to swiftly remove harmful content, and the penalty for inciting genocide could be life imprisonment.

The Canadian Online News Act (Bill C-18)The Canadian Online News Act, also known as Bill C-18, is a piece of legislation that requires tech companies like Google and Meta to compensate news outlets for sharing links to their pages. The law received royal assent on June 22, 2023, and it is slated to take effect "no later than 180 days" after that date."

In response to this act, Meta, the parent company of Facebook and Instagram, has confirmed that it will end access to news content for all Canadian users before Bill C-18 comes into force. The company will begin to block news for Canadian users over the next few months, and this change will not be immediate. Meta's decision aligns with the requirement for tech giants to pay news outlets for posting their journalism on their platforms.

The Department of Canadian Heritage will draft regulations specifying the application of the act and provide guidance on implementing it. It is expected that it will take approximately six months for Bill C-18 to fully come into force. Canadian Heritage Minister Pablo Rodriguez emphasized the importance of a free and independent press, stating that the law levels the playing field by ensuring fair compensation for news businesses.

Despite Meta's announcement, Rodriguez clarified that the company currently has no obligations under the act, and the federal government will engage in a "regulatory and implementation process" following royal assent of Bill C-18. The government aims to stand up for Canadians against tech giants and ensure fair compensation for news content.

The Canadian Online News Act aims to create a fair compensation framework for news outlets, and Meta's response involves blocking news content for Canadian users in compliance with the law.

OCDSB's Lawsuit Against Social Media Giants

Ottawa's largest school board, along with others in Ontario, is suing social media giants for alleged facilitation of cyberbullying, hate speech, and misinformation, claiming a link to escalating conflicts in schools. The lawsuit, seeking $4.5 billion in damages, aims to address concerns about the negative impact of social media on youth mental health. Experts suggest the lawsuit is part of a broader effort to regulate social media, citing similar cases in the United States and emphasizing the addictive nature of these platforms. They argue that social media usage contributes to lower academic achievement, increased anxiety and depression among teens, and shifts in social dynamics within schools. The lawsuit highlights long-standing concerns and underscores the urgency of addressing the issue.***

These legal actions reflect Canada's efforts to address online safety, and content regulation, and combat harmful behavior on social media platforms.

Similar Regulations in Other Countries Around the World

Several countries around the world have been considering or implementing legislation to address issues similar to those covered by the DSA in the EU. While the specifics may vary, the general aim is to regulate digital platforms, promote online safety, and address concerns related to content moderation, user data protection, and competition.[†††]

Here are a few examples:

- **Australia:** the Australian Government has proposed the Online Safety Act, which aims to enhance online safety for Australians. It includes provisions to establish a new Online Safety Commissioner with powers to take enforcement action against online platforms for cyberbullying, revenge porn, and other harmful content.
- **United Kingdom:** the UK Government has introduced the Online Safety Bill, which seeks to tackle harmful content online. It proposes a new regulatory framework to hold social media companies and other online platforms accountable for the content shared on their platforms. The bill includes measures to address illegal content, harmful content, and disinformation.
- **India** has been exploring various measures to regulate digital platforms and address concerns related to content moderation and user data protection. The government has introduced intermediary guidelines under the Information Technology Act, which require social media platforms to comply with certain content moderation requirements and establish grievance redressal mechanisms.
- **Brazil** has proposed legislation similar to the DSA to regulate digital platforms and address issues related to online safety, content moderation, and user data protection. The Brazilian Congress has been considering the *Fake News Bill*, which includes provisions to establish rules for social media

platforms and messaging services to combat misinformation and protect user privacy.

- **South Africa** has implemented the Protection of Personal Information Act (POPIA)[‡‡‡] with equally stringent and rigorous personal data protection controls in place. The Act has undergone several iterations and evolutions since it was first proposed in 2013 and is set to harden the final layers of the Act in July 2021. The privacy laws and protections outlined in POPIA are of as rigorous a standard as those in the GDPR.
- **Bahrain** has a Data Protection Law[§§§] that has the honor of being the first of its kind to be introduced in the Middle East and that provides individuals with rights concerning how their data is collected, processed, and stored.
- **The Philippines** has the Data Privacy Act of 2012,[¶¶¶] which has many of the components that define the EU Data Protection Directive and that ensure the protection of personal information by organizations.
- **Switzerland** has guaranteed its citizens the right to privacy under its constitution and enacted regulations. The Swiss Federal Data Protection Act prohibits personal data processing without the individual's consent the data relates to.

Other international privacy laws for data protection include Angola, the British Virgin Islands, Denmark, Finland, Iceland, Israel, and Nigeria.[****]

These examples illustrate that countries outside of North America and the EU are also taking steps to regulate digital platforms and address challenges in the online environment. Although the specific legislative frameworks may differ, the overarching goal is to promote online safety, protect user rights, and ensure accountability and transparency among digital service providers.[††††]

Foote Note on EU's AI Legislation

The **EU's Artificial Intelligence Act (AI Act), a** significant piece of legislation that regulates artificial intelligence within the EU, took effect in March 2024.

Hereafter are its key points:

- Objective and context
  - o The proposal for the AI Act was introduced by the European Commission on April 21, 2021.
  - o It establishes a **common regulatory and legal framework** for AI across the EU.
  - o The Act addresses both the potential benefits and risks associated with AI technologies.
- Benefits and risks:
  - o AI can bring economic and societal benefits across various industries.
  - o However, it can also pose risks to individuals and society.
  - o The EU aims to strike a balanced approach that preserves technological leadership while ensuring compliance with Union values, fundamental rights, and principles.
- Trustworthy AI framework:
  - o The AI Act focuses on creating an ecosystem of trust.
  - o It proposes a legal framework for trustworthy AI.
  - o Trustworthy AI should adhere to ethical principles, transparency, and accountability.
- Risk categories:
  - o The law categorizes AI applications into three risk levels:
- Unacceptable risk:
  - o Certain applications (e.g., government-run social scoring) are banned.
- High risk:
  - o AI systems in critical sectors (e.g., health care, transport, and energy) must comply with strict requirements.
- Limited risk:
  - o General requirements apply to other AI systems.

- Transparency and accountability:
  - Developers and operators of high-risk AI systems must provide detailed documentation.
  - They must also ensure transparency regarding system behavior and decision making.
- Enforcement and penalties:
  - National authorities will oversee enforcement.
  - Noncompliance can result in substantial fines.

The AI Act represents a significant step toward responsible AI deployment and protection of citizens' rights within the EU.‡‡‡‡

Notes

*Digital-Markets-Act-Explained, www.investopedia.com/digital-markets-act-7097402.

†EUR-Lex. "Regulation (EU) 2022/1925 of the European Parliament and of the Council of 14 September 2022". https://eur-lex.europa.eu/legal-content/EN/TXT/?uri=CELEX%3A32022R1925.

‡American-Innovation-and-Choice-Online-Act, https://en.wikipedia.org/wiki/American_Innovation_and_Choice_Online_Act.

§Open-App-Markets-Act, https://en.wikipedia.org/wiki/Open_App_Markets_Act.

§§§§American-Innovation-and-Choice-Online-Act, https://en.wikipedia.org/wiki/American_Innovation_and_Choice_Online_Act.

¶¶¶¶"Top 10 books about social media"
This compilation traces the effect of Web 2.0 on people's lives delving into both fiction and nonfiction works that explore their relationship with social media. www.theguardian.com/books/2020/sep/23/top-10-books-about-social-media-viral-matthew-sperling.

"Seven Books on Social Connection"
These books touch on networks, connections, and the human need for social interaction. Some are explicitly about networks, while others are stories where characters engage fully with those around them. https://visiblenetworklabs.com/2022/05/03/seven-books-on-social-connection.

"Revealing Books about the Future of Social Media"
These books demystify the enigma of seemingly harmless online activity that led to significant events, including the GameStop situation and the January 6th insurrection. https://en.wikipedia.org/wiki/GameStop_short_squeeze;

www.hachettebookgroup.com/book-list/books-about-the-future-of-social-media-including-twitter/.

"The most recommended social network books"

Drawn up by 26 authors, this list features their favourite books related to social networks, https://shepherd.com/bookshelf/social-networks.

Keeping children safe on social media, https://kitchener.citynews.ca/2024/02/04/keeping-children-safe-on-social-media-what-parents-should-know-to-protect-their-kids/.

Are social media apps dangerous?, https://phys.org/news/2024-02-social-media-apps-dangerous-scholars.html.

Tips for protecting social media account from hackers, https://english.newstracklive.com/news/these-tips-will-be-very-useful-in-protecting-social-media-accounts-from-hackers-sc71-nu371-ta371-1313067-1.html.

Deep dive social media, https://datareportal.com/reports/digital-2024-deep-dive-social-media-is-still-growing.

Social media threats, https://us.norton.com/blog/emerging-threats/social-media-threats

Worst social media platforms, https://thenicheguru.com/blogging/worst-social-media-platforms/.

Meta and other social media giants blocking news, www.cbc.ca/news/science/meta-instagram-canada-online-news-act-explainer-news-1.6914154.

What is Bill C-18? Canada's Online News Act explained | CTV News, www.ctvnews.ca/politics/understanding-bill-c-18-canada-s-online-news-act-and-its-proposed-rules-explained-1.6488532.

Canadians will no longer have access to news content on Facebook, www.cbc.ca/news/politics/online-news-act-meta-facebook-1.6885634.

Online News Act: Police using social media as Meta blocks news, www.ctvnews.ca/politics/police-using-social-media-accounts-as-meta-begins-blocking-news-for-canadians-1.6512383.

Proposed Canadian law to regulate social media companies and streaming giants, www.socialmedialawbulletin.com/2021/07/proposed-canadian-law-to-regulate-social-media-companies-and-streaming-giants/.

Canada introduces sweeping new online safety rules - BBC, www.bbc.com/news/world-us-canada-68409929.

Draft Canada law would force social media companies to quickly remove harmful content, www.reuters.com/world/americas/draft-canada-law-would-force-social-media-companies-quickly-remove-harmful-2024-02-26/.

Canadians will no longer have access to news content on Facebook, www.cbc.ca/news/politics/online-news-act-meta-facebook-1.6885634.

This is the official European Commission website providing information and legislative texts related to the DMA, https://digital-markets-act.ec.europa.eu/legislation_en.

This Investopedia article explains the key aspects and implications of the DMA, www.investopedia.com/digital-markets-act-7097402.

¶¶¶¶ Open-App-Markets-Act, https://en.wikipedia.org/wiki/Open_App_Markets_Act.

¶ Digital-Services-Act-Package, https://digital-strategy.ec.europa.eu/en/policies/digital-services-act-package.

** US-Antitrust-Bills-vs-EU-Digital-Markets-Act, www.pymnts.com/antitrust/2022/us-proposed-antitrust-bills-and-eus-digital-markets-act-have-clear-differences/.

†† Bill C-11: Why is YouTube mad at Canada?, www.bbc.com/news/world-us-canada-65420133.

‡‡ US-Passes-Bipartisan-Antitrust-Bill, https://nationalpost.com/news/canada/liberals-pass-bill-to-regulate-social-media-streaming.

§§ Rights-of-Social-Media-Users-in-Canada, www.ctvnews.ca/politics/rights-of-social-media-users-upheld-in-bill-c-10-department-of-justice-1.5426668.

¶¶ Meta-Instagram-and-Canadas-Online-News-Act. www.cbc.ca/news/science/meta-instagram-canada-online-news-act-explainer-news-1.6914154.

*** School-Board-Sued-Over-Social-Media-Monitoring, www.cbc.ca/news/canada/ottawa/ocdsb-social-media-lawsuit-1.7158899.

††† Data-Protection-Laws-Around-the-World, www.thalesgroup.com/en/markets/digital-identity-and-security/government/magazine/beyond-gdpr-data-protection-around-world.

‡‡‡ South-Africa-Data-Privacy-Law, https://popia.co.za/.

§§§ Bahrain-Data-Protection-Law, www.dlapiperdataprotection.com/index.html?t=law&c=BH.

¶¶¶ Philippines-Data-Privacy-Act, www.privacy.com.ph/compliance-requisites-data-privacy-act-foreign-entities/.t

**** Global-Data-Privacy-Rankings, https://privacyhq.com/news/world-data-privacy-rankings-countries/.

†††† A comprehensive breakdown of the various international privacy laws for data protection across countries and regulations can be found here: https://usercentrics.com/knowledge-hub/review-of-2023-in-data-privacy-around-the-world/ [Last update December. 28, 2023].

‡‡‡‡ EU-Artificial-Intelligence-Act, https://en.wikipedia.org/wiki/Artificial_Intelligence_Act.

About the Author

As a partner of a large consulting firm (CGI) **Dr. Frankl**, MBA, PhD, has managed large-scale systems development projects, conducted numerous information technology (IT), telecommunications, and business re-engineering strategic plans, and played major roles in key systems development initiatives. He has considerable experience in strategic management planning, project management, system development, system metrics and evaluation techniques, system feasibility studies, system quality assurance, and human resource planning. Dr. Frankl is involved in promoting IT at the university level (as an academic) as well as at the industry level (as a research associate) in the areas of systems development techniques and knowledge transfer.

Dr. Frankl held technical, marketing, and management positions with IBM Canada. He later joined the Quebec-based Desjardins Credit Union Confederation as director of clearing systems. While with Desjardins and through CIDA, he spent some time in Latin America, implementing a generalized financial infrastructure project for the Latino-American Cooperative Movement (COLAC) out of Panama City. Next, he joined CGI as a director of consulting services and partner where he participated in a large number of strategic projects in the private and public sectors. After moving to Victoria in the early 1990s he became, respectively, CFO, president, and CEO of several hi-tech Canadian businesses. He is presently a professor emeritus with the University Canada West, a member of the U.K.-based Global University Systems, an adjunct professor with the School of Health Information Science at the University of Victoria, and the program chair of the Master of Information Technology Management at Yorkville University (all in BC, Canada).

Index

OTHER TITLES IN THE SERVICE SYSTEMS AND INNOVATIONS IN BUSINESS AND SOCIETY COLLECTION

Jim Spohrer, IBM, Haluk Demirkan University of Washington, Tacoma, Editors

- *Transformative Strategic Thinking* by Michele Simoni, Eva Panetti and Marco Ferretti
- *Designing Service Processes to Unlock Value, Fourth Edition* by Joy M. Field
- *The Future Is BIG* by Uma Vanka
- *Platform Thinking* by Daniel Trabucchi and Tommaso Buganza
- *Becoming Resilient* by Daniel Schutzer
- *Servitization* by Antonio Pérez Márquez
- *Evolving With Inclusive Business in Emerging Markets* by Rajagopal Rajagopal
- *Hidden Challenges* by Elizabeth Florent Treacy, Fernanda Pomin, James Hennessy, Ricardo Senerman and Ross Emerson
- *Service in the AI Era* by Jim Spohrer, Paul P. Maglio, Stephen L. Vargo and Markus Warg
- *The Emergent Approach to Strategy* by Peter Compo
- *Emerging FinTech* by Paul Taylor
- *The Vice Chairman's Doctrine* by Ian Domowitz
- *Compassion-Driven Innovation* by Nicole Reineke, Hanna Yehuda and Debra Slapak
- *Adoption and Adaption in Digital Business* by Keith Sherringham and Bhuvan Unhelkar

Concise and Applied Business Books

The Collection listed above is one of 30 business subject collections that Business Expert Press has grown to make BEP a premiere publisher of print and digital books. Our concise and applied books are for...

- Professionals and Practitioners
- Faculty who adopt our books for courses
- Librarians who know that BEP's Digital Libraries are a unique way to offer students ebooks to download, not restricted with any digital rights management
- Executive Training Course Leaders
- Business Seminar Organizers

Business Expert Press books are for anyone who needs to dig deeper on business ideas, goals, and solutions to everyday problems. Whether one print book, one ebook, or buying a digital library of 110 ebooks, we remain the affordable and smart way to be business smart. For more information, please visit www.businessexpertpress.com, or contact sales@businessexpertpress.com.

www.ingramcontent.com/pod-product-compliance
Lightning Source LLC
Chambersburg PA
CBHW061134220326
41599CB00025B/4229